Rail Fences
Rolling Pins
and Rainbows

by

Lois Kaiser Costomiris

Illustrations by
Larry A. Kaiser

Guild Press of Indiana, Inc.

Guild Press of Indiana, Inc.
6000 Sunset Lane
Indianapolis, IN 46208

Printed in the United States of America

Library of Congress
Catalog Card Number
94-77599

ISBN 1-878208-25-X

Table of Contents

Dedication

For more reasons than I can name, this book is dedicated to my husband and best friend, Edward "Bud" Costomiris, who lived these experiences, as I have, and enjoyed them. He filled in the gaps of my knowledge of conditions in and around Hamilton County. I've not written anything, and I doubt if I ever shall, in which he does not have a part.

Acknowledgments

I wasn't born with inky fingers. There's an adage: You don't pick a writing career—it picks you. I maintain I *had* to write to be heard. My twin brother and I were born into the middle of a family of six children. I remember, as a small child, crying because I could never finish a sentence at the dinner table. Then I married a talker and we had six children. And *then*, eleven grandchildren!

My dream as a small girl was not to write, however. It was to marry a handsome, very ambitious fellow and have six children. My husband and I had three nearly grown daughters, Wanda, Becky, and Toni, when the rest of my dream was fulfilled with our adoption of three little boys, Dennis, John, and Bill. Back then, writing was farthest from my mind.

It was our adoption caseworker, Mrs. Margaret Davis of Richmond, Indiana, who planted the seed. "You *have* to write a book, Lois, the way you write such exciting letters back to us."

Write a book? Why, I didn't even have time to read one!

Before I knew it, Margaret had acquainted me with her good friend, best-selling author Esther Kellner, and I was buying "how-to-write" books. And so, I became a writer through a combination of accident and compulsion—the latter being the need to express myself.

Thus, my deep appreciation to Margaret for persisting, and to Esther for providing me with beginning materials.

Thanks also to Vaughn Rathbun, editor and publisher of the *Tri Town Topics*, Arcadia, Indiana, who saw my potential and launched my professional career with publication of my weekly column, "This 'n' That." And to *Good Old Days*, and its associate editor, Evelyn Schoolcraft, who published a big variety of my old-time stories.

I will be forever grateful to Steve Peters of Ramsay's Printing Company, in Tipton, Indiana, who sold me my word processor. He set about, very patiently, slowly, and articulately, to lead his oldest trainee through endless lessons and "help" calls, teaching her the hardest mental exercises she ever had to learn.

My gratitude goes also to Ramsay's dedicated office workers Eleanor Wallace, Jo Crume, Jim Smith, Kevin Rittenhouse, and Margie Tebo.

I would like to thank my clever, talented illustrator Larry Kaiser, the very popular Midwestern artist from Cicero.

Thanks, too, to Cicero's energetic librarian, Harriett Vestal, for her unfailing interest, encouragement, and assistance; and to Joe Roberts, Hamilton County coroner and funeral director, who provided most of the old photographs in this book.

I want to acknowledge my two dearest proofreaders—my husband Bud and third daughter, Toni Boone, a first-grade teacher and mother of Kim, Kris, and Josh.

And, I extend my appreciation to others, behind the scenes, who have helped this book progress: Patty Park, Dr. Charles Harris, Evelyn Gentry, Carol Willis, and Clarissa Badger. Also, the many, many friends and family, with their ever-present support.

Finally, thanks to publisher/editor Nancy Niblack Baxter at Guild Press of Indiana, who was excited with my book project from the start, and to co-editor Mary Atteberry, who was just as enthusiastic and helpful as Nancy.

Preface

Rail Fences, Rolling Pins, and Rainbows—men's stories, women's stories, and stories of childhood fun and happiness. Browsing through these pages is like taking a journey back through Indiana in the early 1900s, seeing the landscape and the people through the eyes of those who shared the hardships and pleasures.

These historic narratives come from Hamilton County in central Indiana, but they speak for all of those in Heartland, USA—the people who lived on farms and in small towns and villages across the Midwest at the turn of the century. Today Hamilton County is vastly different from the place reflected in these stories. It is one of the most affluent counties in the state and, due to its location directly north of Indianapolis, its towns are popular "bedroom communities" of the state's capital city.

Americans, whether they live in tiny villages or huge cities, have always been intensely proud of their heritage. In today's upwardly mobile society, people nationwide have a need to explore their roots and rediscover old values. Listening to the voices of an older generation, of a life-style and an era vastly different from our own mechanized and computerized society, is one way to connect with the past.

For years I've used oral history to bring the past to life. It started in June of 1970, when I filled in for a vacationing columnist at the *Tri Town Topics*, a weekly newspaper covering Cicero, Arcadia, and Atlanta. Back then, "family anecdote" columns were popular and I wondered whether I'd have enough material in my own family to sustain the column. I began putting down my own recollections of what it was like "back then," and soon people were calling or stopping me on the street to tell me *their* stories. I was amazed at the interest and enthusiasm these kinds of anecdotes generated! As the saying goes, "Without true accounts, the memories of the past, there is no vision for the future."

And so I began interviewing the old-timers of Hamilton County—unpretentious men and women who told their tales in their earthy, homespun style, with humor and barnyard wit. Each of their stories, all presented in first person narrative, had a central theme, whether tuning old pianos, shopping for a corset, or putting up rail fences. As I listened to them, I learned that perhaps the most extensive, untapped resources abundant in our communities today are the minds and memories of its older citizens.

I began seeing my column displayed in showcases at schools. Classes in the lower grades studied these "stories easily understood and enjoyed," as the teachers put it, before going on field trips. Two hundred and fifty copies went out of state each week, to people who wanted to read these old-time accounts.

It seemed the next logical step, then, was to compile some of these accounts into a book—this book. I hope you'll find in these pages a window to the past, to a time when most people were growing up in a rural setting, in a close family unit, and the values of integrity, hard work, simplicity, and honesty were especially important. I don't think any section in all of America has a more interesting or picturesque history than here in our Midwest. As you read these stories, I hope you will think so, too.

(above) Lola and Carl Heinzman celebrating their seventy-sixth wedding anniversary in January, 1991 ("Lola and Grace's Milk Route," page 83). (left) Jenny Applegate on her ninety-fifth birthday ("You Are Your Brother's Keeper," page 67).

Part One: Rail Fences

Men's Stories

When the State of Indiana purchased the lands now known as Hamilton County, directly north of Indianapolis, from the Delaware Indians in 1818, only one white man was living within its boundaries. His name was William Conner and he was a fur trader who lived with his Indian wife in a log cabin that doubled as a trading post.

The Conner cabin was located about four miles south of present-day Noblesville, on the east side of White River. At that time, the area was nothing but wilderness, abundant with deer, wolves, bears, and other wild animals. The only "roads" were Indian paths, or White River, which was navigable then. A white settlement was sixty miles to the southeast, where Conner's brother and supplier, John, operated another trading post at what is now Connersville in Fayette County.

After the state acquired the new Indian lands through the Treaty of Saint Mary's, other white settlers almost immediately began filtering into Hamilton County, even though the Indians were given three years to leave. Many of the original settlers came from Connersville. As a rule, the men arrived first, carrying only a few tools and personal belongings on pack horses. They were accompanied by few livestock, typically some cattle, sheep, and one or two brood sows. They cooperated in clearing land, planting crops, building fences and constructing cabins before retrieving the rest of their families.

The first men (and some women) arrived in March and April of 1819, and settled in a horseshoe-shaped area embraced by the White River, two miles southwest of Noblesville. The families who had stayed behind joined "Horseshoe Prairie" that fall. As farming took root, so did businesses to support it. Two of the settlers, John and Israel Finch, set up a horse mill to grind corn in the fall of 1819, and the next year they opened a blacksmith shop. By the end of 1820, the settlers had their first school, first church services, and first Fourth of July celebration, and their county seat had been established at Noblesville.

Those early settlers and those who followed through the rest of the 1800s prized this rich, fertile land. Well into the twentieth century, the farm economy in Hamilton County thrived on corn, wheat, oats, and livestock. The farmer's life was rough, but his forbearance was great, as was his spirit of comradeship with other farmers.

Back then, the farmers and the townspeople knew each other. Folks would drop in to visit of an evening, when the work was done, to admire a new colt, look over the hay crop or the garden, sit on the front porch, and have a cup of coffee and a piece of pie. Men could identify every horse and rig around, and later every automobile. Boys knew what each mount would do, and its worth.

The age of the "family farm" as we used to know it is over: those days when the milk hauler stopped at every farm along the country road, and front barnyards were filled with chickens, turkeys, ducks, geese, and guineas.

Today, only remnants of the old barnsteads remain as farms gradually fall victim to the bulldozer. About the only reminders of the men's lives are the stories of all the things they did back then to keep their families going, from cleaning the outhouses ("honey-dipping"), to moving livestock to market, to building rail fences.

Rail Fences

by
Alvin "Punkin" Hunter

Punkin Hunter, along with his wife, Margaret, told this story in the early 1980s. He was an Arcadia, Indiana, yarn-spinner. "Rail Fences" is the first of two of his accounts in this book.

When I was a little squirt, three years old, I liked pumpkin pie so well my uncle nicknamed me "Punkin." That nickname carried all through my life!

Are you wanting a story about rail fences? You've come to the right man for that—old Punkin Hunter!

I was born in 1905. Most all were rail fences then. I did some rail-splitting when I was a kid, but not as much as splittin' fence *posts*, here where we live east of Arcadia.

Rail fences were all along this road. We kids knew every fence corner between here and school, every apple tree and every hickory nut tree and every pear tree.

Coming home from school, we knew what time Mom would have supper ready, and we were always starved, like all kids that time of day, so we'd fill our pockets full of apples and pears from our neighbors' trees out next to the road or in the side ditch. They never cared how many we took. And I won't tell you how many a rotten apple was thrown against the head of an unsuspecting lad!

The first school hacks were horse-drawn, and no one living under a mile from school could ride it. We lived ten rod this side and had to walk, which was a pleasure. All the neighborhood kids, a big bunch of us, congregated and walked down the road together.

Coming from school we'd walk the top rails of that zig-zag fence, seeing who could stay up the longest.

In 1918, November 11, they let school out to celebrate. World War I had ended! They told us the Armistice had been signed, and we'd have the rest of the day off. I was the one chosen to ring the schoolhouse bell for a half-hour. I just kept the old bell a-going! That day I walked home alone. The others beat it as soon as the teacher let them go!

When considering a farm to buy, a farmer looked the rail fences over good. Usually he wasn't interested in buying it if fences were in doubtful repair.

Dad was never one for putting a crop in before he'd repaired or built a fence. All the time, Dad was checking and he'd replace rotted rails with new ones.

They were laid a little better than a ninety-degree angle, so every fencerow you had, it took up a lot of space, and created wasteland.

Now I never laid a fence up, but I helped Dad. You've heard of the old ten-rail fence? That's how they were, ten rails high. Most farmers took great pride in building a good rail fence.

To make a rail fence, first we took a heavy, binder twine string, stretched it out tight, and made it straight from one end of the field to the other. All rails were cut the same length and then split the same size as nearly as possible. We laid the rails in the pattern, two rails high, the full length. That was the basic start of the fence. Then, back in the barnlot, we loaded up our rails on the wagon, brought them to the field, and went ahead and finished our job. The fence was put up so as to be of uniform height to adequately serve its purpose and to make the best appearance.

A rail fence wasn't good around the barns and stock lots. Board fences were built there. They were made of rough lumber, reaching from post to post, and were firmly nailed from the inside to prevent stock from pushing the boards loose.

Garden fences were made of high pickets which had been sawed out of straight-grain pine trees and were nailed to two-by-fours which led from post to post. A rail fence would not do around a garden, as the cracks between the rails were large enough to let in chickens and rabbits, nor around the stock lot, because it was too easy to push down. Chickens could easily fly to the tops of rail fences and go on over into a garden.

In late spring, after the corn came up, we boys always had to take a hoe and a pocketful of corn and go out and plant where the corn was missing. Our other pocket was full of pumpkin seeds, to be planted alongside stalks of corn. All the boys in the community had that detestable job to do for their dads. We bellyached and complained — to ourselves, of course — on those first hot days. We wanted time off to go swimming or fishing!

After the corn in the field was way up there, look in the fence corners and you'd see a bunch of pumpkins coming up through, or big clusters of corn. Those fence corners were where we'd go, dig a hole, and dump all the corn and pumpkin seeds to get that hateful job done in a hurry!

However, we did that only once! Oh, boy, we knew just as soon as we saw Dad's face, as he was coming from the house after laying the corn by, that he was onto our misdeeds! I remember, we stood way back, hearing Dad roaring, "For cripes sakes!" And Mother's, "Mercy, mercy!" As I said, we only did that once!

In those secluded corners, it was an attraction for children to "play house," but they had to watch out for snakes and wasps.

Best danged fish bait under the bottom rails—grub worms, fishing worms. It was a good place for 'possum or 'coon to run, so hunters enjoyed that.

Mowing those rail fence corners—whew! Only way was with an old mowing scythe, all hard hand-work, in the hottest part of summer, of course. Boy, it was impossible to keep clean! Every time we had an extra minute, we'd cut weeds. Blackberry and raspberry briars were a mess to keep out. Nobody liked to mow weeds around a row of them as they scratched you so bad and they'd tear at our clothes. And bull nettles, crime-a-netley! Dangdest stingingest things—itched you. Whew!

It was just work, work, work, all summer long. I heard Ed Venable laugh, saying, "Old Man Frost can kill more weeds in one night than I can cut down all summer long!"

Unless the fence corners were kept clean, they would grow up in briars and weeds, they'd look bad, and they'd create a fire hazard in the late, dry summer. All those weeds go to seed, the wind would carry them all over the fields. We spent plenty of time on the end of a hoe, chopping those things out! A farmer in our community was rated as good or bad by the way in which he kept up his fences.

Some of the old rails were hollow. A woodpecker or a yellow-hammer would drill a hole into it, to find bugs and worms, and I've seen black snakes make a nest in a rail. I kept away from them!

And I've seen a black snake sunning itself up on the top rail. But that's something you seldom ever saw. A snake usually would see you before you saw it, and was gone!

Black snakes devoured the birds' eggs along the fencerows. Little ground sparrows built there. Red-winged blackbirds will usually make their nests up in the top of a sturdy white-top or ironweed, right out in the middle of the pasture field. Most quail nest in fencerows. An old guinea hen likes to hide her nest away in there, too. Wild animals—skunks, fox, even rats—they'll watch until the eggs are ready to hatch, then tear into one, eating the unborn chick, shell, and all, even the hen or bird on her nest!

Speaking of eggs, did you ever hear this one? The story of the tramp in the chicken house stealing eggs for his supper: He'd crack one on his head, it'd slide down into his mouth; he'd crack another and it'd slide down. After the last crack, "Cheep, cheep, cheep," pipped the chick in the egg. "You spoke too late," and down it went into his mouth!

Winds would blow those fences down. Cattle and horses could knock them over. Got so we'd have to put barbed wire up on each side of it to keep the stock from pushing off those top rails.

Late summer, we'd work on fences on free days. There were broken rails and rotted ones. These were replaced and the fence corners cleaned out good. After that Dad would start sowing wheat.

Dad never said "barbed wire" but pronounced it "bob-wa'r." Cleaning up the trash in the fencerows, we'd stack it, and he'd say, "You cain put a match to that-there pile and then watch the *far* till it's burned down so it don't git out of control. *Dreckly* we cain go to the house to eat."

Every spring we had to go around and rebuild each one of our fences. In winter, livestock, 'coon hunters, rabbit hunters—they'd climb over them and break them down. A cry, "Your cattle is out!" sent everyone in the family hurrying out to get the cattle rounded up and the fence mended. Bad, cold, and rainy days, hogs would invariably get out. They're like a bunch of kids on disagreeable days, not knowing what to do with themselves.

Hogs would hunt a bad rail and root through. The only time rail fences were good for hogs, summertime, the old sow would get into a pasture field fence corner, bed down, and have her babies. We'd put rails over the top and throw straw on them to make a shade. Kids liked to play under that, too, after the sows and their families were moved to another field!

A rail fence would hold shoats and feeding hogs pretty well, but when it came to little pigs, it took a pretty tight fence to keep them under control. So, we usually penned them in the back barnlot, where we'd built board fences, until they got up to about sixty pounds each.

I've seen a windstorm come along and blow down five rods of fence. That even happened in the summertime, as well as winter. The reason why you see some rails forming an X in each fence corner over the rail: That was to tie it so the windstorm couldn't blow them down. They used to set the broken rails on each end of an X and they'd take some wire and wrap around that at the corner so the wind couldn't roll the rails off.

I can remember when there were rail fences on both sides of the road past here. In March, 1914, my grandfather died. The snow was over four feet deep all the way up his road. It had to be scooped out—yep, plain ol' scoop shovel and muscle power! Every neighbor pitched in to help get the road opened up for the funeral.

The same rails used for fences were stacked very firmly to build corn cribs. It was open on top. Air circulated through there so the ears wouldn't mold if they weren't completely dry. Dad covered the support posts, at ground level, with tin so the rats couldn't climb up and get into the corn bin. Still some of them made it in. We were fighting rats all the time! A lot of cobs were always lying around where the rats had eaten off the corn. That was a good place for boys' corncob fights!

February, when the sap is down, is the month to cut trees for rail fences, cribs, and posts. There's that much moisture you don't have to dry out. After the sap comes up, that's where you get into the rails drying crooked. August is another good time to cut trees. All the sap is up in the extreme top, in the leaves and branches.

Back in those days, about the only good timber left was oak, ash, and some poplar. Poplar was best, as they are lighter in weight. As long as they were above the ground they'd last a long, long time, but poplar wasn't a timber you could bury in the ground, as for fence posts.

Red elm made a good rail. It was a straight-grained timber and it would split straight. Hedgeapple was a tough wood. You can't break it—it'll tear before it will break. Ironwood is the same way. It's tough but so stringy you can't break it. No good for rails or posts, either one.

The best fence-post material you could get was mulberry and locust. Practically all the old-timers used to cut mulberry for end posts because they would last forever—just wouldn't rot underground. Some have been there over sixty or seventy years and still solid.

The worst trouble with mulberry, you couldn't split them; they are a stringy timber. The only thing you could do was cut them for end posts. Made good stove wood—any fruit tree is good for that. Oak would rot out in thirty years. It got to the place that even good oak wouldn't last. Then they started selling the red cedar posts.

The best wood for line posts was locust. The worst trouble with it, it is as crooked as a dog's hind leg. Occasionally you see the locust groves that people planted just for the purpose of using them for posts. Out through Missouri you'll see a lot of fences using the locust crooked posts, even along the highway. Locust don't grow very big. It's scrubby, small. Could go out and cut lots of posts off in one day. It was more or less a volunteer tree; comes up on the same plan as the thorn tree.

I never did find anything a thorn tree was good for. It has such a root system, you can't hardly kill them out. One man said he had some sticks of it down in his damp basement, to burn in the furnace, and they started sending up sprouts!

Many a farm had the hedgeapple fencerows. They'd grow so thick even a rabbit couldn't get through. The hedge grew rank and was hard to trim. Our hands bloodied from the long, sharp old thorns sticking us so!

When we were kids, we'd play with those big, nubby-green hedgeapples. They looked like they were covered with huge warts and were the size of a big orange. They made the best balls when playing hockey. They were plentiful. Dad cut our perfectly shaped hockey sticks from hedgeapple limbs. Had many a neighborhood hockey game out in our barnyard.

Ma had a small basket of them in our one-and-only closet. She claimed they kept out moths.

When the automobiles first appeared, Dad avoided going past one of those hedgeapple fencerows. They shed thorns that punctured tires. He no more than got one flat fixed and he had another one!

The wire fences, they started coming in around 1920, reduced the fencerows, and made about six feet more ground to plant down through fields. Was easier to control weeds.

A farm boy could make spending money helping neighbors put up new wire fences. We'd find rusty plowshares thrown in a fencerow. Negligent farmers pitched old buckets or other farm trash there. Oh, what a mess that was!

It got so, with rail fences, it was hard to keep livestock off the public highway when automobiles made their entrance. Then the line fences and the road fences were the first ones farmers built of wire. The rail fences stayed on the back end of the farm until they passed on out, too.

In later years, the old rails went for cookstove wood. The bucksaw was used to saw them up in exact cookstove lengths. Then farmers started getting buzz saws and hooked them to their tractors with belts, and that eliminated the bucksaw. Before the tractor, some enterprising farm boys jacked up a wheel on the automobile, using it with a leather belt.

Rails were dry and burned well. The cook liked those! Otherwise we went to the woods, and cut and split timber for the cookstoves. And the heating stoves.

Thirty years ago every farm had a big woods lot. The trees got old, and gradually they were cut down or blown over. Or the greedy took big bulldozers in and leveled them off to make more farm ground.

There were a number of things I liked about rail fences: You could lean on one, sit on top, or prop up against it, and visit and talk. You can't very well lean on, prop against, or sit on a wire fence with a barbed wire stretched on top. A rail fence was easy to climb up on or to climb over, while it is difficult, even dangerous, to climb a wire fence. The top rail of one was a good place to sit and rest and chew a wad of tobacco! It furnished a good vantage point to look over a growing crop or pasture field. Because it was easy to climb, you could cross a rail fence anywhere, enabling you to take short cuts. The old rail fence was easy to climb because there was a good foothold between the rails.

Dad always said good fences made good neighbors. You respect another man's claim to boundaries, and he'll respect yours.

Our whole family was so proud of the new wire fences all around the farm. It was hard work, digging post holes, then stretching the fence just so. I never saw anybody who could stretch barbed wire tight like Dad did. You could play a tune on it! Our hands were always bloodied from barb wire scratches.

An expertly built wire fence would last a generation.

There was maintenance to these, too. We'd check for loose or leaning posts. Hunters cut low wires for their coon dogs to climb through, and a field of hogs found the spot the next morning and were soon out running all over. A real aggravation!

Dad's gates were made and hung on good hinges, just so! No sagging, dragging. Latches were secure.

Later on, some farmers put up a quick-temporary electric fence. Remember the first time you took hold of an electric fence—about knock your teeth loose! Could be fatal if the ground was wet.

Nowadays, all through here, you'll see farmers who have all field crops—no livestock and no fences. Still remaining are the big cement posts dating back to just after the turn of the century. They are fascinating to me: most were formed so different in appearance from any other. A wooden form was made over a very deep hole where the farmer wanted to put the post. Many old-timers offered fence-building advice by saying, "End post-holes (cement or wooden) should be digger-handle deep, approximately five feet, plus another foot for good measure." The wooden form for the cement posts was then filled with concrete. Some of these were said to weigh over a ton. That's probably why most of them are still standing!

Four cement posts are across the front yard out on the old Schildmeier farm, west of Cicero, where the Bill Beechlers live. On top of each one is a big round ball. Beechlers give these a new coat of orange paint each year—a friendly landmark. Pumpkin Corner!

Dad had no time for a man who neglected the upkeep of his rail fences, or *any* of his fences. A properly made one was a beauty to behold!

—Originally published in the Tri Town Topics in 1980, this story has also appeared in Good Old Days magazine and Cicero, Indiana: 1834–1984.

Ada's Papa: Hard-Shell Baptist Preacher

by
Ada McConnell

Ada McConnell, her Papa, and all the Worley family have all been Cicero natives. Their cemetery plot is on one corner of the Worley farm.

Papa, a "hard-shell" Baptist preacher, brought up his children with the strict disciplines of his church. He said he was training us to develop strength and character.

Ours was the traditional rural setting where the values of integrity, hard work, honesty, and simplicity were especially important. Family and religious life were treasured.

Constantly Papa talked the scriptures. All the time. At night, for hours, he read the Bible. The coal oil lamp on the library table made a dim circle of light around him. I always liked the smell of warm oil that permeated the room.

When dusting the library table, I'd touch Papa's Sunday Bible, with its smooth, black leather cover, and the gold-edged pages. I wondered, would I ever own such a beautiful book?

How could Papa read the Bible endlessly? As a child I didn't understand the verses unless it was Jonah and the Whale, or Baby Moses or Baby Jesus.

After dark he'd retire to the barn to say his prayers, where he thundered them up to the rafters. Us kids used to delight in hiding in the hay where we could listen. He would be sure to get all the transgressors' names in when he was asking for their forgiveness.

We noticed, usually before he got off to a good start, he reached way down under, in the hay, in Old Nell's manger. Out came a liquor bottle! He'd take a long and mighty drought from it. "Ah," he always said to himself, "good f'r the stomach."

I couldn't understand Papa doing such a thing. In his church sermons he decried the evils of drinking: "Drinkin' kills! The Devil in a bottle! One man had his head in a jug most of the time. And I says, 'A fine way to send your boy to his Maker! He'll follow your example—his breath foul with likker. Won't be no likker in Heaven! Lord save their souls from Hell, that's all I ask! We don't want that old Devil in the driver's seat.' " Tears would run down his cheeks and he shook all over, bawling so hard during his sermon. The evils of gambling! Smoking! Bad women!

Seeing him drink from the bottle, I worried. Would the kids around town laugh about Papa, like they did the town drunks? "Here comes old cherry-nose Worley." Oh, no, not Papa!

"If you want to keep a dead man, put him in whiskey," Dr. Wendell Hansen once said. "If you want to kill a living man, put whiskey in him!"

Early one morning, as I was getting seated under old Ruth, ready to milk her, I cautiously said, "Papa, I assume you were a trifle tiddly last night when you were practicing your sermon."

Suddenly I knew I should never have said that. He roared over the back of the cow he was milking, "I don't know what you're making reference to. Why were you in the barn at that hour?" Then he continued, "A child ought not to say such things of her own father, no matter what his faults. God doesn't mind if a Christian man pulls the cork now and then, as long as he treats his family and neighbors fine. Christian men don't go around likkered up all day."

I decided he was not the sort of man to keep booze in the house— oh, no! The barn didn't count.

I enjoyed his stories, illustrating points to ponder. This was one of his favorites, told to him by his father: "You ever hear the story about the two frogs in the milk? Well, I'm goin' to tell it to you. Seems there was these two frogs that fell into a pail of milk and they been swimmin' and swimmin' for hours and there don't seem to be no way to git out, the lip of the pail bein' higher than they can reach with their webbed feet. Things are lookin' bad. They're both powerful tired, they feel like their legs are about to drop off, and one of 'em says he jist cain't make it no more, he jist cain't, and without no more talk, he sinks right to the bottom of the pail.

"Now the other'n, he's jist as tired as the first but he keeps goin' anyhow, jist keeps on keepin' on, till he's 'bout knocked out. An' when he wakes up next mornin', there he is, settin' on a pad of butter on top of the milk. So he ups and jumps out! Ain't that a good story? Don't ever give up!"

When I was the age to keep company with the fellows, I never left the house before I had to go through the usual period of questioning:

"Where are you going? Who with? Who's his folks? Where does he go to church? How old is he? What time will you be home?" A girl who was reputed to drink or run with questionable fellows lost her reputation fast. Papa would have none of that. Young ladies always had to avoid the temptations of evil.

When I was fifteen, well-developed, my cousin Helen, she later got the title of "Dirty Helen" because she kept whispered company with Chicago's gangland leader, Al Capone, and other famous men—even had a big book about "Dirty Helen"—she came back to Cicero to visit relatives. How I admired her with her fine clothes and refined ways. She was painted and powdered, bedecked with rings and chains and beauty pins. She wore her yellow hair in a high pompadour, crowned with a gorgeous picture hat. I yearned to be the image of Cousin Helen!

She said to Papa, "Uncle Ell, why don't you let me take Ada back with me? I could do a lot for her."

"No," he shook his head and I knew what he was thinking. "No, indeed."

Later I said, "But, Papa, I could make a lot of money. She wants to give me an education. Why not? What does she do, really? She seems so happy."

"She's a lady of the night, supplying the needs of lonely men. She is not a person to pattern after." To make his point, he added emphatically, "Anybody knows when a red barn is on fire, the first thing that peels off is the paint. You understand what I mean? That's the end of that."

Really, Papa was a farmer. He seldom got paid for preaching. The farm where we lived was cleared by Grandpa Worley about the time of the Civil War. He had a stepson who was called up for the draft when he was sixteen. Grandpa paid forty dollars to keep him out of the war.

We lived a mile east of Cicero in a huge white house: The rich Worleys, with their big house and barn—Papa's pride. Most affluent farmers put all their money back into the farming business, thinking the more farmland they had, the bigger the impression.

"That's where ya make the money," they'd say, letting their wives do without, or at best, get by. Most women had to nag to get any home improvement. Not Mama. Papa loved Mama and wanted her to be happy, too. Papa always said there were so many love promises before marriage, but soon forgotten by the men afterward.

Our big, two-storied farmhouse was cozily placed in the center of a rambling, terraced lawn and it was enclosed by an artistically designed iron fence. The buildings and farm fences were painted spotless white, and the grounds neatly kept. Even the strawstack in the barnlot was tidy and solid, built as carefully in its way as any of the sheds.

Papa bought a pair of peacocks to walk around in the front yard. Peacocks have long been the symbol of splendor, possibly the reason for Papa's purchase. We all loved to watch them strut. "Proud as a peacock," the old saying goes. Oh, their brilliant plumage, the metallic shades of bronze, blue, green, and gold, and a crest adorning their heads. They'd fly to the comb of the barn and shout their calls, heard clear to Cicero.

Sarah and I didn't have many clothes but Mama saw to it we had the very best. Miss Stearate came out and stayed with us a week at a time and did the sewing. We had a good Sunday winter and summer dress, and two or three calico or ginghams for school. Miss Stearate made Sunday and everyday dresses for Mama, and my brothers' shirts, and all our nightwear.

Papa bought me a baby grand piano when I was ten years old. It occupied one room. I took lessons but I never played very well. I'd come into town with my pony hitched to its buggy and pick up the music teacher and bring her to our house. After my lesson, Mama would put on a clean housedress and she'd come in and sit and have the teacher play for her.

No, no, I never played for church. They didn't believe in instrumental music. Everybody could sing the hymns by heart. We had a leader, at one time it was Papa, or whoever knew the tune, would start the song.

I sang all my life. I was in the glee club. When we presented our programs, the music teacher, she'd stand facing us, we were facing the audience, she wore a real pretty white dress with a big butterfly bow in the back. She wanted to look pretty with her posterior to the audience.

The night the glass factory burned, Christmas Eve, 1908, a mile south of Cicero, we lived two miles from it, I remember Mama saying, as we stood on our balcony on the west side of the house, the fire was so intense she could thread a needle by the light from it. They thought it was arson. Why? The gas failed, gas companies were going bankrupt, and they think it was burned down to collect the insurance, but there was never any proof.

We lost our mother of apoplexy. She was so young, forty-five. I was twelve; Sarah, nine; Floyd, fourteen; and Tootsie, our little brother, was two. Mama was such a dear person. How we all grieved. I thought Papa couldn't get over it.

After a while Papa took up with Mary, an old maid from Kentucky he'd met at one of the church meetings. From then on our lives were so different.

Mary was fifty and Papa was fifty five. Mary had never had children, and then to inherit all of us. I imagine Tootsie was quite a handful 'cause we all babied him.

Mary was so old-maidey. She wanted to be the only one Papa cared for. But we loved him, too.

I learned to milk at an early age. As many as seven cows, night and morning. Floyd did his share of chores and milking. Sarah was afraid of cows so she stayed inside and helped Mary with the housework. Sarah just loved to dust.

We were all up at five and had a big breakfast. Biscuits with syrup and all. Farmers got up early. Papa didn't believe in wasting good time sleeping. Sarah never did like to get up early, but we all had our work to do before starting to school by seven-thirty. Mary saw to that.

Mama had sent the washing out to be done. Papa bought Mary a washing machine. She didn't want to waste money paying someone else for doing it. I had to stay home and help or get up real early so it was all done before I went to school.

Mary didn't think the washing machine got the clothes clean enough so she'd make me give the badly stained ones an extra rub on the washboard. I wore off the skin down to my knuckles rubbing those things on that rigid metal board through that hot, sudsy water. My hands were always red, chapped, cracked, and bleeding, especially in the winter.

Tuesday morning, before school, I had to iron all my clothes, and some of Tootsie's and Floyd's.

Long before Papa ever become a preacher, he took care of so many of the church people. Buried I don't know how many, just because he was a member of the Old Church.

We had this very big house and Papa'd haul in all the elderly who were down on their luck or had bad health. We'd take care of them. He did this while Mama was living, too. Both Papa's wives, and all us kids, were willing to help the poor souls out. The new wife was religious, and she, as Papa, felt it a duty to care for the down-and-out.

Tootsie was six when he died of membranous croup. Membrane filled up his lungs. It just grew and grew, and he slowly wasted away. I remember he didn't cry; he just lay there, Papa holding his hand on one side, Mary on the other. I cried every night for a year, I missed him so. His death just seemed to haunt me.

I tell you, I saw more people die when I was a kid. Papa would take me with him whenever a person was on the deathbed and I'd stand there and watch them depart. He thought it was a part of life that could not be ignored. The sick always wanted Papa to come and sit beside them and pray with them to the very end.

One time, I guess I was five, I slipped in and watched when Papa didn't know. The old lady swallowed her tongue. You never saw such nervous excitement. A woman hurried out to the kitchen and came back with a spoon, pushed it down into the lady's throat, and brought the tongue back so she could catch hold with her fingers. She pulled it back out and clung to it. The lady died a bit later.

All this time I hung onto the foot of the bed in terror! I knew I could walk on out, but I was too mesmerized to move. Mama would never have allowed me in there. Death, in the home, was commonplace.

After all the fatalities, Sarah and I were afraid of our shadows at night. Floyd made fun of us. Fraidy cats, he'd say. We'd have to go upstairs in that big house, carrying the coal oil lamp, our huge grotesque shadows following us along the stairway. We were petrified when we hit the bed!

How did people, even kids like us, manage carrying the lamps all about, without dropping them and causing house fires? We realized, when quite young, to be very careful.

Floyd and Mary didn't hit it off from the start. He'd taken Mama's death so hard and didn't want a replacement. Boys knew, when they were sixteen years old they could quit school and strike out on their own. "Out West" lured him, as it had many young men from these parts, and one day he was missing from the breakfast table. I wonder if he'd even talked it over with Papa.

Once or twice a month we had church, always held in one of the homes. No Sunday School. Services lasted two days, Saturday and Sunday. Sometimes there were three or four preachers and it would go on for hours. They'd get to preaching, then crying and I'd cry, too. There wasn't any extremely loud excitement with shouts, like some denominations, but they'd swing their arms and carry on.

We kids didn't mind all this 'cause there were so many children to play with after the devotions ended.

Baptists addressed each other with a "Brother" or "Sister" greeting. It was "Brother Worley" to Papa. Mama had been a Methodist and she never joined the Baptists, so she was called "Jenny" but she always went along with Papa and his religion. It was "Sister Mary," my stepmother.

Papa joined the Baptists when he was nineteen years old. That was considered quite young to have his belief established. Most were much older, confirmed "dyed in the wool" to their concepts. He'd laugh and say, "I didn't know how to pray until I was eighteen, unless I mashed my finger."

Preachers were called "Elder." It was their belief: There's only one Reverend and that's God.

Our favorite was Elder Smoot, from Occoquan, Virginia. He was the most outstanding and smartest Baptist. He published a Baptist magazine for our religious group that was sent all over the country.

A collection plate was never passed. Those who could afford it, gave privately to the preacher or the needy.

The larger Baptist meetings were just once a year, in August, on Friday, Saturday, and Sunday. About seventy-five would attend. They came from Fortville, Maxwell, Pendleton, and Indianapolis. I remember one held as far away as Ohio.

They'd stay overnight, if they weren't close enough to go home. I remember Mama trying to figure out where she'd put all those people. She'd tell Sarah and I about when she was a little girl going to camp meetings. They'd spread oil cloth on the ground for a table near a campfire. Wood smoke filled the air, and how good their food tasted when it was cooked over the open flames. At night, women and children slept in the wagons and men made beds on the ground under wagons or trees.

It took a lot of work getting ready for Papa's church people. From Monday morning till Thursday night the house buzzed with preparations. Aunt Mattie, Papa's sister, lived with us. She was a hard worker and very strong. She could chop wood like a man. We used a lot of wood to cook and heat with. All day long we could hear her scurrying to and fro, beating up pillows and feather beds, flapping towels, jingling crockery, singing all the while, accompanied by—or maybe it was in competition with—our caged canary bird.

No one brought any food with them for the overnight stays. Papa furnished the whole business. Mama, and later Mary, cooked for them all. We had lots of chickens to dress and hams to bake. We always had fried ham or bacon and eggs for breakfast, pancakes, or biscuits.

We made new bedticks out of heavy ticking goods. The day before everyone was to arrive we went to the straw stack and filled them with new straw, then we put them down on the floors for everyone to sleep on.

When the barn was new, Papa put straw ticks all around inside the corn crib, and men slept out there. The women slept upstairs in the house.

It took a special knack to make up a bed. The beds had ticks of straw placed on wooden bed slats; over these were spread the feather beds. The feather mattresses were left on year-round and were terribly warm, in winter and summer.

Mary was particular about bed-making and wanted the top cover-let to be smooth. The only way this could be achieved was to pass a broom handle back and forth over the feathers to rearrange them into a flat surface. No one ever dared sit on a made-up bed.

Papa hired Gertrude Cornelius, a young Cicero girl, to help. We made the beds together. She, bigger than we were, would be on one side of a bed, and Sarah and I on the other.

Gertrude said Mama taught her everything she knew. She was al-ways laughing and carrying on, singing, hurrying about her work. In each room there were starched, freshly ironed scarves to lay across the dusted bureaus. Hand-embroidered linen towels hung on the rack of the washstands. There was a heavy hand-painted china pitcher, wash bowl, and soap dish, sparkling clean, on each washstand. A cake of transpar-ent Pear's soap and matches for lighting lamps were laid out. Clean cot-ton crocheted rugs were on the floors. All the furniture was gone over with an oiled dustrag. We cooked, cleaned, and polished until the house bloomed like Aunt Mattie's summer flower garden.

Gertrude made an exciting adventure of every task that had to be done. Oh, the dishes! She washed them; Sarah and I dried, giggling to ourselves over the funny way one of the women talked and walked, twisting her bottom. Then we mimicked her the rest of the day.

One woman, so big and fat, waddled like a duck. I'd imitate her. Gertrude was the husband, so tall and thin. Sarah was the child. Why is it big, fat women always have skinny men? They eat the same food!

One man walked like a frozen-toed rooster and we made-believe our feet hurt just as his must have.

One time, when we spent the day strutting like peacocks, I saw Mary frown at us but we pretended we didn't notice.

We'd take warm water upstairs in the tea kettle to each wash bowl and pitcher when the guests arrived. One old maid was so finicky she bathed fully every night. This lady would take one of the bowls and sit down over in the corner, with her back to the ladies. My goodness, everyone else took a bath just once a week in a big wash tub in the kitchen, then take spit baths in between, using the bowl and pitcher.

At night I watched all the ladies take out the hairpins, brush through their manes, then braid their hair in one long, loose braid. Next morning they'd do it up in a knot on the back of their heads. Women who had naturally curly hair were at an advantage. They didn't have to put it up on kid curlers every time they washed it.

Before retiring, after dark, the women walked out to the toilet. We had pots under every bed and a slop jar in each room to use during the night.

Next morning, we girls and Gertrude had to take the slop jars around to each room and empty the pots into them, then carry the slop jars out to the privy. We girls had to do that—not company. We thought they should empty their own, but we were never allowed an opinion.

Gertrude laughed at anything distasteful. Those pots—she'd look down inside and squint up her face something awful. She'd squeeze her thumb and forefinger over her nose, "Peee-yeeew!" Together we three marched down the stairsteps, like soldiers off to war, raising our feet high, singing, one as proud as the other, with armored pots in hand, off through the house, out the back door, down the steps, and over the path beyond the garden.

Each morning, after the beds were made and the pots taken out and emptied, rinsed with water from the yard pump, then tilted by the garden fence to sun, Gertrude called everyone to breakfast.

The church services were held inside the house. We had two huge parlors with a double-door opening between. On the other side of the big hall was a large dining room. Sometimes we used it as a sitting room. At mealtime Papa announced, "Welcome to the Lord's house. You come on over here now and get in line and take your plates. Let's all bow our heads and thank the Good Lord for this food he has provided us."

The adults ate their meals at the first table. Kids later. We thought we'd die of hunger before it was our turn! Prayers were always too long. I remember kneeling down, along with the other children, so hungry. I must have been there on my knees for half an hour. Long enough to know that soup beans had been a poor choice for supper the night before.

Mary died with the flu, the first case in Cicero, only four years after she and Papa married. The whole country suffered terrible losses from that influenza epidemic.

Then Papa married Emma Marguerite Jones. She was a widow, had several children, and she was real nice to all of us. We couldn't tell the difference between her children and Papa's; she treated us all alike.

Papa was sixty-five when he got to be a real preacher. He had no special schooling for it. He rejected all offers of cash payment, saying, "You don't owe me anything; the only way you can pay me back is for you to help someone else who is in trouble." Papa was always trying to help someone out of a hole—a hole that was often self-dug, it seemed to me.

Once when Papa had typhoid fever the doctor said to him, "Sometime I'm going to come out here and set till I crack that shell of yours." The doctor knew what that shell was—Papa's odd religious belief, predestination and all, like nobody believed at that time. Thus, "hardshell" Baptist.

He stressed predestination to me all the time. What is to be, is to be, and you can't do a thing about it. From the day you're born, God knows everything that's going to happen to you. He preordains it. And as I grew older, it seemed to me that all things were predetermined. I came to feel more and more that whatever happened was the will of God.

Papa lived to be ninety-one. He was always a farmer and preacher. I remember how gnarled his hands were. Above all, I remember how he liked to argue, mostly religion. He outlived three wives.

I loved Papa but I got irritated with him and others who would try to justify a vice as a "right." Papa had a bad temper. He called it his moral deficiency. Sometimes he said it was his character flaw. His bottle in the horse manger? He claimed every man was entitled to a vice or two, and these were his.

But I felt his teachings and beliefs had far-reaching effects, not just for me but for many, many other folks.

—*Originally published in* Tri Town Topics, *February 21 and 28, 1974, and in* Cicero, Indiana: 1834–1984.

The Passing of the Pot

As far back in childhood
As my memory can go,
One household vessel greets me
That wasn't meant to show.

Beneath the bed 'twas anchored,
Where only a few could see.
But it served the entire family
With equal privacy.

Some called the critter "peggy,"
Some the "thunder mug,"
A few called it a "badger,"
Some called it a "jug."

To bring it in at evening
Was bad enough no doubt.
But heaven help the person
Who had to take it out.

On cold and wintry evenings
It was a useful urn.
And we can all remember
How the cold rim seemed to burn.

The big one was enormous
And would accommodate
A watermelon party
Composed of six or eight.

Sometimes when things were
   rushing
And business extra good
Each took his turn at waiting
And did the best he could.

When the moon was hid behind
   the clouds
To our disgust and shame
We fumbled in the darkness
And slightly missed our aim.

Today this "Modernism"
Relieves me a lot,
And only in my memory
I see that homely pot!

—*Unknown*

The Path Out Back

by
Ralph Waterman

Ralph Waterman, a retired farmer east of Noblesville, was living with his wife Lela in 1978, at the time of this interview. The parents of eleven, the Watermans had many humorous stories of how it was "way back then."

I used an outside toilet longer than an inside one. Me and my oldest boy, Jerry, we didn't like a toilet in the house where we ate, but oh, the wife and daughters were happy with that new bathroom.

People usually made this facility right off the kitchen, where the pantry had been. It was the right size and often the only room available.

But then, I guess you want to hear about our outdoor toilets? They always put them down back by the garden, but not too far back, and away from the well—didn't want our drinking water polluted.

Every house had a grape arbor you either walked under going to the privy or it was somewhere nearby. Grab a handful of those grapes on a dewy morning—mmmm! Winter, dried grapes still hung on the snow-covered vines and birds fed on them. Usually there was a sweet-flavored apple tree or a row of raspberries beside the garden, all good eating.

It wasn't too bad going down there on warm nights. Winter, late, cold and bitter, I'd put my coat, boots, hat, and gloves on over my bib overalls and long underwear, light the coal oil lantern, and start out. Sit down on that icy seat—that was enough to take the urge out of you! Put the lantern between my legs, hover around it to get all the heat I could. I'm here to tell you, I didn't tarry long!

Men had side waist-buttons on their overalls to unbutton, and waist buttons in back of their overalls for their galluses, so they didn't have to take off their heavy coat and sweater to drop their pants. Most times, during the day, to save time, men went to a corner in the barn where the cornshucks and corncobs were handy!

When I was a little guy, nine, our toilet was way down backside the garden. I'd go there, be so cold, I'd just kind of squat back on the seat, and that old frigid wind whistling up through there! I'd had the whooping cough earlier and when you had whooping cough, you coughed and whooped the rest of the winter. I'd sit there. Get so cold. I'd cough and strain. Cough and strain.

Ready to go back in the house, I could hardly pull up my overalls, it hurt so bad down in my belly. I finally hobbled to the house with my hand holding tight that spot.

Grandmother and Grandfather lived with us. I started in through the kitchen and Grandma noticed me. She was nice, heart as big as a pumpkin, but a loud, rough-talking old lady. She roared, "Ralph, what's the matter!"

I said, "I don't know, Grandma. It hurts so bad!"

She bellered, "Let me see!" I pulled my pants down and there was a place sticking out there, big as a football. I had ruptured myself.

She roared, "Oh, my Lord! Come in here in the bedroom." She put me to bed with my feet hooked up over the foot. "You lay there and you lay still! Why didn't you use the pot in the pantry 'stead of goin' out there and freezin' your tail off?"

In about two hours it all went back. But I was always ruptured. Fifty years later I had an operation. I spent enough on trusses and rupture locks to have paid for the surgery.

Do you reckon that's the reason so many people had stomach trouble and piles? Wintertime, put off and put off. It's so cold, I'll just wait till morning.

I can see Grandma yet, every morning hobbling down that path carrying her chamber. It was a stone one, looked like a child's potty, with the handle on the side. She always kept it under the corner of her bed.

Lela, my wife, sent me to town once to buy a *combinet*. I went into the dime store and a young woman came to wait on me. I said, "Lela sent me up here to get a combinet."

The lady looked at me so serious, studied me, "A *com-bin-et*?"

"That's what Lela said to ask for, a *com-bin-et*."

She was looking all around and an older clerk came along, said, "Can I help you?"

"Have we got any *com-bin-ets*?"

"Why, yes, them's slop jars!"

Different families had different pet names for them, like our neighbor lady called hers a thunder mug.

Great Uncle George McCoy lived east of Fishers about a mile. Me and Paw, when I was a kid, often took the horse and buggy from home, east of Noblesville, and we visited him and Aunt Beth.

Uncle George was a shrunken morsel of a man. He was so crippled up from arthritis he couldn't hardly help himself. Aunt Beth had to practically dress him, put on his socks and lace and tie his shoes. He was so thin and feeble, fine white hair, skin dry as paper, and tightly drawn over misshapen bones. I couldn't help but notice his Adam's apple—I had always wanted one of those—in his gaunt neck. It heaved convulsively. His lips quivered.

In his weak voice he said, "Been feelin' queer since breakfast and now I'm chillin'."

Aunt Beth scolded him, "Why didn't you come in straightaway after you did up your chores, 'stead of hangin' 'round talkin' to those hog buyers? You know better than to be so foolish! Now you've fired up your rheumatiz again."

Paw sat backwards on a kitchen chair, arms stretched across the back, close to Uncle George's cot behind the stove, to visit. Uncle George claimed it was good and warm back there and it eased up the pain of his rheumatism. The two visited and spun yarns and Aunt Beth got busy making a batch of cookies.

Well, Uncle George got a sharp pain in his middle. When you had the urge to go, you had no time to tarry. He finally got to his feet and tried to stamp the circulation back into his legs. Aunt Beth helped him pull on his roundabout, and his hat; he got his cane, and out the back door he staggered. Down through the yard and the garden he trudged.

Got there. Sat down. Sat there. Nothing. Came back in the house. The old man, all bent over, stood before us, eyes watering, and a water drop frozen at the end of his nose. He took off his roundabout and his hat, laid his cane down, and pulled his galluses off his shoulders so as to rest more comfortably. A leftover dish of brown gravy sat in the middle of the table. Aunt Beth pushed it back, ready to roll out the cookies, and asked me if I'd already "et." I said we ate at dinnertime. I once asked Maw why they said et instead of ate and she said that's the way old folks often talked.

Uncle George crawled back onto the cot, all the time muttering to himself: "All wind. All wind."

Wasn't too long, another pain struck. He and Aunt Beth struggled with his clothes. He went out. Awhile later he was back. "Blame it, all wind. All wind! Bloody hell, it's colder'n a stepmother's tits out there. It's so cold, wonder it didn't freeze me whatzit off. Oh, well, nothin' there 'cept the skin it come in."

"Now, Paw, you hush such talk around the boy," Aunt Beth scolded. All the time I was holding back giggles.

Dad and Uncle George talked on and on. Again, he swung a crippled leg from the daybed. Stood up. He pulled one of his legs way up in the air and I thought for sure he was going into a jig! "All wind, huh!" he bellered, out of patience with himself. "I'll just show you! You're not going to fool me this time! OOO-ooo-OOO." He stood there, flabbergasted!

That was the funniest thing I'd ever seen in all my twelve years! A pained look spread over Aunt Beth's face. I caught the odor. Dad pointed to our coats. We hurried and pulled them on.

I can see Uncle George and Aunt Beth yet, when we were leaving, she fixing a washpan of hot soapy water, peeling his overall straps down, his shirt, and then his long underwear over his bony shoulders. Such a pitiful sight, the crooked body of the wizened old man. Gaunt as a plucked banty rooster, he was, when he bent down to hide his stark, white nakedness.

As we went out the door I could hear the agitated conversation going on between the two of them, each snapping at the other, then Aunt Beth's sympathetic overtones.

Dad and me crawled up in the buggy, he gave a snap of the lines, a "Giddy up!" and I then let loose with the biggest belly laugh in all my born days!

At school there was a girls' toilet and a boys' toilet. Girls here, boys over there. Bethlehem School. Sometimes the boys ran and grabbed a girl's bonnet, then teased, saying they were going to drop it down in the toilet. "I'm gonna tell the teacher! I'm gonna tell!" He'd yell back, "Cry Baby! Cry Baby!"

There was a big, eighth-grade boy, sissy-type, always wore a suit, shirt, and tie. The rest of us wore blue overalls and everyday shirts. One of the boys said, "Let's play a joke on Melvin. Let's play a joke."

"Well, what kind?"

"We'll get out here in the schoolyard and we'll dig a hole and we'll play a game, 'penny-in-the-hole.' "

Instead of putting a penny in the hole, we went over to the toilet and fished some of that out with a coal shovel. We took it and put it

down in the hole we'd dug and covered it all up with loose dirt. Then we
called: "Hey, Melvin, did you ever play penny-in-the-hole?"

"Naw, but if there's a penny in that hole, I'm gonna have it!" He
got right down on his knees, started digging with both hands, clawing
through it as fast as he could!

By that time we'd beat it! Then he realized what we'd done. He
looked all around for us, those hands covered thick with that stuff! Boy,
was he mad, ready to fight! He walked over to the pump and washed off
good. But he never did beat us up like we thought he might.

There was this city boy who came to our school. Nice sort of a kid.
Fine clothes, even wore dress shoes. We had a feeling he kind of looked
down on the country jakes. Us farm boys decided one day we'd initiate
our city friend.

We said to him, "Let's play the game, 'pee-wee-moe.' "

"How do you do that? I'd like to learn—yeah, I would!" He always
wanted to join in on our fun. A good boy.

We blindfolded him. Told him we were all going to stand in a ring
together. He always wore a beanie. We put it in the middle of the ring.
And then we instructed: "You keep saying, louder each time, 'pee-wee-
moe.' "

He started in. "Pee-wee-moe." Louder! "Pee-wee-moe!" *Louder!*
"PEE-WEE-MOE!"

By now he knew what we were doing in his hat and he yanked the
blindfold off! Oh, he cried like a baby, ran to the teacher and told on us,
but I don't remember that she did anything to us.

One day the teacher made an assignment: "Write a short essay
about something you do to help your family." Sally, with rich parents—
she'd been bragging about their new bathroom—stood up and read hers
to the class: "How to Wash Dishes: You can wash dishes in the sink or in
a basin. But don't wash them in the toilet. It might stop it up."

When I was a grown man, an outhouse was pretty nice in the
spring, especially to go down there early on a Sunday morning, before
time to go to Sunday School, maybe read *The Farmer's Guide*. It had soft
pages like the catalogues. I'd look out across all my fields, sit there,
warm sun shining in, and plan what I was going to plant and sow and
how I was going to rotate my crops. Sat there penciling on a privy board
with the stub of a pencil I carried in my breast overall pocket.

Someone said, "I traded with Sears, Roebuck and Monkey Ward
all my life, and to show their appreciation, they started using all those

slick, colored pages!" Before the next catalogue came out, so we could take the outdated ones from the house, oftentimes that was all that was left, pretty to look at but not for swabbing. I'd sit there and keep wadding it up, to soften it for use, but still there was no softening the slick sheets!

The toilet's side ledges were good to place my work gloves, where they wouldn't fall down the hole.

I'll tell you what was frustrating when I was a kid. When someone kept me waiting outside the door. You're out there yellin' and jumpin' like a frog, while someone's sitting in there reading last year's catalogue. Can't you hurry? You're just sitting there on purpose so I can't come in!

Cal Socks and his nephew, Joe, they lived in Indianapolis, and their job was cleaning out toilets—honey dippers. They'd go down alleys, from one house to the next one. Toilets in towns were usually sandwiched between a woodhouse and a small barn. Most of them had back openings.

One Saturday Joe was down inside there, stooping over, dipping. This old lady rented. She didn't know someone was coming to clean it out and, of course, she couldn't see around back. She ran out there the first thing that morning like her Epsom Salts were chasing her. She sat down. And then!

Joe come out of there yelling and cussing! About that time she saw what was happening and she jumped up and away she ran. If she hadn't, he'd have surely hit her backside with that shovel!

There's this man, he probably wouldn't want me to tell you his name, he came in from the toilet one morning when it was way below zero. "Just about froze my whatsit off!" he complained. "Why didn't you hold it?" his wife laughed. "I did, with both hands like ya hold a baseball bat, but it was what was left over that benumbed me!" he groaned, all the time shaking from the cold. She chuckled, shaking her head in disbelief, "My soul and body!"

When the Roosevelt toilets came along, no flies, no odors. But, only one hole. I think they cost around twenty-five dollars to build. Harvey Johnson built them all through here. Good job. Had to be built according to government specifications.

The pit was so much deeper than the old ones. At least five feet. When they got full to the top, they'd just dig another hole and move it over.

Most people only had them five, ten years, then they were getting bathrooms. And they were put in the pantry, and that's why I didn't use ours for a long, long time—didn't like eating in a room so close to one of them!

Like the little kid, ran home to his parents and shouted, "They have a flusher next door and it's right where the old pantry was. They're doing it in there!" So, when the flusher arrived, the toilet met its doom.

And now, I'm as old, but not as crippled, as Uncle George, about ready to be turned out to pasture, and I'm mighty glad I don't have to hurry down that back path when Mother Nature calls!

—*This story originally appeared in* Tri Town Topics, March 1 *and* 8, *1978, and is included in* Cicero, Indiana: 1834–1984.

Honey Dipping and Manure Hauling

by
Elmer Scherer

Elmer Scherer, at ninety-five, was Cicero's oldest citizen at the time of this interview. He, along with his wife, Edna, told his tale of how sanitation was carried out in the villages during the early part of the century.

Men who went through towns cleaning toilets in the early years were called "honey dippers."

I'm ninety-five, oldest man in Cicero, and I remember them well. I'll bet over half the people reading this have never heard of them—a very important part of a town's sanitation.

The man who cleaned them at Noblesville hauled it out there on the big field where the golf course is at Forest Park now. Oh, that raised the best corn crop every summer. And he had enough business to keep him busy year-round.

Sam Edwards was a honey dipper in Cicero. One time he was cleaning a toilet out up on Cass Street. He dug a bunch of speed wrenches up, the kind they used in garages. He said to me, "Elmer, know where these came from?" He went ahead telling me the boy's name that stole 'em from Whistler's Garage, and the law was about to catch him so he threw them down in a toilet. Sam said if I'd clean 'em up I could have 'em. Whistler had replaced 'em by now. I've got 'em here yet. Had an antique buyer say if I decided to give 'em up, let him know. I won't tell you the boy's name. He had a wonderful mother.

One time the Lutheran Church had a harvest market up there at Lively's Store. All at once the cigar box of money was gone. Bob Wiggs was town marshal. He put me on the front door, said, "Now, Elmer, don't let nobody in or nobody out. Somebody took the cash box."

That boy was there at the time and they caught him red-handed, and not one of those people in the store had seen him do it!

Sam had a one-horse wagon, looked a whole lot like the drays. He threw a layer of straw in the bottom of the bed to keep it from dripping out along the way. The bed was big enough to hold one job and then he'd go spread it on a farm.

He pulled up close behind each toilet with his horse and wagon. He had a long-handled shovel, like a dipper on the end of it. He'd tip over the toilet, then he'd dip down in there, git a dipper full, lay it over the wagon bed, and dump it. If the toilet was real rickety he'd take off a board from the back and clean it out from there, rather than tip the toilet over. I never knew Sam to leave a mess.

Us boys took shortcuts through town, down alleys. Behind some of them my nose told me which were the dirty ones! Of course, they all smelled bad. Some worse than others. Most folks had a sack of lime sitting there and they'd dip into it and scatter lime all around below. They did that as soon as Sam cleaned out, to keep the odor and flies down.

One time Sam asked Roy Byers, "Will you come and help me do my honey dipping? I pay good. I'm way behind."

Roy took off his hat, scratched his head, said, "I don't know. I'll have to need money a whole lot more than I do now to stomach that!"

Sam said he got used to the foul odors. Like at the rendering company, at Noblesville, why they said those fellers could cut the hide off a horse, been dead for several days, and sit down beside it, and eat their dinner!

Sam cleaned toilets out once a year, depending on how many in a family and how deep the pit. He charged a dollar.

They never put that on gardens. Claimed lettuce and cabbage picked up the taste. Onions rot bad. Too rich.

One time, when I was a kid, we were down there about Allisonville, driving home in our horse and buggy. One of my sisters nudged Mama and cried, "I have to go to the toilet bad!" Always, on the way back, someone would be sure to have to go and they couldn't wait. Papa, in a hurry to get home, didn't want to stop. Tears were rolling down her cheeks. "If we don't find a toilet, I'll wet my pants!"

When we came up to a farmhouse, Mother ran in and asked the lady if we could use their privy. "Why, sure, honey, help yourself!" she said, in such a kind voice. Folks always did that on trips.

There was no catalogue to tear sheets out of to wipe with, but down on the floor was a box of corncobs. They used to say they put red and white cobs both in the box. Red cobs came from yellow corn and white cobs from white corn. They used the red cob first, then the white cob to see if they needed to use another red cob.

I suppose with four kids they'd have spent most of the trip back home stopping on the way. One neighbor solved the problem. Her parents lived several miles from them. She pushed aside the piece of old carpeting in the back of the buggy, and she lifted a thin, flat piece of tin that covered a hole on the floor. Then, propping both carpet and cover back with her foot, she motioned each to take a turn. She'd pull the baby's diaper down and hold him over the raggedy hole. Why, of course, if all the others were taking their turn, the baby wanted to take his. All the while the others were looking back, down the graveled road, to see what had passed on through that hole.

Folks traveling through on trips looked ahead for toilets out in the open at schoolhouses or churches.

The ultimate in elegance was a laid-brick or poured-concrete foundation. When the deep cavity had reached its capacity, a new hole was dug by the men of the family, and with their own muscle power, they lifted the wooden building from its former station and placed it over a freshly dug pit. They filled up the old site with dirt to the ground level. That spot became an Eden for growing flowers.

Womenfolk always wanted a honeysuckle vining up over it 'cause the white blossoms smelled so sweet and knocked out the foul odors. But honeysuckle draws bees—hundreds of 'em! No, don't plant honeysuckle, not with the activity at the family toilet, or the comings and goings of little feet.

I'd hurry to the toilet, door hooked inside. "It's only me. Please hurry!" I'd cry. One or the other sisters spent a lot of time out there. When Mom caught them lingering, I can hear her: "What's taking you so long? What ails you?"

Pop used the mud boat to clean our toilet. One year he went down along the south side of the house, in the wheat, throwing loads of it by hand across the field. When that wheat headed out, it was the prettiest red color. It looked just like a bordered rug with the long, red ridge, four-five feet wide, around the field where that had been spread. The wheat grew much taller and the heads were a lot heavier. Oh, that stuff was rich!

I s'pect I was twelve when I started hauling manure for Pop. We used a four-tined pitchfork. The manure wouldn't slip and fall through the prongs. It was easy to pitch up on the wagon. Now, if we used a five-tined fork, we'd have a forkful so heavy we'd have trouble lifting it or getting it to slip off.

I was feeding the cattle one night inside the box stall. Pop had a young bull. He came in and when I turned around, the bull looked at me and went Brr! He missed me. I might not be here today to tell you about it if he hadn't! I yelled and Pop came running with the pitchfork. I tell you, Pop loosened that bull's ribs up for him! Never, ever trust a bull! They've killed or crippled more than one man or boy. Now a male cow was a very necessary animal on a farm and we learned early to respect and be on guard around him.

Mom and the women of the family never said the word "bull." It was "the gentleman cow"—and then, only in the privacy of our home.

We boys always cleaned out the ammonia-smelly litter from the chicken house. That'd open your head up if you had a cold! Pop made roosts to raise and we'd scoop out from under them. If they were lousy, and they always were, the lice crawled all over us and we'd be an itchy mess. After we had cleaned them, we painted all the roosts and the back walls with Black Flag louse killer. Then, that night (it was usually Saturday when we were out of school) we took a hot bath with lye soap.

We used a gravel bed to haul out the manure. We'd take it to the high knolls, pitch it off by hand, spreading it to cover the farm. What a job, day after day!

When Pop bought a new Studebaker farm wagon, they gave him a big umbrella to hook onto it, to make a shade. Us boys went up in the haymow, crawled out on the comb of the roof. Brother Harry, the aggressor, went first. He gave a big jump down with the umbrella, like it was a parachute. The thing turned wrong-side-out and Harry lit knee-deep, unhurt, in the manure pile. Dad repaired the umbrella and we were able to enjoy its wonderful shade while in the hot sun, working in the fields.

Bob Myers came and dynamited the stumps out of the new ground. Pop had us there with a crosscut saw, sawing the wood up in stove lengths. Bob said, "No wonder boys leave the farm if that's what they've always got to do. Such drudgery!"

I guess Pop got to thinking about the manure. When Bob had a farm sale and sold all his tools, Pop bought his Kemp manure spreader. Boy! We could just load that thing up, drive around the field with the team of horses, and it unloaded itself automatically! Then hauling manure wasn't so bad, when we could look forward to that easy ride!

Cornstalk bedding matted down. It took a mattock to tear it away. It didn't lie there long enough to rot good, and they just kept throwing on more when it was needed, and oh, try to pull that loose!

Rye straw didn't deteriorate like oats straw. It was stringy and hard to handle. Rye grows much taller than oats or wheat. Oats is soft and is the best. Wheat is a good deal like rye, but not as tough.

Pop used the straw from the strawpile to bed with. We'd go out and pull it loose and bring in a load to the barn and bed the mangers.

We built a cattle shed, eighteen-by-twelve-by-eight feet tall, using poles all around. The cattle could get under there for winter protection, or Pop could pull a wagon or tools underneath. Fixed it to face south for the winter sun, and so they could drive a team through. They thrashed straw on top, making better protection.

One winter our cattle kept reaching way up and out from one side, until finally the whole stack rolled over and caught a coupla cows. Fortunately they were close enough to the edge, they didn't smother.

We hauled away rotted straw from around the strawpile each spring, where the cattle had run it down. That wasn't as hard to manage as stable manure. Cooler out there, too.

Noah, my young brother, shoved a pitchfork through his big toe when we were hauling manure. Pop took him to the house and got some brook water and Mom mixed lye in it. She used good wood ashes to make the lye. Noah put his foot in there to soak so he wouldn't get blood poison. Never did even get sore!

All us boys went barefoot in summertime till we were real good size. That juicy brown manure oozed up through our toes and we got toe itch. Toes'd get real sore, raw underneath, crack and bleed, skin peel off. That smarted!

After we washed our feet at night, Mom would take a strand of wool yarn rubbed in tallow, tie it around the toe, up through that groove where it was cracked, so that it would have a chance to heal. Put a clean yarn on each night till it was all well.

When you think back, you could get a real good pair of work shoes for four-fifty. That sounds like they were cheap, but I'd work for a whole month for ten dollars! Half a month's pay today would make shoes quite expensive!

No kid wore shoes from May Day to Labor Day, except on Sunday, and then only under noisy protest. By late August and September, the bottoms of our feet were so tough they could stand almost anything. Just before school started, Ma took us to the shoe store. Following the bare-foot summer days, the new shoes were like hasps on my feet, but in their tissue wrappings, in that nice shoe box, how good the shoes smelled!

I have such precious childhood memories to live out my life! But when I think back, the toilet flies and odors, the catalogues and the newspapers, straw or wheat bedding, days on end of manure-hauling— I've had enough of the smell of that. I don't ever want to go back to those "good old days," only to reminisce!

—*This story originally appeared in* Tri Town Topics, *January 11,1979, and is included in* Cicero, Indiana: 1834–1984.

My Dad, the Piano Tuner

by
Monroe Whitmoyer

The Fred Whitmoyers farmed along the Noblesville-Cicero Pike just af-
ter the turn of the century. Fred added to his income by tuning the many pi-
anos in homes, churches, and schools in Hamilton County.

My dad, Fred Whitmoyer, first became interested in piano tuning
when he was around forty, just after the turn of the century.

He'd bought my mother a new, expensive piano. As I remember, it
cost between four to five hundred dollars. It was very heavy, made of
oak, ornately carved, with beautiful gold letters on the front just over
the keyboard spelling out *American Home, Sears, Roebuck & Co.*

There were two reasons for its purchase: first, Mama was musical;
second, in those years of the early 1900s, children who did not take music lessons were castigated. It was never Mama's intention to have her
children criticized. Other luxuries a struggling farm family could do
without, but they were going to have a musical education!

More than anything, though, Mama had wanted a piano ever since
she and Dad had been married. She sang endlessly while doing all her
household tasks.

While Dad was trying to figure out where the money would come
from to buy a piano, I heard him and a neighbor talking. The man
frowned, shook his head, and complained, "My wife is always wanting
money. Last week she wanted fifty dollars. This week she is asking for
seventy." Dad asked, "What does she do with all that?"

"I don't know," the husband replied, "I never give it to her!"

Dad hauled the piano home from the Noblesville freight office on
the farm wagon pulled by his team of horses. Mama cried, "My cup
runneth over!"

Mama didn't know one note of music from another, but she could
play anything she heard, by ear. The next week or two, every time I
walked in the back door from school, or was doing my chores, I'd hear

her rippling flourishes over the mother-of-pearl keys of her beautiful new piano.

Dad grumbled he didn't have a clean shirt for three weeks after he brought that piano home, and that he ate so much mush and milk his brains turned soft.

"Music is food for the soul," Mother announced loftily. Dad's mouth folded in a determined line, and he said tartly, "Tell the Lord it don't do much for my empty stomach!"

This piano had a bench, a nice place to keep all the music. Pianos that had no benches, had stools. When I first started taking lessons, over at Grandma's, I'd wind the stool up almost as high as it would go, to reach the keyboard. Teacher beat time as I played. My feet dangled.

We cousins all loved to whirl on that stool. "My turn," even the littlest would say, to be first, and he usually got his way. I'd belly-flop across the stool, stretched out flat, then someone would give my legs a big push, to give a fast spin.

Once my sister, Anna, went flying off the stool, clear across the room, and banged her head against the wall. She hurt bad, I know, but she didn't cry very loud for fear we'd be banished from the room. "You did it on purpose," she was crying, accusing me in whispers. "You wanted to throw me off!" I really hadn't, but sometimes boys get carried away!

Dad wondered how he was going to meet that added expense after he bought it. Lately he had been worrying—what could he do to supplement his farm income? He picked up the newspaper at noon one day. I still have that big half-page advertisement: "Niles-Bryant School of Piano Tuning, Correspondence Courses, Niles, Michigan." Pictured there was a man tuning, with family members gathered all around him.

Dad sent for the course of study. He answered the questions and sent them back in. They were graded, then he'd get his papers back, with another assignment and questions, about every two or three weeks.

It took a year to do it all. He graduated and got a diploma. I ought to have that diploma here somewhere....

I wouldn't have any idea what the course cost. Wouldn't think it was over fifty dollars, if that much.

Dad could chord. That was exciting 'cause we didn't usually see grown men playing a piano. My sister, Anna, and I took lessons from Blanche Brock, an old maid. We went to her home. Later she married a man by the name of Moore. We also took lessons from Mrs. Gray. And I took singing lessons. I tried everything!

Dad used to go in and sit down and chord—sing and play. One song he always sang was "Gooseberry pie, says I/Since the time of the war/Nothing so good, and delicious/As gooseberry pie!"

All little girls, and a few boys, took piano lessons as a matter of course. Probably cost a quarter, not more than fifty cents per lesson. By the time the girls were old enough to be wearing their hair up and their dresses down to their ankles, they were playing for school and church programs.

After Dad got his diploma Mother said, "Fred, I don't think you ought to practice the tuning on our new piano."

So he went out and bought a cheap old Kurtzman, I think it was, one of those great, big, old, square pianos—looked like a baby grand, but square, had four massive legs under it. Cost fifteen dollars. The strings ran flat, instead of up and down. He kept it in the dining room over in a corner, and that's what he learned his tuning on.

Most people would write him a note on a penny postcard: "Come and tune my piano the first chance you get." Folks nearby would phone. Not long distance. That was for emergencies and cost extra. We had a Deming phone. Deming was an independent phone company, owned by Marvin Jessup. Three dollars a month with the privilege of talking free to Noblesville and Cicero.

Dad tuned pianos all over this county, in homes, churches, and schools. And some, way down in Rush County where his niece lived. She was a piano teacher.

Seems to me like he charged three-dollars-fifty for a tuning. He was an honest man. If it didn't need tuning, he told them so, but they usually waited until it was badly out-of-key. He could work-over three pianos a day and he made big money. Ten dollars a day!

He was kept busy early in the year when the ladies did their spring housecleaning. He still farmed, so he did the tuning on rainy days when he couldn't be in the fields, and some through the winter.

Kids liked to stand around and watch as he went about his job, always back out of his way. It was a fascination for them, seeing him work with the big solid front boards off the piano and all those wires inside.

If he was there at the noon hour, the family wanted him to come on to the kitchen and sit down and eat dinner with them. Kids'd argue over who'd get to sit next to him! Our family questioned Dad when he got home that night: "What did you have for dinner?" I could always expect a good meal, too, when I went along. Sometimes, after a long day, on the way home, we'd eat the food Mama prepared for us, in case we weren't asked to join them. That night, after the chores were done up, we were ready for Mama's big supper.

Dad came home one night, after tuning a piano in Noblesville, and sat down to eat supper. He said he'd been invited to eat with the family at noon. After they'd washed up, the husband was looking out the kitchen window when he said, "There goes that woman our next-door neighbor is so crazy about!" The man's wife flew to the window to look. "Why," she said, "that's his wife!"

"Of course!" he laughed.

When Dad first started tuning pianos, he went by horse and buggy. We had a car by the time he was going to Rushville, but he never learned to drive, so I drove for him. We went early and worked late.

All those sounding boards are made out of hard maple. The pins are tapered as they go into that wood and they fit real tight. When you tighten them down, they stay there. In time, they will loosen up a bit. Sometimes if a piano sits against an outside wall or in a cold room all winter, that will cause them to go down. And you didn't want to set one where the sun would hit it. That weakened the works and damaged the surface.

One Noblesville rich man called Dad late in April. He said, "I have just come back from wintering in Florida with a married woman. Had a big time!" Dad was startled and asked shyly, "Well, well, who was she?" His reply: "My wife!"

Did you ever see one of these? It's Dad's tuning fork. I think this one is C. Looks like a big dinner fork with two, heavy, three-inch prongs. Hit that, and now, listen. Perfect C pitch every time. Singers and school teachers used a tuning fork when they didn't have a piano to tune to.

Dad would start on C on the piano and tune it by the tuning fork, then he'd know how to tune each key a little bit higher or lower. I think he had another fork but don't remember what key it was.

Rainy, or hot-humid summer weather, a certain note or two would stick and it wouldn't play. That really irritated a musician. Dad fixed it. Years later, when folks got electricity, women put an electric light bulb down in there to take care of the moisture.

The felts, where they hit the strings, would eventually get kind of hard. He had a little tool, with tiny sharp-like needles on it, and he would prick to bring the felt out again.

He threaded a felt through the strings to deaden the sound on the other keys while he was working. There's other red felt threaded back there. Mice or moths liked to get in and chew away. That had to be replaced.

Oh, how upset Mama got when mice crawled through the little holes under the foot pedals, carried in paper and trash, made nests and had their families! Mama would take off the big bottom front board, clean the nests out—that smelled bad— then she'd dust good-smelling talcum powder down in there, and plug up the pedal holes with corncobs. I'd set traps there to catch the mice who'd automatically go back to their nesting place. Women had mice and moths to constantly contend with. They were glad when they could buy moth spray to use inside there. Some put moth balls or crystals, but that always stunk the whole room up.

And, some places Dad took the whole action out, the inside works of the piano, and pulled it into the room, to work on it. He'd take the front off, unscrew a few screws and it would all lift out. There's certain things he did to get way back behind it, like maybe put in a new hammer.

Dad brought all kinds of news and stories home at night to tell us. One man always said, "I see you're back workin' on our *pie-anner.*" A lady laughed, "I didn't expect you quite so soon after I sent my penny postcard for you to come and tune our *pie-annie.*"

There was a little boy, as full of rebellion as Uncle John's old mules, every time his mother asked him to perform, he'd stumble through the simplest pieces and jump up and run off the minute he could escape. Or he'd use the loud pedal, banging out "Chopsticks," until his distraught mother sent him out to hoe in the garden. "I'll never be able to tickle the ivories," he'd grumble.

At one house a dainty little girl, whose mother was a piano teacher, was always sitting on the stool doing scales and finger exercises when Dad went in. The mother would give Dad a recital, after he'd finished tuning. Her fingers, enormously arched, swept up and down the keyboard. She amazed him!

It's been over sixty years since Dad tuned pianos and I don't remember it all. He stayed at it for a couple of decades. It's a nerve-wracking job and he began getting irritable. Mama finally told him, "Now, Fred, you're just going to have to quit." He hated to, because he loved the work and he met and enjoyed so many people through his piano tuning business. As for me, piano practice never made perfect, nor even a really good musician of me, but it did suffice to give me many hours of pleasure during my lifetime!

More than anything, I remember the enjoyment our whole family got, Dad and Mama each on a piano, and Anna and I joining in singing, at our very frequent music sessions!

—*This story originally appeared in* Tri Town Topics, *December 11 and 18, 1975.*

A Wake: Vigil Over a Corpse Before Burial
A Conversation Around the Kitchen Table

by
**Ada and Harold Knapp, Pauline and Edgar Evans,
and Lois and Edward "Bud" Costomiris**

*In the late 1980s, Pauline and Edgar Evans, sisters Ada Knapp and
Lois Costomiris, and their husbands, Harold Knapp and Bud Costomiris,
described the old pioneer custom, now long-gone, of vigils held after deaths in
farm and village homes.*

Pauline: Way back, when a person died, first, they stopped all the
striking clocks. The undertaker came and hung a wreath of flowers on
the front door. Folks going by knew someone had died there.

Edgar: They tied the wreath with a big ribbon—white for the
young, and a purple or black for the old folks.

Lois: In real early days, as soon as there was a death, neighbor
women came in. There was frenzied activity as they covered all the
looking glasses, turned the wicks of the lamps down low in respect for
the dead, stopped the clocks, emptied vases—the belief that if water is
left in them, the soul of the dead may drown before it reaches purgatory.
They watched the chimney smoke; the direction it drifted showed the
place of the next death. When a person was "very low" they always felt,
if he could last till the sun came up, he'd have a better chance to pull
through. Oh, those trying, dark, night hours of waiting!

Pauline: They always embalmed them at home, but they did go to
the undertakers to pick out the casket. Whenever anyone died, neighbors would come in, make room, usually clearing out a corner in the
parlor, and set the casket there. Sometimes they'd use a downstairs bedroom, take down the bed, move furniture out, and bring in church or
funeral home folding chairs. A small house, everyone helped take everything from one bedroom and pile stuff into another.

Edgar: I can shut my eyes and see my grandfather, he died in 1918,
see him laid out across the corner of that bedroom.

The family would always go on to bed. Neighbors or relatives sat up
all night to watch that cats and flies didn't get in under the mosquito
netting, to the corpse. I don't know why they never closed the lid. They

lay there three days. At a wake, the hours passed with agonizing slowness.

Pauline: Seems there were funerals all the time! Child mortality was high. Most persons died in their own homes, surrounded by friends and relatives. TB was common. When any of us went to set up for the wake or funeral, Pop would remind us: "Now don't you dare drink no water. Tuberculosis is in that old dug well there. You drink before you go, and when you make coffee, boil it until it's thick enough to cut. Then it's safe."

Neighbors cooked food and brought it. At the wake, 'long about midnight, one of 'em would go to the kitchen and make a pot of coffee and then everybody would eat pie and cake. About every twenty minutes or so, go in to see if cats were in the coffin. For some reason, especially before the days of embalming, cats seemed to be attracted to a corpse—even the barnyard cats.

My first time, I reckon I was fourteen, Mother's health wasn't good, so I went along with Dad. It was an old woman in the coffin and we had to keep talking or we'd go to sleep. We'd visit, tell stories. Old folks always talked about the "olden days." After that first time, I enjoyed it.

Lois: Every few weeks was overhung with sadness. Death was everywhere, and visited young and in-between as often as old. Consumption, fits, diphtheria, growths, pneumonia, blood poisoning, apoplexy, heart trouble. Like the old preacher said, "There are a lot of mysteries in life we don't understand. We have to live by God's timetable."

I was concerned about deaths of the young; why does God claim youth? I read this once: "There's a reaper whose name is Death/And with his sickle keen/He reaps the bearded grain at a breath/And the flowers that grow in-between."

Grandma Venable always said, "I want someone to cry at my funeral, even if they have to sprinkle black pepper around. I want flowers, even if it is a bouquet of dandelions!"

Her son, Andrew, a good Christian fellow, died suddenly from a heart attack when he was only seventeen. Why? Why? With his whole life ahead of him. A few days after the funeral a tribe of gypsies came to her door. They could see she was grieving. When told she'd lost her son, they consoled her: "It rained and rained, didn't it? He's saved. Those were tears from Heaven. Blessed is the corpse the rain falls on. May you rest in peace!" Grandma had a kinder feeling toward gypsies after that.

Pauline: A cousin of Pop's, Albert Miller, was going with a Catholic girl. Her brother died and Albert went to the wake. I guess the Irish Catholics used to carry on, drink, dance, sing. Long about midnight they all got to drinking, most of 'em pretty well polluted, and they said, "Well, let's go in the parlor now and celebrate." Albert was a little late arriving. He told us later, "When I went in there, they had that guy standing up in the corner, straight as a rifle barrel. With a flourish, they introduced me to him! My skin was covered with goosebumps, from my toes to my scalp, hair bristled. Right then I took my hat and coat and I headed West!"

Harold: Ada put all three of our little boys in their red wagon and pulled them over across the road to Blackfords' to visit with their boy, David, when he was real sick. Wasn't it a ruptured appendix he died from? He enjoyed watching Don, Fred, and Dennis playing. After he died, summertime, us men sat outdoors at the wake. Ada stayed home with our sons and prepared food for the next day. We probably got loud, talking, anything to keep awake.

Pauline: We'd get breakfast for the family the next morning, then clean up the kitchen and go home. Someone else would come and look after the other meals during the day. It was a job, to get the work all done, callers coming and going. Most all the funerals were in the homes. A few in the church. Then, after the services, some of us went in and put everything back in place and cleaned up. There was generally washing to do. And ironing.

Lois: I was twelve when our neighbor lady died during childbirth. Her first. Mother walked us kids up the road to call. They whispered that her baby was tucked under her arm. I'd have wanted my baby tucked up in my arm. Heartbreaking! I remember once seeing this engraving on a stone at the graveyard, "Beloved Wife. Died Giving Life."

Harder to understand were the "useless deaths," as with Clyde Adams and his little four-year-old son, Carsie. A man driving at high speed ran a red light, hit the Adams' car broadside, killing the two instantly. Left to mourn was his doting wife, Beulah, and Jim, Becky, Annie, Joe, and Barbara.

I was in the home when a loudmouth came shoving his way through. Supposedly a preacher. He sat down at the kitchen table with the sobbing family, demanding they quit their grieving. "You all should be happy! They are in the hands of the Lord. Their work on earth is over." And on and on he went. I turned and saw Clyde's and Carsie's gum boots sitting side-by-side on the back porch. Sad memories all around. How could anyone be so uncaring?

Ada: Each woman braced herself against the day she would have to see a little grave in the family plot at the cemetery.

Harold: Wayne and Joanne Nightenhelser's baby, he must have been six months old. He was such a pretty little thing.

Lois: Do you remember what happened to him? Mother said women always worried about losing a child until he passed his second summer. Summer complaint.

Edgar: I made hay with a neighbor, Charlie Crooks' boy, Howard, on Saturday. On Sunday evening, driving past there, we saw a lot of cars parked around in the barnyard. They said Howard and Myron Thompson went swimming up at Bishop Park and Howard drowned. Myron never got over it.

Pauline: They always had flower girls, usually neighbors, Sunday School kids, and cousins, to take the flowers after the service from the room to the hearse, then from hearse to the grave. Six adult or young men, usually family members or neighbors, carried the heavy casket.

Ada: There were flowers, yes, but not as many as today. Women saved baskets from other funerals and, in summertime, someone in the neighborhood usually had garden flowers and made up bouquets. Helen McGill's dad raised acres of the most gorgeous gladioluses. People took their baskets and he made arrangements for a small fee. Later, and even yet, we'd go around to the neighbors and take up money for flowers, then buy them from a florist. Sprays back then had huge lavender, blue, or pink ribbons with gold printing: *Sister...Beloved Mother...Rest in Peace.*

Lois: Women took those beautiful satin ribbons and made them into a crazy quilt, using fancy embroidery stitches around each block after they were sewn together. In most homes where there were older people, I'd see one of those throws spread over a corner of the sofa in the parlor.

When I collected flower money, one old man was always willing to give. He'd say, "Never know when I'll be next."

Seems like they usually took up a dime or a quarter at each house in earlier times. Get a pretty spray or basket of flowers for around two dollars.

For the burial, a dead child was usually dressed in white. Men were clothed in their one-and-only dark Sunday suit. Women in their best dress, or something pretty picked out at the store or undertaker's. Sometimes it was a robe. I was glad we didn't have to be in mourning for a year afterward, and have to wear black, like in the olden days. The men had a black band around their hat.

In 1944, when I was twenty-three, Ada Hull, Mother's cousin, asked me to make a white velvet robe to be ready for her very elderly mother's burial, thinking she'd be needing it in a couple of months. I picked out a suitable pattern and the fabric. It was a loose, belted wrap-around—there was no way she could be fitted. She looked so nice in the white robe, with her beautiful white hair. Wanda, three, saw me mulling over in my mind how I'd use up the leftover scraps. She kept insisting, "Make me one like that lady's, Mommy!"

I was told that sometimes a family was so terribly poor or had had so many misfortunes, they didn't have anything decent to be buried in. Some in the community furnished them, or helped to make something. The garment was often made from cloth donated by friends or neighbors, then a seamstress went to work.

They said if a man belonged to the Masons when he died, the Masons looked after his family—got them money to live on, food, and clothing. The community people, seeing them in need, took turns helping out. "Oh, it affected everyone," one lady said. "We were close to everybody that died."

Edgar: Raymond Shaffer's dad was the undertaker at Arcadia. He also owned the furniture store. Only man in town who always wore a necktie and shaved everyday. He had a big old horse-drawn hearse. I remember seeing the men, in their black suits and big, old, black top hats, sitting up high on the seat on top of that, drawn by his beautiful black team, swinging black tassles on their heads, going west past our house to West Grove or Hinkle Creek cemeteries. The long processions of carriages, moving so slow, creaking of wheels and harness, were a common sight and sound, up to about the early twenties.

Ada: What did the hearse look like at that time?

Harold: The sides and back-end were glass, big, heavy buggy wheels rolled along on springs, tongue in front with two beautiful horses hitched to it. Black curtains tied back from its glass windows. Some had dark red velvet curtains. Fancy-work all around the top. Probably had room enough for all the flowers inside with the corpse. They said Shaffer had two high-stepping teams. One was glossy black with white-starred foreheads, and the other snow white, sporting a highly polished leather harness, with its silver and gold trim.

Pauline: I remember seeing a lady passenger riding inside, her face covered by a long, black veil. She laid it back with both of her black-gloved hands when she saw us, and waved her white lacy hanky at us.

Lois: Bud and I had six kids; three were teenagers with summer jobs and after-school activities. We were in desperate need of a second vehicle. One day I saw a nice, long, white hearse in Cicero's used-car lot, its price painted in black, bold numbers across the windshield— very reasonable. I pointed it out to the girls, Wanda, Becky, and Toni. They about died! The look on their faces conveyed the thought, what will Mom think of next? The three little boys, Dennis, John, and Bill yelled, "Yeah, Mom, yay!" No one knew, at the time, it was a forerunner of the "soon to appear" station wagon! Needless to say, we didn't buy it. Not much later, and for years, we had station wagons piled with kids— ours and neighbors'.

Edgar: One bald-headed man in our neighborhood, he'd been real sick, went down in their cellar, put a rifle in his mouth, and shot himself through his skull. At the time we were in a back field cutting wheat. Somebody come running, said, "Gotta get over there quick, right quick, something's happened!" So we quit cutting wheat and went. Bob Ross and Albert Leap, they were working on the thrashing machine, they went. Bob Ross hurried down into the cellar, said he opened the door, and the man's dog, an Airedale, made a lunge at him. Scared him to half to death!

I watched as Frank Evans, the undertaker, pumped that blood out and then the embalming fluid into his veins. My first experience. Then, when the embalming fluid started coming out where the blood was, he knew the fluid had been all 'round. He had some trouble at the bullet hole, packing that so it would go on through and not run out. All done, the man on the cooling board, four, five of us took him upstairs.

As he worked, Frank was telling me that he'd always come just as soon as he got the word—had to get it done before rigor mortis set in. You see, after the body'd get stiff, it was awful hard to do anything. Then, go right away to dressing the corpse. If it was a man, usually the wife or sons wanted to dress him. And women, some of the ladies— daughters, friends. A mother always wanted one last chance to care for her child.

Frank said they'd massage the person's cheeks to get the eyes closed, and then put a silver coin over each eye, under the eyelid, to keep 'em shut. Lot of times, with the homemade fixing and the jostling laying him in the coffin, then taking to graveyard, the eyes'd pop open. Silver coins were preferred 'cause copper might turn the skin green.

Bud: Grandpa said that no matter what anyone was doing, when they heard of a death in the neighborhood, everyone quit and went to help. Hear dinner bells ringing other than at mealtime, it meant an emergency—someone was needing help or had died. Grandpa Venable told me that when the horses heard that dinner bell gonging, they knew and they turned right around there in the field where they were, and headed for home. The men didn't go back to the fields until after the burial.

He told me that in town the church bells tolled. The number of times the bell rang depended on the age of the person who had died. You'd count the bells tolling, oh, so s-l-o-w, dong-dong-dong, and you'd know exactly how old that person was. It took a long time when the person was old, and sometimes they'd lose count.

On a farm, the cows were still there, needing to be milked, the sheep, chickens, and hogs fed. Neighbor men came at feeding time. Several sat around the kitchen table, drinking coffee, and remembering the man's or woman's kindnesses, lamenting the death.

I'd always heard how a dog would carry on when his master passed away, but I questioned it. When Grandpa died, his tiny dog—he was Grandpa's little buddy—he just howled and howled, a cry unlike that of his normal bark. He whined something terrible until they took him clear away and gave him to someone. They were afraid, if they brought him back later, he'd still miss Grandpa so much.

Ward Applegate told about several men sitting up at a wake. He didn't say who'd died. There was Elmer Heinzman, Al Jacobs, and Ward, and I don't remember who else was there. Old Al Jacobs ran out of chewing tobacco and he found some Prince Albert pipe tobacco up on top of the kitchen cabinet. He poured a bit into the palm of his hand, then rolled it into a wad and took it to chew. Ward whispered to Elmer, "Let's fix him up some good chewin'!" They walked out to the barn, got some dried horse manure and pulverized it real fine between their fingers, then went into the house and put it into the Prince Albert can, shook it up good. I guess Al had been in with the corpse while this was going on. Next time Al took a chew, he'd spit, sputter, but he never did catch on. He was the kind of man who liked nothing better than pulling a playful joke on a friend. Now the prank was on him.

Many superstitions and ghost stories had their beginnings at old-time wakes. The doctor would hold a looking glass over a person's mouth, to see if there was life. If it didn't fog over, he was pronounced dead. Before the time of embalming, some of the dead suddenly woke up at the church, to live on for several years. He told of a neighbor who was shot during a fight and died with his eyes open.

I remember reading about General Lee being born after his mother had died. Folks, looking in on her the next day, saw that she had moved. She came out of the coma and lived for years.

Lois: Charlie Gilkey, Bob Gilkey's dad, told about sitting up when a neighbor's young wife died. They had several small children. After the man had been in bed awhile, they heard him carrying on so in his bedroom, moaning and groaning so frightful. Thinking he was sick, they went in to see. He cried, "I was justa worryin', me with all these little ones, if I should git married again right away."

Bud: There was a wreck over by Sheridan. A man plowed his automobile head-on into the front of a hearse. On impact, the coffin rolled out the back and the corpse slid onto the gravel road. Folks going by stopped, backed up, and looked in shocked disbelief!

Even when they did start embalming, so many couldn't afford it, so a corpse could be kept only one day. Someone told me about this young lady that died. Carrying her out on a stretcher to the horse-drawn wagon, they bumped the gate post. Then she moved, as though finding a better resting position. She wasn't dead! Years later, when she did die, they were again carrying her out. Her husband called, "Watch you don't bump the gate post!"

Pauline: One farmer was so exasperated when the ambulance took his very sick wife away. Folks back then only went to the hospital to die. He brooded, "I cain't figger why she got so sick; she's never been off the place!"

Lois: Agnes Haworth, our sweet little old neighbor, was full of local lore. She told about one lady always going to the viewing of a woman corpse. She'd talk sympathetically with the widower; then, as he turned to speak to someone else, she'd slip this note in the man's coat pocket: "When you get lonesome, come and see me!" For so long people wondered why a new widower was seen so soon with this woman.

Harold: Early years, they put two poles across the grave and placed the coffin on them. They put plow lines or ropes under the coffin and four men let it all down into the grave. When it was in place, the lines were withdrawn. The preacher scooped up a handful of soil, and sprinkled it on top of the big gray box, and he said, "Ashes to ashes, dust to dust. The Lord giveth and the Lord taketh away. Blessed be the name of the Lord." The grave diggers then picked up their shovels and began throwing heaps of dirt into the hole while the family stood by watching, crying helplessly, until the last shovelful.

Really, I think the greatest thing that ever happened was when they started taking the bodies to a funeral home. The family, if they couldn't sleep, would relax at home. The graveside services aren't as long, now. They fill the hole after the mourners leave.

Pauline: When one of the Cooks up here died, it was late March and we'd had a freak snowstorm. High drifts everywhere. The undertaker laid down rail fences to get around the drifting in the roads, driving his horse and buggy through the fields. Farmers took their teams and plowed out the roads, so people could get there for the funeral. Yes, weather played a big part in deaths.

Lois: Nothing worse than a funeral in a downpour. An old saying: "Rain or snow in the open grave, it is a sign that another burial will take place soon."

Ada: Funeral music was always so sad. I remember four songs they'd either play on piano or organ, or there'd be singers: "Beyond The Sunset," "Going Home, Going Home," "What a Friend We Have in Jesus," and "Nearer My God To Thee." I don't know how anyone can sing at a funeral.

Pauline: When they had services at the church, the preacher was up front and two men seated everybody. They'd take the casket to the pulpit and open it. If the person was old, the service was long. If a younger one, it'd be short. The preacher'd read a chapter in the Bible, then his sermon. Passing through a last time, the neighbors, they went around and viewed. The closest relation was next to see 'em. Then the family, who had been sitting in the front rows, they went last. And all the children went. Children that weren't big enough to look into the coffin, someone'd pick 'em up and say, "That's Grandma," or "That's Grandpa." If one of your neighbor's children died, somebody'd take care of her other children and take 'em around and show 'em.

Bud: The Cicero undertaker, Dan Wenger, a young man just starting up, he hailed me down one day as I was going through town. "Bud," he said, "you got any work out there on your farm I could do to earn a few bucks?" I said to Dan, "What's the matter? I thought people died, hard times or not!"

"No," Dan said, "during a Depression people take better care of themselves. They cut down on the drinking, smoking, carelessness, and they don't overeat. I've been two weeks without a funeral or an ambulance call."

I said, "I have a field of hay down, ready to make. When hay's ready to put up, doesn't matter how hot it is, it's got to be baled. But, Dan, it's pretty hard work for someone who's not used to it. Suit yourself." Dan laughed, "Don't worry about old Dan. I can take it." One hundred-three degrees that afternoon, in the shade. He drove out in his ambulance and parked it alongside the road under a big tree, to be ready if he got an emergency call. All afternoon people stopped, seeing the ambulance, thinking someone had been overcome by the heat, or there'd been an accident. Lois got all kinds of phone calls at the house, "Did someone get hurt when they were baling your hay?"

It's been said, over and over again, that death has been, is, and always will be one of the sure things of life.

Pauline: Sitting up at a wake can be a very sad occasion, yet it's a good time to get to knowing your neighbors better—and hear their tall tales!

—This "Around the Kitchen Table" session was held in the author's home: September, 1988.

Moving Livestock to Market

by
Alvin "Punkin" Hunter

*"Punkin" Hunter and his wife, Margaret, were living on their home-
stead east of Arcadia when he related this story.*

My dad, Cardon Hunter, was a livestock buyer. I helped him from
the time I was knee-high to a duck, working it in with farming, with no
pay. That was my part of our family livelihood.

Dad was sick for years with stomach ulcers and he couldn't do
heavy farm work, so he went out and bought full barnlots of livestock to
resell.

It was my job to drive them home. That kept me busy the biggest
part of the time. I've driven cattle in here, two miles east of Arcadia,
from as far away as Noblesville, Ekin, Tipton.

Two of us, maybe three, drove them down the road. That was the
only mode of transporting animals in those days, driving 'em on foot to
market.

The real trouble we had was when we got ready to cross this big,
old, steel bridge. After we got the first two, three on it, they'd start, then
the others would follow. Oh, that rattling-sounding metal bridge scared
them, going across, made such a racket, like a thundering herd! As a
small boy, I was afraid a couple of cows would start fighting and one
would butt the other over the steel railings, into the creek way down
below, break its neck, or drown.

Us boys, unbeknownst to Mom, when small, would sneak away
and climb high up on top of those metal sides. Fished off the side many
a time.

A carload at the train depot was usually sixty hogs. We'd wait till
late afternoon, summertime, when it began to get cool, drive them into
Arcadia and intend to be there when the sun was going down. A hog
suffers from heat. The Arcadia streets were a moving cloud of dust in
the summer, as riders and wagons traveled back and forth.

We had a time keeping the hogs out of people's lawns in town. Going in, all the farmyards and gardens were well-fenced, so that posed no problem. While most of the town yards were fenced, we watched them closely or hogs would root under, or get to scuffling around, and break down fences or rub their rumps on corner posts. By the time we got them to town they were getting so tired we could pretty much control them.

Saddest of all was when the time came to sell our pet pig, who had spent her first weeks wrapped in a gunny sack in the warm woodbox beside the kitchen stove. A runt, it was, when first born. Dad wondered if it would even live, or if it did, ever amount to anything. The family took turns getting up during the night to feed the baby—very carefully at first, with an eye dropper; later with a nippled baby bottle. She soon fleshed out and her skin turned a healthy pink under her black and white bristling hair. She continued to enjoy the warm milk, table scraps, dishwater-slop, and all our family attention, until the day she was shipped out. She wouldn't have known how to fend for herself with the other hogs out in the barnlot.

That woodbox—it held many forms of tiny animals struggling for a foothold on life! Chickens, geese, ducks, and baby lambs. Sometimes even a big newborn calf.

Worse trouble we had, rains, the old dirt streets turned to mud, full of mudholes, and all the hogs, hot and tired, lying down in them. We couldn't prod them on. Had to let them have time to cool off.

Once a great big hog got tired and lay down in a mudhole right there in front of where Oleine Kakasuleff's Dime Store is now, in Arcadia. We told my little brother to stay with him till we got back. We'd take the rest of the hogs on to the stockyards down by the old glass factory.

We got them all there. Came back to get this old hog and he was gone! My brother was sound asleep. We finally found the hog. He'd wandered on to town and was devouring a long, old rattlesnake! Hogs loved snakes and there were so many we had to watch out for.

Sheep are easier to drive than hogs or cattle. When one lead sheep goes, they all go. They have to be handled carefully. A leg can be easily broken, or if they pile up, they'll soon smother.

Usually there was only one farmer's stock in the depot at a time, so as not to have mix-ups. We'd gone earlier, in the horse and buggy, from our farm home in the country east of Arcadia, to order a boxcar brought in. Then they'd tell us when that local was expected. We'd wait for it, then we loaded, and they'd head out.

We counted on twenty pounds shrinkage per hog, driving them the two miles from home, because of the extra exertion. After they got to Indianapolis, thirty miles away, they were given ear corn and water.

Later, the interurban started hauling our livestock but that only lasted five, six years. The interurban was faster because they went direct to Indianapolis, with few stops. The freight train stopped at every town, picked up more cars, freight, and they dumped off empty cars.

The biggest deal I ever drove was four carloads of sheep. Brood ewes. An Ohio buyer came and Dad took him, miles and miles, all over, buying sheep. Dad put 'em all in the east field until he had the full quota bargained for.

Then one afternoon we drove them all to town. We could figure around fifty head of sheep to a car. Dad had two hundred for the Ohioan, four carloads.

On the way we kept them divided, fifty to a pack, then a dividing space, fifty more. Two men on each pack. The reason we did that, people passing on horse and buggy, and a few automobiles, we'd have to let them through. Our road, going directly into Arcadia from the east, was heavily traveled.

Cattle are the hardest animals to drive. They want to run the first mile or so, just like mischievous boys, and we'd let 'em. It took three men at a crossroads, one on each side to keep 'em from going down another road, and one driving 'em from behind. But usually after you've driven cattle two-three miles, they begin to wear down and won't run. They might pause along the way and eat grass!

Many a time I've ridden a horse alongside. With hogs, we had a horse with us, pulling a spring wagon full of loose straw, to bed down inside the railroad car.

We also had some bedding in there for sheep, but not as much as for cattle. You had to have something to keep sheep from slipping and sliding. Hogs'll lie down but sheep won't, nor cattle. They'll stand all the way.

When I was sixteen we got a truck. The truck business took the railroad cars out of action pretty fast. This also stopped about all the driving of livestock on the roads.

Our solid-tire truck would carry twenty, thirty head hogs to the load. We trucked for every farmer around. Me and Dad made the trip to

Union Stockyards on Kentucky Avenue in Indianapolis. We'd start from home before daylight to gather up cattle, hogs, and sheep that were market-bound. Most of the farms were small and we might have to make several stops to get a full load. We wired up gates to block each farmer's stock from the next one's.

Pigs, fattened for market, were driven up a chute which led into the truck. The homemade chute had a lattice flooring, so hoofs wouldn't slip as they made their way up.

Unloading, we finally got the hogs moving along. They'd all try getting through the opening at the same time, shoving, grunting, and squealing, making the side racks bulge way out. Sometimes I wondered if it would break down under all that weight.

It puzzled me to see cows get right up to the gate, to unload, and walk down the chute—right to the jumping-off place and then not want to go any farther. It took a lot of hollering, hooting, and hazing to make them jump on down to the receiving pens at the stockyards.

Long before we were in sight of the huge, sprawling stockyards, our noses picked up the strong smells of hogs and the sounds of bawling cattle! As the saying goes, "Pigs don't stink, they smell of money!"

Charlie Gilkey had a big old boar he wanted to sell, but since he wasn't castrated, he knew he'd be badly docked. Charlie reached through the truck's wooden racks with his tree trimmers and clipped those things off and sent the boar on! He'd make a lot of sausage!

(Here's a newspaper clipping Mom's had in her Bible all these years: "March, 1889, T.H. Hunter"—that's my dad—"of Jackson Township, shipped 82 head of hogs this past weekend.")

We had to watch where we loaded the porkers on the farms. Barnyards were muddy places in wet weather—an awful mess in spring! Always getting hung up.

It took three hours to go to Indianapolis and four hours to return. That sounds unreasonable, doesn't it, take longer to come home than to go with a full load? The trucks only ran about fifteen, eighteen miles per hour. When one of 'em was loaded, you could drive and get there faster, but empty, the old rough roads like they were, so darned bumpy, it took longer to get home and we were sure shook up!

The solid, hard, rubber tires made really rocky riding. Didn't have to worry about flat tires but we had to worry about hanging up on account you get even a little patch of wet grass and you're stuck. They were worse than steel-wheel wagons.

Get hung up, either had to find a team of horses to pull her out or we'd have to unload, and what a horrible mess getting the livestock all back in after the truck was through that bad spot. Sometimes they scattered from here to Kingdom Come! Then, trying to count each one of them to see if we got 'em all, or sorting one man's stock from the next. Sometimes one got clear away and we'd have to search all over for him. A farmer depended on his hog check—the mortgage lifter!

In the spring of the year, I've seen fellows out there on the old Range Line Road, the state highway from Kokomo to Indianapolis, with a string of horses. They made a good living pulling automobiles out. They charged anywhere from five to ten dollars a pull for my truck. In fact, it was better to run our animals over to the depot in wet weather.

Other times there'd be ankle-deep dust or mud from side ditch to side ditch. I've seen Arcadia streets that-a-way, before they bricked 'em.

Hogs were marketed at two-twenty-five to two hundred and fifty pounds, just like today, but it took pretty near a year to produce that size hog. They were all fed yellow corn, grass and water, some tankage, that was it. Tankage? That's a beneficial supplement made from processed dead animal meat and ground bone meal.

When trucks came in, you waited till the roads got fit. We just re-timed things.

That reminds me of the first time I took a truckload of hogs to the stockyards. Feller there looked my new truck all over, front to back. What a beauty! He told about this new car with a husband and wife in it. They arrived at the main highway. As the husband started to make a left turn onto the heavily traveled road, he said to his wife, "Gander out your side. Do you see any cars a-comin'?"

She looked and looked, said, "No. Don't see any." As he stepped on the gas to make his turn, she added, "Only a big truck."

Mom was so uneasy when Dad took a job hauling a mean bull or a kicking cow. She worried from the time he left home until he returned.

Dad would always remind her of the Quaker's kicking cow who'd as soon kick your head off as look at you. One day the ever-patient Quaker said to his cow, after she'd sent him whirling—full bucket of milk dumped all over him, "Thee knows I can't beat thee, but what thee doesn't know—I can sell thee to the Baptist down the road who can!"

My kids always liked to hear me tell this one: A farmer came in one morning and told his wife, "Old Bessie had twins last night. We'll give one to the Lord and keep one." Months went by. The calves grew and grew. One morning he sat down at the breakfast table, said, "I have bad news. The Lord's twin died last night."

I look back, my, my, the changes that have taken place in the livestock business since I was a boy in the early 1900s!

—*This story was first published in the* Tri Town Topics *on May 29, 1980, and appeared in* Good Old Days, July 1984. *It is also included in* Cicero, Indiana: 1834–1984.

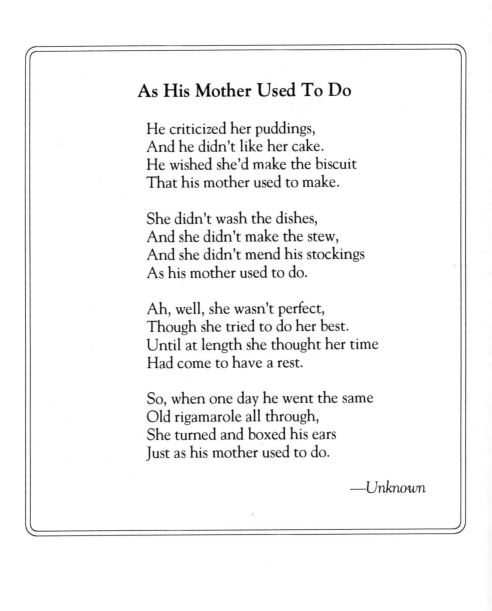

As His Mother Used To Do

He criticized her puddings,
And he didn't like her cake.
He wished she'd make the biscuit
That his mother used to make.

She didn't wash the dishes,
And she didn't make the stew,
And she didn't mend his stockings
As his mother used to do.

Ah, well, she wasn't perfect,
Though she tried to do her best.
Until at length she thought her time
Had come to have a rest.

So, when one day he went the same
Old rigamarole all through,
She turned and boxed his ears
Just as his mother used to do.

—Unknown

Part Two: Rolling Pins

Women's Stories

In April of 1819, Solomon and Sarah Finch set out from Connersville with their three daughters and two sons to begin a new life in the Hamilton County wilderness. The very first women settlers soon learned how difficult their new life would be.

Their party journeyed for nineteen days before reaching Noblesville, sixty miles to the northwest, and it rained or snowed almost daily. At one point they had to build a bridge to get across rain-swollen Blue River—a delay that took them two days. After reaching White River, south of present-day Noblesville, and ferrying their supplies across to the west side, they camped for the night before moving to higher ground, where they planned to build their cabins and start farming. Before they could begin work, however, a severe storm blew up, and a limb cracked off a tree and crashed down onto Mrs. Finch's dishes, destroying nearly all of them. They were the only dishes in camp.

These women learned to endure many other hardships as their families eked out a living in "Horseshoe Prairie." They were nothing if not resourceful. With the nearest "store" being a trading post in Connersville, they learned how to make warm clothing from animal skins and sheep's wool. In summer, they discovered that they could cut and cure nettles culled from river and creek bottoms to make a flax-like material for lighter-weight clothing.

As new Hamilton County settlements flourished, hardships eased. Shops opened. Brick dwellings replaced log cabins; cookstoves supplanted fireplaces. But even at the turn of the twentieth century, farming was still the main livelihood, supported by small towns and villages.

The stories in "Rolling Pins" provide details about the lives of ordinary rural and town women that were rarely written down. Laughter and tears often mingle as we read of the simple, everyday happenings in the life of loveable characters who lived in an age that had so much to teach us about hard work and perseverance, family bonds, and neighborliness.

Plates

A plate don't look like very much,
Just china dabbed with paint an' such.
But all the same, they sort of keep
A family record of long, happy years,
An' then, plum lonesomeness, an' tears.

Start out, young married people do,
By settin' plates out just for two.
Then, 'fore they know it, seems to me,
They start in layin' plates for three.
And after that, might say, the rate
Mounts up till they is six or eight!

At first, just two plates ain't so bad,
Folks never miss what they ain't had.
But after plates has once been set
The saddest task discovered yet
Is pickin' them up, one by one,
Till you've got back to where you begun.

Two plates, when six or eight was there,
An' noise an' clatter everywhere,
Small youngsters, hollow to their toes,
An' short on manners, goodness knows,
Just babies, an' then children grown,
Then two plates settin' all alone.

A plate don't look like very much,
But they hold memories, an' such.
Love wove in every flowered wreath,
An' every nick dear past belief.
Worst task I know, under the sun,
Is pickin' plates up, one by one.

—*Author Unknown*

You Are Your Brother's Keeper

by
Jenny Applegate

Jenny Applegate, widowed for several years, made her home with her stepdaughter and her husband, the Leland Carsons, west of Cicero. She was interviewed in the early 1970s.

My parents had a soft spot for any unfortunate person that came along. Like it mentions in the Bible, they felt we were our brother's keeper. It's the neighborly thing. They'd quote this Biblical verse: "Forget not to show love to strangers, for thereby some have entertained angels unawares."

Old Granny Pike and her little Johnny walked in off the road one summer day—she in her run-over shoes, skimpy, faded dress, large mole on the nose, straight, sun-faded greasy hair hooked behind the ears—and announcing that she and her barefoot boy, in his torn, faded bib overalls, had come to stay a spell.

"I'm stayin'," Old Granny said, with spirit. Us kids hated those words, "I'm stayin'," but we were never allowed to speak disrespectfully of anyone. Papa always said, "God placed a bit of good in us all. If you can't say something good about a person, don't say anything!" But there was little good about Granny.

We kids thought Granny was awful old 'cause she looked it. Women were old at forty or fifty. Just think, I'm ninety-six! What would they think of me?

She'd stay awhile at our house. First thing, Mama took down the washtub and then had to insist they take baths. Mama washed and mended Granny's clothes and would make her a new dress and buy undergarments and shoes and stockings for her and her boy, just like she did for all of her own.

Granny would get up one morning, after being with us several weeks, and announce, "I'm goin'," and she and Johnny took off walking down the road, to Lord knows where. Maybe the next neighbor's. That's the way she spent her whole life—one house to another. I don't know if her husband had died, or if she was ever married.

She wouldn't do a lick of work, never, wouldn't wash a dish, sweep a floor, or dust. She just sat around and ate and we had to furnish her and her boy a bed, until they up and moved on.

Johnny was nice, a good sport, but they made a lot of extra work for all of us. A farmer's life was supposed to be hard. Sacrifices and doing without was what it was all about. We felt Mama or Papa could have informed her of her duties, right at the beginning, but they didn't. We resented that! Oh, well, you can't light a fire with a wet match!

Papa happened to hear us kids complaining once and he quoted, "The Bible says the poor are with us always." He felt this was our God-given duty to take care of Granny and Johnny, and any others of misfortune. What happened to the Biblical injunction that if you don't work you don't eat?

One Sunday the preacher's sermon, I have it right here in my Bible, let me read it to you, Second Thessalonians, 3:8: *Nor did we eat anyone's bread without paying for it, but with labor and hardship we kept working night and day so that we might not be a burden to any of you.*

I pointed it out to Mama and Papa; didn't matter.

I got so I just couldn't bear that old lady. Even as little tots we had many family chores and responsibilities.

She caused me to get a licking once. I needed it. My bedroom was narrow, with just enough room at the foot to go through. It accommodated all us youngsters.

A Monday, it was raining, and Mama was washing. Dora and Cash and I were jumping from the big bed to the trundle bed, back and forth, back and forth. That was fun!

Granny told on us. Mama gave us a licking and while she was thrashing each of us, all except Dora—she was crippled and she always got out of that—Old Granny was sitting right there rocking, insisting, "Well, now, Reddie"—Reddie, that's Mama's name—"Reddie, give 'em a goodun while you're at it! Give 'em a goodun!"

I wanted to shout back, "Reddie, give Granny a goodun, and make her get out of that rocker and help with the work! Papa works hard farmin' the fields and Mama works her fingers to the bone to care for all of us. We each do our share around here. What are you a-doin'?"

One night we were all sitting around in the living room, eating juicy pears, while Papa read aloud from the Bible. Granny ate hers, pear juice running from her mouth, down her chin, all over. After she finished, rather than go to the kitchen to get a washrag to wipe up with, she crossed each arm across her front to her armpits and dried them off!

Mama wasn't any bigger than I am—I'm a little over four feet tall and weigh ninety pounds. Papa was six feet. They made a curious couple.

Our home was a log cabin with one great big room along the east side, and a lean-to kitchen. The loft-bedroom for us all was above, and a small room to the side.

Mama's hand-loomed rag carpet was on the big downstairs floor. She didn't run it up to the fireplace like it should have been because the menfolk chewed tobacco and spit into the fire, and often they missed.

One fellow, he'd go up real close and squirt his juice square into the fire. What a s-s-s-sizzle! While he didn't miss, I couldn't abide the smell of that burning tobacco spit.

We always knew when Papa was about to spit. He would sit in his rocking chair, and he'd rock, rock, going a little faster, faster, working up closer. All of a sudden he'd WHOOSH! way over into the fire!

Sometimes the men wouldn't hit the spot, and after it had dried, us girls had to scrub and scrub the dark stains off the stone and wood. The steaming odors from the homemade soap and tobacco juice made me puke. I've been mad enough to throw those men into the fire. Why couldn't they clean up their own mess? I never dared say a word.

One man, each time, he got up, went outdoors and spit, never hitting the porch or steps. We girls admired his cleanliness. Still, it was just a filthy habit, and we vowed when we grew up and got married, our husbands wouldn't be chewers and we wouldn't allow it in the house. And we never did.

A Dutchman we knew had no home. He stayed with us a long time. Joe was shipped over here from Germany with a bunch of orphan children. They did that years ago when the Germans got too many kids, mostly orphans they couldn't support; they came to the States, and we found homes for them.

Old Joe was one of them and a good worker. He always came into the house singing, and sat down and wound his long legs each around the other. We listened wide-eyed as he told tales of his homeland. He could make or repair a kite or play a game of checkers. He praised Mama's cooking. Anything needing to be done, Joe jumped up and did it. He'd say, "I see your Papa has no time for idlers. I intend to do my share." Good thing he didn't know Granny.

In wintertime, when there wasn't much work, he ate his breakfast, got on his coat and hat, went out, took the wedges and saw, threw an ax over his shoulder, and then went to the woods. He stayed most of the day, sawed the limbs off a tree, and when he got down to the trunk, he sawed it down. Then he cut up all that wood for the fireplace.

The fireplace was for heating and cooking our food. Mama was always wishing she had one of those new iron cookstoves with a real oven to bake in.

Winter or summer, Joe took his coat with him. "A wise man always takes a wrap in case the weather turns off bad," he'd relate. And it often did!

He worked for his room and board and Papa gave him spending money. We kids all liked him—oh it was a pleasant house with Joe in it! We were so sorry when he decided he'd go on West, maybe to a ranch.

One man, we called him Old Pete, he had been a soldier and drew a pension. I don't know how it came about for him to live with us. He wasn't related. He just walked in off the road one day and said, "I got me a misery in my back that don't much like farm workin', so I'm reckonin' I'll jest take me a bed here awhile." Obviously he meant it. He did nothing more physical than dip his pen in the ink bottle or poke his fork into a plate piled high with food.

We washed and ironed for him, furnished his bed and board, and he wouldn't lead a horse to drink. Never turned a hand. He and Granny Pike would have made a good team. Wonder they didn't run into each other.

He was an authority on everything. Us kids would get so tired of his endless yammering—on and on. I wanted Papa to tell him like he did us kids when we all got to talking at once, "If God had wanted us to talk more, he'd given us two mouths and one ear."

He'd be chewing, shift his tobacco from one cheek to the other one, and resume his conversation. He'd let tobacco juice fly with a line of dark spit that missed the fireplace, spattering against the sides, causing a sizzling sound and a putrid odor. He'd mop up the overflow of tobacco juice that ran down the corners of his mouth with the back of his hand or sleeve, and went right on. Washday, Mama had me scrubbing those tobacco-stained sleeves on the washboard!

Old Pete didn't offer the folks a penny of the pension money for his keep. In the wintertime he'd go to the Soldiers' Home, then was back to our house summers. He was always and forever worrying about his bowels.

One hot day, haymaking time, Papa and the boys were out working in the hayfield. This old fellow—I say old, but Pete probably wasn't more than fifty—was sitting in the front room reading. He was a great hand to read. Usually the big worn family Bible on the library table. We kids often wondered why he didn't put some of its Biblical teachings to work in his own life! Papa, all excited, ran in the back door, yelling, "Pete, it's going to be a bad storm and I don't want my hay to get wet. Come and help us!"

"I ain't none ambitious in that direction myself, I told ya when I comed here. I don't have to work!" he answered boldly.

"No, nor do I have to keep you. Git out! Don't you ever come back!" He never did and we were surely glad!

A real nice Indian family lived east of us. Only Indians I ever knew. If any of the neighbors needed help, the Indian and his squaw were both willing. When they were moving away the Indian said to Mama, "Well, I'm sorry to go. We're leaving some mighty fine neighbors."

Mama was crying, "And you're taking an awfully good neighbor with you! We're going to miss you all so much."

I look back and I think, even as a small child, I learned a lot about life from those unfortunates that lived with us. Most of all, I'd work for my keep and be clean, and not be a burden to others! There was an old saying, "You can pull a duck's neck all you want, but it still ain't gonna end up a swan!" It reminded me of Granny and Pete. Mostly, though, we did enjoy having the others, if it weren't for all the extra work.

—*This story originally appeared in* Tri Town Topics, *May 18 and 25, 1972, and appears in* Cicero, Indiana: 1834–1984.

From the Flopper-Stopper to the Hinder-Binder
"Oh, Mama, You Really Look Nice!"

by
Myrtle Witham

Myrtle Witham was a mother, grandmother, and wife of Vance Witham, Hamilton County sheep shearer. She was a telephone operator for fifteen years in the little town of Atlanta, in the forties and early fifties.

There was a time when a woman not only needed a pretty dress to look nice, she depended on that all important foundation garment, the corset, to make her *really* look nice.

Joyce Newby, my daughter, and I were talking the other day. She said, "I liked to watch you and Grandmother get ready for Eastern Star. Mesmerized, I'd watch you dress for the festivities. How nice and trim you both looked when you came out with your formals on! The corsets drew up your bosoms to giddy heights, pinched in your waists, and flared out your derrieres! The low-cut fronts revealed the milky whiteness of your flesh. I learned, at a very young age, a woman with a successful husband was supposed to carry herself proudly, and much depended upon the effect of that all important garment, the corset!"

Sara Fippen had a severe back condition that practically bent her double. Women had very heavy work to do. They were always on their feet, washing, ironing, cleaning, canning, raising chickens, and doing farm chores. They needed good support! Someone was selling the Trixie corset. Sara bought one and it helped her so much, she was soon back on her feet. That prompted her to sell corsets.

The first thing a lady put on when she arose and the last thing she removed at night was her corset. It was a great trial to her to be without her stays. She felt undressed and indecent. It was believed that going without a corset was very bad for the health, besides being immoral in some way.

Sometimes we'd hear a lady say she'd never wear one because it just killed her every time she put one on!

Way back, in Mother's day, a lady had many trappings to put on before she could finish with her dress. First there was a cotton undershirt. Next came a long corset that laced in the back with strings pulled as tight as her body could endure. What a sight to see Mother straining and pulling her waist in. Remember the cartoon where the husband had ahold of the strings in the back of his wife's corset, his foot clamped on her waist so she couldn't move, she ahold of the bedpost, all the while he was pulling the strings tighter and tighter, taut enough to satisfy her. Some, but a very few, bragged about their eighteen-inch waistline.

The strings were then tied around her now-small waist. A fancy corset cover went over that to cover the vest and corset down to the waist. It was a thing of beauty, full of lacy ruffles.

The bloomers came next, and they were made of white muslin, full and gathered at the knee, with elastic. The black cotton stockings and the high-top button shoes, hooked with a long button hook, were then put on. Two long ruffled petticoats came next and a big thing called a bustle, when they were in style, was tied around her waist and worn in the back. Finally a frilly white shirtwaist, with a long black skirt, made up her costume.

All those undergarments were worn for Sunday best and also for everyday, with a calico dress. Think how hot that was in summer!

You can't imagine the impatience of us kids, waiting for Mama to finally get ready. But, oh, she looked so pretty!

No lady, in Mama's time, left her front door without wearing a hat, gloves, silk stockings, and often carrying an umbrella or a parasol. Handbags were small. She had a handkerchief, pair of gloves, and some small change.

Papa would tell us, when I was a girl, that ladies, in his day, did not have legs; they were supported by "lower limbs." It was an exciting thrill if a summer breeze would lift the long skirt and show the ankle above a low slipper! The ankle was the only possible erotic zone and drew all male eyes, even when encased in a heavy dark stocking! There could be no other erotic zones, he laughed, with all those layers of clothing covering them!

Sara measured each of her customers exactly, then sent the measurements away. When the garment was ready, I went to Indianapolis to try it on, to see if it fit properly and to pay for it.

It was Vance's custom—Vance, he's my husband—to refer to slim women as "skinny" or to accuse them of "tight lacing!" Of the heavy ladies, he'd remark, "Her rear is ax-handle wide!"

"From the flopper-stopper to the hinder-binder," he'd tease as I prepared for my scheduled Indianapolis trips.

As in any town, Atlanta had a well-to-do couple. I was envious of the wife, and apparently it showed. Vance couldn't understand my concern. He said, "Oh, shoot. She gets her wash rained on the same as you do."

The first time I went to Indianapolis to get fitted, my children, Joyce and V.E., went with me. A month ahead, one or the other marked off the days on our calendar. They pictured it vaguely as a vast city of towers and castles, ladies with elegant silk dresses, and romantic gentlemen, like in storybooks.

How excited they were with their first interurban ride, for they had never in their lives been beyond Atlanta and the bordering towns. They were fascinated with the smiling conductor who walked along the platform that ran the length of the car on the outside. He seemed so happy as he collected our tickets.

Once, going around the bend at Forest Park, the conductor lost his balance and fell out over me. We all laughed! The interurban creaked and groaned as it sped along. The children imitated its sounds—click, click, clickclickclickety—clicketyclickclick—as we rode along. Then the clickety-clack of the wheels on the rails as it went slower and slower, nearing Arcadia, then Cicero, and Noblesville, on to Carmel, then Indianapolis.

The passing scene just outside the window—it was so new to them, such fun, to be sailing along. Seemed like flying to them, for the telegraph poles went by almost faster than they could count them. Farmhouses no more than came into sight before we had flashed past. The kids pointed to the time on the court house clock in Noblesville. They admired the magnificent Victorian homes, with their gas pipe fences, climbing red rambler roses, in full bloom.

Joyce looked around at lady passengers, then whispered to me which ones were tightly corseted. V.E. drew pictures on the dusty windowpane. If I heard it once, I heard it a dozen times: "Are we almost there? Are we almost there?"

When we entered the city, the car screeched and swayed and bumped along the ties. The two kids would drunkenly tilt back and forth in their seats.

We walked, a lady hand-in-hand with her two anxious little children who had never been to the big city before, from the interurban station to the Monument Circle. I cautioned them, "Do not interrupt an adult conversation at any time. Don't touch a single thing. Say please and thank you. Speak only when spoken to."

Several of the buildings had their first floors built up above the sidewalk level, so you had to climb five or six steps to reach the front doors.

There were numerous areaways with steps leading down. One was to a shoeshine parlor and repair shop. Another provided access to a barbershop, marked by a red-and-white striped pole.

Lots of the stores had molded tin ceilings, embossed with elaborate designs and then painted. Many of the city houses had such ceilings in the kitchens and bathrooms, they said.

We stepped into the store's elevator. I told the nicely-dressed attendant which floor we wanted to go to—I can't, for the life of me, remember now. It about took our breath away, going up, and so exciting!

We were greeted enthusiastically. "Mrs. Vance Witham, all the way from Atlanta? Ah these yore darlin' chil-lun? Come this way, deah, and we'll all get started."

We soon found ourselves in a large, queerly furnished waiting room, like a rich family's parlor. Large gilt-framed mirrors hung all around reflecting everyone and everything which took place there.

Walking to the fitting room I caught the rich pleasant odors of spice, burning incense, and flowery perfume. On the wall hung an embroidered picture: *A well-dressed woman contributes to the beauty of the world.*

Once in a while my two kids pulled back the curtain to see what the fitter was doing in there to their mother! When I was finally properly fitted, I walked out. I saw, standing there in the doorway, their faces mirroring the happiness and pleasure they derived from my new look.

We'd hear all kinds of conversations as we walked along the booths: "Will you like being all bound up, do you think?" That was probably her first corset. When each came out, the figure, under the tight bodice of her dress, was so feminine! Once my children pointed out two very stylish old ladies, smelling of lavender talcum powder, as being so nice! Joyce, with her inquiring mind, had asked them their names, where they lived, how many children and grandchildren, husbands, and their foundation-garment history!

Each time we went there, my kids stood spellbound, staring out the window overlooking the Circle, the street that goes around the Soldiers' and Sailors' Monument in the center of downtown Indianapolis. Some-

thing exciting was always going on. One time they were demolishing
the English Theater. Next visit, they watched J.C. Penney's being built
in that spot. The Flying Wallendas had a tightrope stretched from
Penney's over to the Monument, on the Circle, and they'd walk it if the
wind wasn't blowing too hard. One time we heard the fire sirens come
to the next building. Smoke was rolling! We didn't want to take the elevator in case we got trapped in it, so we walked down all those steps.

They excitedly watched the massively strong brewery wagons,
drawn by powerful draft horses, or a street fight, a runaway, saw a bal-
loon man with his gas-filled balloons, the newsboys walking the streets
shouting, "EXTRA! READ ALL ABOUT IT!"

We always made a day of it. Bought our lunch. If somebody needed
their eyes tested, we went to Kernel's. Woolworth's dime store had real
nice dress goods. I made all our clothing.

In earlier years the department stores had only a few items out on
display. The customer sat on a stool in front of the counter and a bejew-
eled clerk looked in a drawer for the item requested. Most women wore
kid dress gloves. When buying a new pair I sat down on a chair. The
sales clerk, her hand festooned with heavy rings, spoke sweetly to Joyce,
then winked at V.E., "No well-dressed lady appears in public without
gloves." She showed me a pair to inspect, then fitted the gloves onto
each hand, gently smoothing them over each finger, working and working to get them on.

In making the desired selection, sometimes I had to try on several
pair. When the clerk took off each glove from my hand, she held it open
to blow into it, before laying it flat and putting it back into the drawer.
Joyce and V.E. giggled and giggled! Wintertime, at home, they'd do that
with their woolen gloves.

There were no cash registers in the individual departments. V.E.
and Joyce looked on, so excited, as the change baskets traveled on a
network of wires that criss-crossed below the ceiling and led to a little
balcony office back in a corner. A clerk put a large bill and the sales slip
in a small metal basket and pulled a long cord which hung from the
wires. This raised the basket onto the cable network, rang a bell, and
sent the basket whizzing along the wires to the balcony office. There a
teller counted out the change, prepared the customer's copy of the
saleslip and sent those items whizzing back to the point-of-sale in that
interesting basket! When it arrived, the bell rang and a tug on the dan-
gling cord dropped the basket down to the level where the clerk then

handed me my change, along with my purchased package. Already I could see Joyce and V.E. figuring out how they'd do that back home.

Joyce remembered one saleslady who wore her glasses on her nose. They were attached to a thin gold chain that was pinned to the bosom of her dark, serge dress. Oh, my, she was impressive!

When all our purchases were made, the store sent them home by mail, postpaid. Of course, the kids carried theirs with them, to show off to their friends at home.

The trip back on the trolley was a wordless one. Joyce and V.E. slept.

The neighborhood kids were envious of Joyce and V.E. going clear down to Indianapolis on the Circle! They'd hurry over as soon as we got home, anxious to hear a running commentary, from getting on the interurban in Atlanta, until they got home that night.

They huddled all around on the grass under the apple tree in the back yard, listening to Joyce and V.E. imitating the sales lady. "Hullo, Mrs. Witham. Ah these yore dahling chill-run? Have you come do-own to-own to our big city? My deah"—she 'my deared' everybody—"you may come with me now-el."

I remember one particular garment. It had the laces tied in place. They could be adjusted once, and that was it. Then there were the hooks to hook it together, a zipper over that. It had an extra piece here on the side, and that lifted the bosoms up!

We got extra supporters to use when the first ones wore out. How happy I was with the new elastic and spandex. I forgot the corsets with their stays!

Those metal things would work through when the corset got old and they'd stab a person. I'd reach down and pull it on out. Boys used their mothers' old stays for flippers.

The garters hooked to the stockings and held the foundation down and wouldn't let it ride up. If you happened to get a long-length one, with long stockings, then you were in for trouble! Either your stockings would wrinkle around your ankles or the girdle would ride way up.

It had three supporters on each side. The back one, you could hardly reach way around to get it fastened. Bend over, reach between the legs, and get in all kinds of positions. Joyce always laughed at me! Stockings had dark seams up the back of them. The supporters had to be fastened just so, or the seams wouldn't stay straight.

The big fat women poked all that extra flesh in. Then they really looked nice. Joyce worried how those women would ever get to the bathroom in time in all that contraption.

My mother's corsets lasted much longer than mine, as she wore cotton underwear under hers. I did that with the one I kept for Sunday; then I didn't have to wash it often.

In proper circles this was called "the garment." On Mondays it was laundered and hung on the clothesline, discreetly covered with a towel, and when the wind blew, the kids, and men, could catch a glimpse of this wondrous piece of clothing. By the time I had children, women weren't embarrassed by hanging them out.

Mondays, coming home from school, Joyce and V.E. giggled when they'd see them hanging out on the clotheslines all around town. Those and men's long underwear flapping in the wind. When our teasing neighbor fellow had his wash on the line, they'd tie his underwear and trouser legs together, to devil him back.

V.E. was as big a cut-up as his father. He'd say, "Get a load of Aunt Tillie's tiddy bags hangin' out there on her clothesline!"

Children delighted in dressing up in Mama's old corsets. Men joked about them. Women were envious of other women's figures—the look they got from a new foundation.

Corsets later came proportioned for the short, medium, tall, fat, skinny. At Vance's insistence I ordered a long-line proportioned one out of the catalogue. The brassiere and girdle were all in one piece. I was more comfortable than I'd been in the others. More support, and my dress looked prettier over it.

Joyce noticed every lady, especially those with the big stomachs, or if they wore skirts that were rump-sprung. She'd say, "She's so big her bottom wobbles when she walks! Mother, now she'd look nice in a garment if she'd just wear one."

The corset garment is almost a thing of the past. There got to be a lot of discussion about tight lacing causing deformed babies. One lady they told about, her baby was born with her hands attached at the elbows. Folks said she had laced too tight. That baby grew to womanhood, was happily married, and had children. She could diaper her babies as quickly as anyone. She worked her head off all her life, doing for her family and unfortunate people!

Women don't do the heavy work they once did, so there isn't the demand for a good support. Joyce never quite understood how all of

Mama got into it, but my elegant, beautiful appearance on Sundays and Eastern Star nights attested to the fact I did! Everyone she'd see, after an Indianapolis trip, she'd say, "Mama's wearing her new corset!"

As a child, my highest ambition was to wear such a garment and become a beautiful woman. Finally I did.

I always felt so charming when I came out all dressed up in my formal for Eastern Star. Joyce would be so thrilled, "Oh, Mama, you really look nice!"

—This story appeared in Tri Town Topics, *June 21 and 28, 1979; was published in* Good Old Days, *January, 1980; and is included in* Cicero, Indiana: 1834–1984.

Lola and Grace's Milk Route

by
Lola Heinzman

In 1914, Lola and her sister-in-law had a country milk route which showed them as independent women in a time when that wasn't common. Lola is still an independent woman and yarn-spinner, at the age of ninety-eight, in today's Hamilton County.

We didn't have a name for it back in 1913, but just the same, some women got out and did the things men were always accustomed to doing, and they didn't make a big to-do of it!

My brother, Willard Tash, his wife, Grace, and their two-year-old son Forest, lived with her mother, Mrs. Long, on her thirty-five acre farm down south of Cicero. That wasn't very much land for a young man to make a living on or to keep himself busy, so Willard took a milk route.

He bought a spring wagon, then built a cab up over the front like the storm buggies had. It was pulled by his team. The wagon bed held fifteen eight-gallon metal milk cans.

A new receiving station for the farmers' milk was going up at Cicero. From there the milk would be shipped on the interurban to Polk's Milk Company in Indianapolis.

They asked Willard to do all that carpenter work to build the station. Grace suggested, since Willard could make good wages doing that, why not let her and me take over the milk route; then Willard and Grace could get a good start in life.

Real early each morning Willard fed, watered, and hitched up the two gentle old work horses, ready for us.

Mrs. Long prepared a big breakfast at five o'clock, seven days a week, as cows were milked twice a day and their milk was hauled in every day. She fried potatoes and meat and made gravy. Then she cared for Forest.

We started our route just after sun-up. Winters, of course, we made our stops later than in the summertime.

At ten, halfway through the route, we stopped at Lee Fleming's grocery at Clare for a dime's worth of baloney, nickel's worth of crackers, and that, with our pie from home, made all two people could eat. We rode along and ate.

Some of the farmers where we stopped, as I remember, were Charles Roudebush, George Roudebush, Henry Burkhardt, Ed Griffin—he lived in the log cabin at Clare—Charlie Robey, and Mr. McClintock.

One time at Ed Griffin's, no one was home, so I stuck their milk check partly in under the lid so it wouldn't blow away. Farmers were paid on the first and fifteenth of each month. When Griffins returned home, all they ever found of that check was a corner. The goat had eaten it! The milk company issued another, of course.

We rode along to the background music of the bumping milk cans, the jingle, jingle, creak, creaking horse harness, and the clop, clop of the horses. We'd pull over on those narrow dirt roads, so buggies or other wagons could pass. We never took chances of upsetting our load. We'd give everyone we passed a neighborly wave and hello-yell!

The route was several miles long. We passed country churches with all their tombstones, and we'd wave to kids playing in the schoolyards.

Sometimes we'd drive in bad weather but that was no bother. In summer we didn't like a storm, but a shower didn't amount to anything. Hard rains, we'd pull under a big tree for protection for ourselves and the horses. Bad lightning, the farmer hailed us into an empty wagon shed. Grace and I sat in there in the dry, reading.

I always kept a dime novel beside me, or *McCall's* or *Ladies Home Companion*. We'd drive along after the rain let up a bit, then get out and hurry to take the empty milk cans in and bring full ones out, so we could make it to the plant at Sheridan on time.

In winter we kept warm in our long wool coats, wool dresses, and two or three flannel petticoats, long underwear, black cotton stockings, and rubber boots pulled over our shoes. Mrs. Long knitted our heavy woolen gloves and hats. We started out with flannel-covered heated rocks to our feet, but they soon cooled down. If we got real cold we'd get off and run alongside the wagon. Frigid weather, farm wives invited us in to get warmed beside their heating stoves and they'd hand us cups of real hot coffee or cocoa.

Zero weather, the night's milk froze almost through, and it was hard to pour out when we got to the milk station. The dirt roads were

narrow and rough, ruts frozen solid. Us girls and the milk cans bounced around in there like cream in a churn!

Willard had rubber blankets to cover the horses if a sleet storm came up. We'd throw them over their heads. There was a place in front for their ears and nose to come through. A couple snaps underneath held them on good. Cold air blew in the slot in the front where the lines pulled through so we'd poke rags around that. Didn't have to use the lines, anyway. The horses knew the way, when to stop and when to start up or pull over.

Warm weather, between stops, we sewed on quilt blocks or we crocheted. We'd pull on gloves before we'd load the milk, then riding back down the road, we'd take them off and start our nice, clean handiwork again.

People always recognized us coming, by the rumbling cans and our singing—oh, how we'd sing!

'Most every farm had a field gate we had to stop and open; one of us would drive the team on through, then the other close it—we took turns. At one farm we went through a gate, then around and out a back gate to another road. The farmer fussed, "It's a nuisance having all those buggies and wagons cutting through all the time, a short-cut to the pike. Somebody's always leaving a gate open—you two never do—and the cows and hogs get out." Oh, we understood chasing livestock back to where they belonged. Done it many-a-time at home when they broke down a rail fence.

Around the back porches of most farm houses were lush growths of morning glories and mole beans planted there for summer shade and privacy. Mole beans grew up tall during the summer, like trees, with such beautiful foliage. Most women thought the planting of mole beans would distract moles from the area.

Everyone had a woodshed just out the back door, to keep their wood in the dry all winter. One lady had her back fences covered with gourd vines. Late fall they'd bear long-handled gourds. She said they made handy dippers for washday. The large round ones, she cut the tops off and they made vessels for holding soft soap. The small curved-handled ones, good drinking dippers, hung near the pump. Those pretty little yellow striped ones—they were cute baby rattles, as the seeds stay in until they are opened up. Gourds will last and last, won't dent, and never rust!

There was always something going on at the back door of every house. Mondays, women were standing at the clothesline hanging out their family's weekly wash; a mamma cat sunning and nursing a lapful of baby kittens; a lady bending over a pen of baby chicks; a fighty rooster sparring up to the fence at us—but we weren't afraid as long as he was on the other side!

We'd get to visiting, the kitchen-door friends, a man, a woman, kids, and always the family dog. They came out to chat a minute, to get any news we'd collected along the way. When we were ready to go, there'd be old hens scratching for grains of corn and oats in the deposits made by our horses. They'd squawk and fly to safety when we took off.

Men talked of weather, their crops, or any political issues, but usually they didn't think young women cared much about politics. Grace didn't but I did.

"We can use rain for the corn, but it won't rain till that wind gets around to the east...It's about time the rain let up so's we can get in the fields...Men's all out in field today...."

One man admitted his impatience with the uncertainty of the weather, getting his crops into the ground, or harvested. If he cuts the hay and it rains, it's ruined; but then, it has to be cut down before it can cure, then be put up. One day he was so beside himself, then laughed when he saw my teasing look, and he said, "I'm rarin' to go but I can't go for rarin'!"

One of the wheels of our wagon was making an odd racket and a farmer came out to inspect. "That's a hungry wagon hub," he said, as he paddled thick grease into it. "Takes lots of grease, don't she? Willard musta missed it."

They were always handy to tell us jokes or tales, to see us laugh. "An Atlanta bachelor," said one farmer (I can still see him as he tongued his cud of tobacco from one jaw to the other—most men chewed), "says one of the funniest things in life is how sweet a girl can look in the evening and how plain the same girl appears to the milkman. Young man, grab that woman! One that arises in time to meet the milkman was made to be married!"

"Kissing a man without a mustache is like eating an egg without salt!" laughed one man after he'd asked me all about my beau, Carl.

In most houses, a grandparent or two, or old maid sisters, hired men, usually lived with them, and they took time to talk, bits and pieces of chitchat. Edith Voss was telling about the time her brother came running in, yelling, "Ma! Ma! A wagon just run over my liddle brudder! Over his neck! Don't worry, he ain't dead yit!" I think he lived to be quite old!

Flies were everywhere in the summer, horses tails swishing at them, flies around milk cans. Occasionally they'd get inside the cans and we'd reach in and pick 'em out. They didn't hurt anything, but the milk inspector would have had a fit!

One house, Sunday mornings, farm chores done, the whole family were always out on the front porch, singing and playing instruments, before getting ready for church.

April Fools', we had to watch out for pranks when there were young sprouts in the family. They'd apply grease or even cow manure to the underside of the handles of the milk cans!

Oh, those tantalizing odors coming out of back doors, especially on holiday mornings! We'd often get treats to take along with us.

Girl milk haulers. We got all kinds of objections along the way. Men, brought up to be gentlemen, came out and wanted to load the milk cans for us. We had trouble there for we aimed to do it ourselves. One stop, the wife was in her garden violently attacking weeds. It was so hot, the sweat poured down her red, red face. The husband insisted on helping us. He said it was too hard work for a couple of little women. We both knew he never, ever offered his wife any assistance! We learned a lot about people. Men went through life virtually oblivious to their wives' feelings and needs. To him she was handy for preparing a good meal, warming his bed on cold nights, and fulfilling his physical needs.

We'd stand behind the wagon, with a can full of milk, each one of us taking hold of the can on the side handles, and giving it a swing way up, slick as a knife cutting into butter. We were both five-two, a hundred-ten pounds. We could climb up over those wheels like a couple of squirrels, on up inside the open wagon to arrange the cans in proper order for easy handling.

Each patron's milk cans had a number. We could look at a can and identify it immediately, like "8" painted in black on the side, that's Griffin's. Sometimes we talked in numbers to each other. "Did you hear that 12's daughter is keeping company with 4's boy?"

"They got a new girl at 5's last night!"

We were always kind of afraid we'd stumble as we threw the can up and if we did, the lid would pop off, we'd have milk all over us, and those people wouldn't get their pay for that milk. Farm families were so poor, so we were real careful.

Dogs at every farm barked or they nipped at our heels, but we ignored them. Springtime, we had all kinds of puppy or kitten offers. We were often led to the barn by an eager child, to see a new colt or calf.

The grass along the side of the road was always thick and green and tall. Whenever we stopped, the horses had their noses busily searching out the richest growth. With bits in their mouths, they couldn't eat much. When it was time to go, we'd give the reins a reminder flip. Like kids, they'd reach for another mouthful, they'd shake their ears when we'd give the lines another jerk, then walk on.

One place, a widow woman wanted to know what I was going to do when I quit driving the route, when brother Willard came back. I told her, "I'm going to marry Carl Heinzman. Lola Tash—Lola Heinzman. Yes, I like that!" I said to her.

Grace laughed and joined in, "It's like the Grandpa tells his grandson, 'When you fall in love you'll know it. She'll hit you over the head with a frying pan!' Carl's been hit over the head!"

Oh, that woman just had a fit! "Well, I wouldn't get married," she stormed. "I'd get out and get me some money, if it weren't for that thing," she nodded in the direction of her little daughter. The girl was a pretty thing who cowed and looked down at her bare feet when her mother was talking. The woman went on—you notice I didn't call her a *lady*—she went on saying, "If I didn't have her, I could git me a job, five dollars a week! I'd look for ads in the paper if I was you."

Everyone had definite opinions about her. Said one neighbor lady, "I think she was afraid of dying an old maid, so she married the first man, probably the only one, who ever went with her, and he was out for her inheritance. He didn't live long and now she regrets getting married."

One lady was distressed when the subject was brought up, and whispered as if someone might hear her, "She had often been the subject of gossip, even before matrimony; she scandalized the neighborhood by her masculine proclivities. She ran the farm, marketed the produce, and raised both cattle and hogs. She was seen in town with clinging skirts spattered with mud, striding about with a buggy whip in her hand. Her poke bonnet concealed the roughness of her hair, and she always wore gloves to cover the cracks and scars of her hands. After she married, she didn't give a dang. She even wore men's overalls! Women in men's clothing? Why it's against the teachings of the Good Book!"

The farmer-husband wasn't whispering when he added his two cents' worth. "She was one of those women born wantin' to be a man. At first, neighbors felt sorry for her when her husband died. It takes a strong man to work a farm. How could a woman manage? She didn't want no sympathy—always sour as vinegar. Ever time ya tried to be neighborly, like when her husband lived, we'd help him if a fence broke down, animals git out; but helpin' her, she ordered everbody 'round as if she were a army sergeant about to take the next hill, and all the time she raised her voice in its never-endin' vendetta against men. Us neighbors soon got a bellyful of that!"

Me and Grace were thinking what a lonely life she must live— never went to church, revival meetings, or the Fall Festival, nothing at all. One day I said to her, "You should get out and mingle a little more."

"What! Let people think I'm out lookin' for a man! It'll be a cold day in hell! I had one man, and that was a-plenty. Once bitten, twice shy. I'll never marry again!"

She had one child, eighty acres paid for, and money in the bank. She was rich! And, I suppose, in her own way, happy.

Riding along, me and Grace, still thinking about that farm woman, we were remembering when we double-dated, we went to the Chautauqua down at Noblesville. Old Maid jokes were favorites. The comedian was telling this one: "The old maid laughed at anyone who suggested that it was too bad she didn't have a husband, and she said: 'I have a dog that growls, a parrot that swears, a fireplace that smokes, and a cat that stays out all night. Now, why should I want a husband?' "

An attractive lady, when asked why she never married, explained, "I would rather go through life wanting something I don't have than having something I don't want."

"Grandma," asked the girl, "what kind of husband should I get?"

"Take my advice," said Grandma, "and leave the husbands alone. Get yourself a single man."

At one of our milk stops I felt something bumping down inside as we were carrying it to the wagon. A can of milk has a certain feel and sound, like the difference of rain or sleet on a window. We stopped and took the lid off. This woman had dressed a chicken and I just knew she'd sent a kid out to throw a dishpan of that stuff over the fence into the chickenlot, but he'd dumped it into the milk can, to save steps. I had brothers. I knew their tricks! I just reached down, took those entrails out, threw them over to the dog, and we went on. Oh, that lady was always so particular, they were so poor, and needed the pay check bad.

It humiliated one lady when we showed her a swelled-up dead mouse floating in the milk. The can had been sitting on the back porch next to a table and they'd forgotten to put the lid on. She yelled to her husband. He came and carried the milk out and poured it in the hog trough for hogs to drink. No, a mouse we'd never reach in and throw out! That might make illnesses.

Most of the places we went, they had the cans cooling in an ordinary washtub of cold water there by the back porch or woodshed. We lifted the milk can with a suck from the water and set it down on the grass to drain off. Just by lifting their milk can, we knew if the cows were off their feed, drying up before calving, if a touchy cow kicked over the bucket, or if the family had ice cream the night before. We'd usually see the ice cream freezer bucket with some floating ice inside, sitting nearby. When all the cans were full to the top, cows had freshened. Boy, when the cans were full, we got a bigger check, and so did they. Springtime, when the farmers were the busiest, then's when cows freshened, so milking time took much longer.

One lady was continuously complaining about their milk test. The price of milk was determined by the test. No cream—low test, smaller pay check. Everyone at that house enjoyed whipped cream. She was always skimming off heavy cream for rich desserts and ice cream. She had the nerve to complain!

We were sorry to have to return a can of milk because it tested sour at the factory. We got no pay for hauling it, and they didn't get paid for it. When delivered, we'd draw the lady's attention to it. "Doesn't matter if the milk is a little blinky for ice cream," she'd say, after a quick taste, to which the kids rejoiced! If it was real sour, she'd let it sit so the cream could rise good, then skim it off to make butter and use the clabber milk for cottage cheese. The whey from the cottage cheese went into hog slop. Nothing was wasted.

Seems we'd always expect sour milk after a hot, stormy night. Thunder sours milk was the consensus of most. One time a family kept having sour milk. Finally each cow was tested at milking time. One cow, I don't know why, but she was giving sour milk. They had to send her to the stockyards.

Another time, two sticks of stovewood started to roll out at the milk station. I hurried and got them before anyone could see. Those little buggers back there at Griffins' did that! They were always up to something.

Farm ladies, with their Hoosier thrift, grabbed at a chance to send correspondence to a neighbor or a relative on down the road, without paying for a two-cent stamp. We didn't mind.

There was a pump and tin cup at every farm, and we knew which one had the best drinking water. We occasionally needed that little house out back.

One fellow at the milk station was very accommodating, and Grace said it looked like he was sweet on me. I took a three-by-five picture of Carl and put it up on the front dash. He got the hint!

One little girl, probably four or five, would hurry out, catch a ride with us, to go spend a few hours at her grandparents' on down the road. We'd pick her up on the return trip. Going through Red Bridge west of Cicero, with a load of empty milk cans—rumble, tumble, shake—she thought that was the greatest fun!

She always treated us to the funniest running commentaries throughout a trip, talking nonstop: "When you were liddle, like me, did you play on top of the rails, run along, swinging your arms, then seeing how long you could stay up before falling into the leaves? Mama always warns me of snakes hiding down in there. And Mama told me about Ruby Venable, when she was a liddle girl, they had company and someone asked Ruby if they had any cows. What are the cows' names, did she know? Ruby said, yes, she knew, her paw named them—they are all sons-o-bitches! An' when people talk about that widder lady, the one that wears men's pants, Papa always says he be durned if he knew what to make of it—her broad rump packed into tight overalls like two shoats in a sack. Hear that? Jays are noisy birds, ain't they? Always hollerin' about nothin.' Them two folks that lives there, Mama says they quarrel right smart much but Papa says they fight like two stray cats in a rain barrel. There at that farm, they got a mean bull and Ma says they outta git rid of it—it'll kill somebody yet, but Paw says it's a goodun. Did you ever hear this joke? 'Up she jumps, out she runs, down she squats, out it comes.' What is it? Give up? Little Dutch Maid out milking, ha ha! Ain't that funny?"

"Goodness sake, you can talk the ear off a tea cup!" I'd tell her. Just after Christmas one year she brought out her autograph book for me and Grace to write in. I don't remember what Grace penned, but the little girl laughed and laughed when she read mine: *He met her in the meadow when the sun was sinking low/They strolled along together in the twilight's afterglow/She neither smiled nor thanked him as he lowered all the bars/For she knew not how/For he was just a farmer and she a Jersey cow!*

Holidays, summers, over at Riverwood, was a place for all-day fishing, swimming, boat racing, and horseback riding. Me and Grace were always anxious to go, and we had informed the patrons the day before that we'd be a half-hour early the next morning. You can be sure we didn't stop to visit along the way! By early afternoon, we were on our way to see the celebrations!

Our daily schedules never varied. After arriving home from our route around one, Forest came running out the back door to hug his mama, then he'd ride with us to the barn. We quickly unhitched the horses, led them out of their shafts to the water trough for a drink, and into their stalls in the stable, unharnessed them, threw forkfuls of hay into the mangers, and a scoopful of oats into the feed boxes, stroked their noses a few times, then headed for the house. Mrs. Long insisted we eat another meal, then to bed for an afternoon nap. We needed our rest, she said, after such a long, hard day.

Sometimes we cleaned up and went into town in the afternoon. Most women thought harnessing a horse to the buggy was really hard work and they wouldn't try it, but I always managed by climbing over, under, and around the animal.

It seems to me the three of us—me, Grace and Willard—divided our check three ways; I just don't remember for sure. I was having a great time!

Through those many, many miles of milk hauling, Grace and I gained a real close kinship to so many good people that followed us throughout life!

(Lola and Carl's romance was a lifetime relationship of pleasures and some perils. They celebrated seventy-six years together before his passing, four months before his one hundredth birthday. Lola still lives alone at ninety-eight, is mentally active, reading many books a week, does handwork, and is a regular churchgoer. Her response when asked about living a long married life? She laughs, "We disagreed agreeably.")

—This story originally appeared in Tri Town Topics, *January 1 and 8, 1981, and in* Good Old Days, *August, 1984; it is also included in* Cicero Indiana: 1834-1984.

When Pa Is Sick

When Pa is sick
He's scared to death,
An' Ma an' us
Just holds our breath.

He crawls to bed
An' puffs and grunts,
An' does all kinds
Of crazy stunts.

He wants Doc Brown
An' mighty quick;
For when Pa's ill
He's awful sick.

He gasps and groans
An' sort o' sighs,
He talks queer
An' rolls his eyes.

Ma jumps an' runs
An' all of us
An' all the house
Is in a fuss.

An' peace an' joy
Is mighty skeerce.
When Pa is sick
It's somethin' fierce.

When Ma Is Sick

When Ma is sick
She pegs away.
She's quiet though,
Not much to say.

She goes right on
A-doin' things,
An' sometimes laughs
Or even sings.

She says she don't
Feel extra well,
But then it's just
A kind o' spell.

She'll be all right
Tomorrow sure.
A good old sleep
Will be the cure.

An' Pa, he sniffs
An' makes a kick,
Says woman-folks
Is always sick.

An' Ma, she smiles,
Lets on she's glad.
When Ma is sick
It ain't so bad.

—Unknown

Zula, Traveling Dressmaker

by
Zula Cammack

Zula Cammack was born, grew up, and faithfully served most of her long existence in the Deming and Cicero area. Her turn-of-the-century account, given in the 1970s, details the life of a visiting dressmaker.

You should have seen the waves of excitement that filled a house when the mother of a family of several girls announced that I, Zula Cammack, the dressmaker, was coming for a week to make their dresses. I'm ninety-five. My feet have peddled many-a-mile on one of those old treadle sewing machines, before and after the turn of the century.

I managed to support myself quite well with my needle. Back then, virtually all of the family's clothing was sewn by hand, in homes, since ready-made clothes were generally unavailable or unreasonably priced. Many households didn't have sewing machines, so each little stitch was put in a garment by a mother with a needle, thread, patience, and a whole lot of loving care.

I was booked up solid every week. I lived with my parents, Clark and Margaret Cammack. There was a big family of us at home and Zula did all the sewing, for Mama was always so busy with other things. I don't even remember when I learned to sew. Mama didn't sew, not to speak of. I took after Grandma. She always had needle-marked fingers, a lap full of mending whenever she rested in her rocker or she was bent over a quilting frame. She'd whip me up a new dress in no time, with just a needle and thread.

I was taught at Grandma's knee. She put an embroidery hoop in my hands at age five, I was only toadstool high, and was given my first lesson in fancywork. Grandma said, when Mama was a little girl, she would rather have her hands in a mixing bowl!

As I went from house to house, I always had bits of news and stories to impart. They liked having me. A traveling dressmaker spent the bulk of her days, most of her life, in other people's homes. She knew everything about nearly everyone in and around the community because of

her peripatetic life. Yet I never gossiped in an unkind way, or said an unkind thing about one family to another. "Zula is a perfect lady," one woman said. And I added, "A dog that brings a bone will carry a bone." If I gossip, they'll gossip about me!

Most of us sewing women were old maids like me. Or widow ladies.

I remember Grandma telling me: "If work baskets were gifted with powers of speech, they could tell stories more true and tender than any we read!" Women often sewed the tragedy or comedy of life into their work as they sat at home, thinking, living whole-heart histories, and praying prayers, while they embroidered pretty trifles, or did the weekly mending and sewing. Or patching or darning. What piles of darning.

When someone made a garment and it didn't fit too well—a few women were terribly careless—someone would be sure to remark, "She must have fitted it on the ash-hopper!" And not-too-neat buttonholes were called "hog eyes" or "cat eyes." Long stitches in quilting, someone'd remind them that "your old man will snag his toenails in them."

Grandma told me that when they first took a quilt out of the frames, the young girls would hold the four corners, put the family cat in the center, and shake it up and down. Whichever side the cat ran out indicated the first girl to get married! I guess the cat never ran out my side.

"Actually, I have nothing to wear," would begin a call to me or a note on a penny postcard. "I've been too busy to think or care till now, but here it is nearly summer and I have hardly a decent rag to wear on my back. Usually I just go to Zula and tell her what I want, and here I am!"

So I took care of all the needs of our community in and around Cicero and Deming—I lived not far from Deming, a town of fifteen people and forty dogs.

A neighboring farmer who despised loafers, smokers, and drunks, had no taste for reading. He ran his wife's sewing machine after long hours in the fields. It beat all—he enjoyed it! Said it was restful work. And that was a big help when almost all clothing was home-sewn. He was such a good family man. While most husbands in the homes where I worked were good people and providing, there usually wasn't much respect for his hard-working wife—he was forever cutting her down or making snide remarks. I soon picked up on that.

Once Grandma and Mama were discussing fashion pictures in ladies' magazines. "I wonder if the time will ever come that one can walk into a store and buy a dress all made up," Mama pondered.

That nettled Grandma. "Good land, no! They'll never just go into a store and buy those fancy duds or order 'em outta a catalogue. There ain't no two sets o' hips 'n' busts 'n' shoulders in the whole wide world alike. No, that's one thing ain't never goin' to be invented by nobody. Till the end of the world folks has got to have dresses made for ev'ry separate one. And if a woman is an old maid or widah, she can make a good livin' dressmakin'."

Grandma, I can still hear and see her, she'd measure an arm's length of thread, then bite it in two, then thread her needle—holding it way out and squinting to be able to see to do it. She'd talk incessantly while she worked, her mouth full of pins, and her red strawberry pin-cushion stuck full of pins nearby. She'd measure a yard of goods from her nose to the tip of her fingers. When I asked her how she knew it were a true measurement, she told me that the legal yard in the time of King Henry I of England was the distance from the King's nose, arm outstretched, to the end of his thumb. She always carried facts in her head, and that's the way she measured. One day when she left the room I sneaked her tape measure and measured for myself. It didn't hold true for me—I was too young, I suppose.

She would lay out a newspaper or a length of leftover wallpaper on the floor, get down on her knees and begin to measure, then carefully cut out a pattern to fit me. I don't know how she did it but she never missed in her measurements! I can still hear the sound of her scissors, cutting away, sharp and brisk, whisk, whisk, whisk!

When my dress was all sewed up, she'd call me in every five minutes to try it on, but I wanted to play. I'd have to take off my everyday dress each time. "Hold still fur a minute, wiggle worm!" she'd say. "Now, go in yonder…turn around—I want to see if that-there hem hangs even. Stand over side that door and turn slowly," she was waving me around. Sometimes I'd get so hot I thought I'd faint, especially when she'd say, "Oh, my, I think that's whopper-jawed!"

Why did it have to be so perfect? "Hurry, Grandma, somebody might see me without my dress!"

"I cain't hurry lessen you hold still!" When it was all finished, I strutted peacock-proud, before all the members of the family. Mama was delighted. What fun it was to turn around in front of the looking glass, Grandma and Mama beaming approval.

Papa was always more fussy and concerned about the length of his maturing daughters' dresses, not how pretty we looked. He'd have a big frown, "Girls, you better push them hemlines down and the necklines up. I don't want any ankles or breast works showing in this-here house." That bothered me. He never had anything nice to say of how we looked.

Children's clothing was made large enough to allow for shrinkage and growth. Always, at least a four inch hem. When they finally fit, they were faded and worn out!

After hours of sewing, Grandma'd remove her spectacles and pinch the bridge of her nose to ease it. I couldn't wait till I was grown and could wear spectacles. What tiny details register in my mind at such a time and remain through the years.

The very day I tried out my first sewing machine, I ran the needle through my fingernail down to the bone! I sucked on it good, then soaked it in hot Epsom salts water, bandaged it in a strip of clean white rag, tied it with a string, and forgot to be afraid of the sewing machine needle thereafter.

Dellie Applegate! Yes, how well I remember. I used to go there and stay a week at a time. They had five boys and five girls. Dellie had been an only child, never learned to sew, and when she had so many children, she needed Zula.

I made a dollar a day, and that was pretty good wages. I never did make more than two dollars a day, six days a week. Stayed a week, yes I did! I sewed for all the Applegate girls, but I don't remember in particular that I made anything for the boys, don't remember that I did, but all five of the girls I did.

Dellie would drive her horse and buggy to town and buy up a big stack of yard goods and the patterns I needed. Patterns were on a rack and they cost five cents, ten cents, maybe fifteen. There were no printed instructions on them, just the three holes meaning to lay it on the fold, and the notches you matched along the sides. There was no printed guide—you just knew how it all went together.

I had a cotton bag full of patterns from other households with girls these sizes, cut out of newspapers, each rolled together separately and tied with bits of goods—ribbon, gingham, or silk. Patterns were passed from one friend to another.

I'd take along my own scissors 'cause women who didn't sew, theirs wouldn't cut hot butter. Even if they sewed, in a big family they were always lost or they were dull from the children cutting paper. The kids would even try to sneak mine out.

Dellie would buy the yard goods at Leo Lively's in Cicero, or Osborne's at Noblesville, where Willits are now, or Clark and Brocks, on the other corner. Not at Craycrafts. They catered to the fashion plates. More expensive.

Most didn't believe in spending a lot on clothes when a child was still growing, especially when there was no one to hand things down to.

Some of those I sewed for, with money, gave me their scraps of left-over goods and I kept a supply on hand for those who were very poor. Sometimes there was enough for a little dress. I often made gifts for these children, like doll dresses and blankets for the little girls. Boys, too. Once I made a baseball out of a pair of worn-out heavy corduroy knickers—the backs of the legs still pretty good. Or I'd make 'em gun holsters.

Dellie, she'd buy this great big stack of goods and have it all ready for me to start in on. I think it was Waltz Applegate, that was one of the older boys, I was talking to him awhile back, and he said, "I remember how I used to hitch up the horse and buggy and come out and get you early on Monday morning. And the purring of the sewing machine all day long. The whole family looked forward to your appearances. It meant fancier dishes of food, more unusual desserts, and a festive time in general. Mama would usually outdo herself so that you'd carry the tidings along that Della Applegate was a good cook!"

More than likely I slept in a bed with a couple of little kids, 'cause most big families didn't have extra rooms or beds. More than once I woke up wet clear through.

They expected me to take part in the family conversations. One time little Edward asked me if I had a papa and I said yes, and a mama and sisters and brothers. "No!" he scolded, "I mean a papa, you a mama and little kids."

"No," I explained, "I'm a spinster."

"A spinster!" He had such a bewildered look on his face. He and I had the rapt attention of all the family now. I said, "Yes, a spinster. No husband and no children. Years ago mothers put unmarried daughters, living at home, to work at the spinning wheel—hence the term 'spinster.'" Edward still had a confused look. The girls all gave me sympathetic glances, until I hastily added, "You all are my children. And next week and the week after I'll have a new family!"

When I first arrived, the Applegates were all so happy to see me. Oh, they were animated at Dellie's. I tried to make myself heard above the general uproar of questions that everbody was asking and nobody got answered! In such a hubbub, explanations of "What are you making me?" were impossible until Dellie took command of the situation.

At every house we were up at cock-crow, ate a big hearty breakfast with the whole family, and then, as soon as the dishes were cleared off the kitchen table, the oil cloth scrubbed clean, I went to work cutting out dresses, or stitching 'em up. I stopped only for meals or a mid-afternoon cup of tea and cookies or a piece of pie.

Those Applegate girls, thin as paper dolls! They were happy when I brought my latest *Ladies' Home Journal* along. I subscribed to it for its fashions and I could look at one of the illustrations and duplicate it perfectly. "I don't want my dresses to look back country," they'd remind me. Trying on, I'd hear, "Does it pull, pucker, or hike up?"

One lady always sent to *Comfort* magazine for boughten patterns, for her daughters, and all the other girls would want copies of them. She didn't mind. So there was a lot of cutting patterns off the boughten tissue paper ones.

Dresses were hung on hooks in wardrobes or along the bedroom walls. Some of the women took newspapers, rolled 'em into a tight roll, wrapped cotton string around it in the center, then pushed it all through the shoulders, and hung it on a nail. That held a dress in shape pretty well. I just can't remember when hangers came available. They were wooden, and of course, most of us couldn't afford 'em.

One very poor family, the mother wanted her children to have something new, not always the hand-me-downs. So, one time, girls' dresses and boys' shirts were all cut from one bolt of goods, for economy's sake. That was cute, seeing 'em all alike, lined up so proud in their pew each Sunday at church.

There was one little feller who was a "fixer." He was forever carrying around a hammer or a hatchet. Before I started sewing at any house I'd oil the machine so it would run smoother, and I'd adjust the tension. Then I'd take an old rag and wipe away any excess oil so as not to damage a garment. One day we were eating dinner, maybe it was at Applegates', or Geigers', a little fellow's chair was empty. We didn't think much about it. After the meal I found him in there with oil can and screwdriver. "I fixt it really dood!" He'd worked it over, all right! It took all of us the blessed afternoon to find lost screws, or loosen those he'd tightened too much, to get the sewing machine back together and wiped clean, after such a generous oiling! I was thankful I hadn't left the dress goods nearby.

I kept my little watch pinned on my bodice, so I'd know the time without waiting till the kitchen clock struck. The tiny kiddies liked to come, in the midst of my sewing, they'd put my watch to an ear and listen to it tick.

I'd sew eight to ten hours at a time. The missus would say, "Well, I think it's time to light the lamps." I'd gather everything up and stack it in a pile. I never sewed at night 'cause after supper was over the children got ready for bed. I took good care of my eyes. Sewing's hard on 'em.

Mr. Applegate had a sister, with a good job in the East, and she'd send great big boxes of fine apparel, her castoffs, and those of her friends, to be made over for the girls. I liked doing that. A lot of good used clothing was given to most families and I was pretty clever at altering, remodeling, and remaking things, so bedtime was for "trying on." Or, I'd look something over from their last season's summer's dresses and say, "Someone better put a brick on your head—you've outgrown all your clothes!"

"You can't wear that this summer; it's tight in the arm's eye."

"This will take a lot of cutting-down; this lady was much more full-figured than you." Many of the dresses necessitated setting over buttons, after a spurt of growth.

I'd have a mouthful of pins while I finished pinning something up, and there'd be one of those little tykes with pins in her mouth, trying to talk around them, pinning scraps together on her doll like I was a-doing.

Usually little boys and girls liked playing on the floor, around my legs, while I sewed. They were fascinated at the speed with which my feet could make the foot pedal fly. Occasionally one would try to catch the pedal or belt, and oh how he'd howl when his finger got caught in the wheel. He'd get a good scolding from the mama!

Every household had a big buttonbox. Buttons were snipped off discarded garments and kept for later use. Children loved playing with them. Now this happened a lot: a child would grab the buttonbox off the table, and spools, thimbles, and buttons went rolling all over the floor, every which way!

I'd get the new dresses all sewed up, then Dellie would do the handwork, the hems, and buttonholes and all. She had picked up enough sewing to get by. With the back-fastening dress styles of the day, she had a lot of buttonholes to make, and buttons to sew on. The boys were always losing buttons off their clothes. She'd sew them securely at the fly front of their pants and on their jackets. Buttons, hooks and eyes, and snaps were used on all openings.

Those Applegate children—they were pretty young when I started in there, and I stayed with 'em for years and years, to when the girls graduated from common school, high school, and were married. They all wanted fancy dresses for those occasions.

How old is Agnes now, past eighty? She came along third in line. I remember we just couldn't get her ready and off to school on time. A long time was spent in buttoning her shoes in the morning, drawing the buttonhook in and out and all the while listening to all the conversation around her. She was always busy doing something else. The whole family worried over her. And she was that way all her life. Every place she went, church, club, or meetings, she tore in, in a hurry, always late! She never walked; she trotted. Jude, her ever-patient husband, would say of her, "She trots herself to death!" Really, she could throw a lot of work!

I remember one morning, before school, the heel of her shoe ripped the hem out of her skirt. She got a thread and needle and was curled up on the floor, trying to hurriedly mend it. I said, "Agnes, did anyone ever tell you it's bad luck to sew up rips when the garment is on you? Hurry up, now, it'll never be noticed on a gallopin' horse anyway!" She hated it when I made that comment to her. Agnes wondered all that day what bad luck was going to befall her.

Dellie said, of all her children, not one had been wanted at the time she first knew they were coming along. And not a one would she give up. "Heaven sent me ten babies," she'd brag. "Ward, Janette, Waltz, Agnes, Carl, Clara, John, Margaret, Edward, and Katherine. They came, boy-girl, boy-girl all the way."

Dellie had a stormy temperament which kept her children on the straight and narrow path. She had reason to get easily provoked with so many, and probably couldn't understand much of their mischief, she being an only child.

Dellie was the one who cultivated the children's minds. They got their discipline, ideals, and standards from their mother. She had each one committing to memory long verses, often animated, for school and church entertainments. I'd get to hear all of these because I was making clothes for a special program the children had to perform in.

Kern loved his family and worked hard making a living for 'em. He took his sons along with him to farm.

Most families I sewed for lived with three generations under one roof. The Applegates had Grandpa.

The children, in most homes, were mannerly-quiet at mealtime. As the expression goes, you're to be seen, not heard! It was a different story at Applegates'.

Every time I went to Applegates', seems there'd been a new baby and the seating arrangement around the table had changed. The young-est sat in his high chair—usually sucking on a greasy chicken bone or bread crust—between Dellie and Kern. The children were seated ac-cording to a system—a little one next to an older one, who was to watch over his behavior, and to see that he got his food. Of course they all fought over who I'd sit by. After each meal, you should have seen the pile of dirty dishes! And the fighting and scrapping would begin again.

Henry Bowman, a close neighbor, asked me how I got along at Applegates'. I said they were the awfullest kids to fight I ever heard tell of. Fight one minute and makin' up the next. Say somethin' ugly, and regret it as soon as it was said. Henry mused, "I stopped by one day when they was eatin' dinner and I never heard so much racket in my life! Everbody talkin' at once. One little fella, Edward, or was it John, three, four year old, I guess, he yelled, 'Pass the tatas!' It was so noisy, 'stead of asking agin, he climbed up on the table, walked the whole length of it, and brought the dishful back to his place, dodging dishes of food."

My very first meal in their house I remember so well. Ward, rising like a jack-in-box to give this lady his seat, and the others on the bench moving over to make a few inches of room for me. These big families, eating three meals a day together, they'd have a long table, with benches on one, two, or three sides. Chairs would take up too much space.

Waltz, when he was little, had a bad habit of not getting to the table to eat. One day he was lying out prone on the floor, screaming. The other kids decided to break him by teasing him that there wouldn't be enough food left for him anyway. "Pass the last of them potatoes in that-there dish." And they laughed about the last piece of chicken and pie. Didn't take him long to find his plate!

The three oldest girls chattered about their fellers amongst them-selves. I'd laugh right along with 'em. I made Janette's clothes when she went away to Minnesota, I believe it was. They could teach up there after high school graduation without a certificate. I guess it was two, three years later Agnes taught up there after her graduation from high school. Maybe Margaret did too. I made all those clothes; all the Applegate girls had stylish notions. Then, before I knew it, I was mak-ing their wedding dresses.

The girls would say to me, "Zula, tell me a funny story." I told 'em about this sewing lady down at Block's in Indianapolis. She used one side of her stuffed bodice as a pincushion! At first, those around her cringed—sticking herself with pins? There was an old saying back then: "What God's forgotten, fill with cotton." Probably what she did.

Another sewing lady kept feeling one of her fronts, then the other, "I know I had one when I started!" She was feeling for her handkerchief, a handy place where women tucked them down their neck when busy.

At one house I was sewing a little girl's dress for her to wear to the last-day-of-school program. The baby sister kept getting in the way. Finally I said, "Honey, if you'll amuse the baby, I'll make a dolly dress for your doll, just like this-here dress for you, out of the dress scraps," which I did.

It was common for a little tyke to crawl around on the floor near my feet. After a while, listening to the hum of the sewing machine, or watching my feet pedal back and forth, the baby would soon be sound asleep on the floor.

Another home, all big people, the gentleman would always say, "I like my hogs, cows, chickens. I likes 'em fat. And that includes me wife! I don't know how you feel about it, Zula, but I wus allus sorta glad the Lord A'mighty used a fair-sized pattern when he was makin' her." She'd laugh and shake all over when he said that! She was always so jolly.

I knew which husband was faithful and kind to his wife—no one had to tell me.

And, there was the Clark and Mag Geiger family. Oh, dear, that was a big clan. A cramped, airtight little three-room house, ten children, filled to the bursting point! Some were married and gone when the little ones come along. There was Bessie and Goldie and Geneva. Was that all the girls? And several boys. Their mother didn't sew either. I walked over there, then home at night—no room to sleep me! I made their school clothes and, of course, their church dresses, then their graduation dresses when they graduated from common school, and any who graduated from high school. Real nice family.

I remember how proud Bessie was of her wedding dress. I said, as I fitted a pattern to her, "Such a tiny waistline! You do draw yourself up with those corset strings. Surely your man's two hands could span you!" The dress was white with a lot of lace insertions, and pinned at the neck with a family heirloom breast pin. The skirt, six yards around the bottom, barely cleared the floor, was complete with rows of tucks, miles of ruffles, yards of lace edging and insertions, dozens of tiny cloth-covered buttons and corresponding button loops, and touches of embroidery here and there. Under the dress were several white cotton ruffled petticoats, an embroidered corset cover, and lace-trimmed drawers.

And I made her in-fair dress, too. You don't know what that was I bet! Well, they had the wedding put on by the bride's parents one day; the second day was the in-fair, a dinner at the groom's parents. That was a nice party, too.

I made her in-fair dress out of blue taffeta with a white silk collar. My, she was pretty! She married Raymond Briles. He was driving a team to the school wagon to Deming, so no time for a honeymoon. Some had honeymoons, but most of 'em around us couldn't afford one.

When Mrs. Geiger died, Mr. Geiger, the father, was set on having a brand new dress for his wife to be buried in. She'd been sick for some time. The Geiger girls went to town and picked out real pretty goods and they stopped by with their horse and buggy and got me and took me home with 'em. Bessie and I had to hurry to have her ready for viewing. I don't know how we did it, but we did. I just know oh, how proud she'd have been of that dress if she could have worn it when she was still living! She had such a few of the worldly possessions. Very seldom a new dress. Always one of the kids needed something worse, or pressing farm expenses. I didn't charge folks for funeral dresses.

There were several makes of sewing machines, but I liked the Singer the best. They didn't all have a sewing machine for me to use. I had one at home. I never did take it with me, oh, mercy no! I suppose those who didn't have their own, borrowed one. I just don't remember. Several I knew did all their stitching by hand! It took me some time to get used to my new electric—push the control and the thing'd almost get away from me!

I sewed all kinds of women's suits and coats.

The Sunday winter clothes for girls were made of nice, dark woolens, and had ruffly white aprons to wear over 'em, to keep the woolens from having to be washed so often. What fun it was to try things on and turn about before the looking glass!

I made my sister Halcie's dress when she played the piano at Mrs. Gray's recital. It was yellow crepe, real full, and scallops all around the bottom. I took yellow satin ribbon, an inch wide, and shirred it and had rows and rows of that on the skirt. She thought it was the prettiest dress there ever was! I made her a wool suit and everyone thought she'd bought it. And, I made her wedding dress—white and oh, so beautiful. Her underthings I made were snow white and lace all over.

Did you know Cora Evans? Well, I made one batch of baby things for her and when she had 'em, they were twins. Edgar and Edna, born

Christmas Day, 1907. I remember that like it was yesterday. She'd been a schoolteacher and didn't marry young. I went back and made another batch.

Those baby things—made 'em all, baby boys dressed like baby girls, dresses and slips and gowns and the diapers and blankets, everything. Cora never had any more children.

Every year Cora had me come the week before Decoration Day and again the week before school started. She dressed the twins exactly alike, only a bloomer showed on Edgar's.

When Edgar started school, all the boys were wearing boys' clothes and from then on he insisted on overalls.

Which reminds me. One neighbor woman said she was useless with a needle. She was handier with a hay fork! She wore men's overalls! Can you imagine that?

Yes, and I used to go to Noblesville and sew at the Brays' and the Heaths'. People with money, Heaths, there by the Masonic Temple. I'd stay sometimes two weeks at a time, and sew for their girls. One lives in Florida now and another in South Africa. I get letters from 'em all the time.

My sister, Beulah Mundy, died of pneumonia, leaving three little children. Josephine was only fifteen months old, Don was five and Mary Alice was three. We took those children right home with us from the funeral. It's real pitiful for children to lose their mother when they're so young, oh mercy! I made all of their clothes, and I often took Mary Alice with me. I'd take care of 'em a lot when I was home, to relieve Mama. Later, the two oldest ones went to live with their father when he remarried. I bought a house in town and Josephine lived with me until she got a husband and home of her own.

Oh, mercy me, there were a lot of different dress goods. There was calico, gingham and, oh, voile, dotted swiss, linen, plushes, and satin. And there was corded and tucked silk. Lots of kinds. Beautiful laces and ribbons.

The organdies made into little girls' dresses were so beautiful! It was stiff when ironed out, and thin, needed a pretty petticoat underneath. It'd scratch around the neck and the arms would often rub raw, but no one seemed to mind because it was elegant!

I remember I made myself a black silk taffeta petticoat that dragged the floor. It had two ruffles on the bottom of it. Oh, girls who had them were the bee's knees! They'd rattle and rustle as you walked and you'd feel so special! I can remember that so well. Yes, I dressed stylish, too.

And I sewed for Emma and Will Johnson and their six kids, and for Sally O'Rear and her family, in our neighborhood. The O'Rears had seven kids. And Dr. Tomlinson's family, in Cicero, a whole lot. Oh, I could just name family after family.

Later, in Cicero, Mrs. Slater and I opened a dress and hat shop. I could sew elaborate dresses just by looking at magazine illustrations, and she created beautiful hats the same way. For fashionable ladies, there would always have to be a new hat to complement the frock. Gladys Applegate, she'd come in our shop. Mercy me, I can't begin to remember them all.

After Josephine married, I went to live with her, and continued going into the homes all week long.

Then I moved in with Mrs. Butler, to be a companion. You remember her? I had my sewing machine right there and they'd bring sewing to me. I had my radio, then later, a TV. It hurt me awful when she died.

Oh, mercy me, I've sewn all my life, about. I know I sewed till I was past ninety for here's a picture of me. I made that dress. Here's a picture of me in a dress I sewed up when I was a girl. I didn't have anybody else to do my sewing!

Before World War I, you couldn't go to the stores and buy readymade clothes hardly. It was after the war, around 1923, that people started buying from the stores when they stocked 'em. But I still had plenty of sewing, after World War II, to do for families because I could do it cheaper.

Just recently someone asked me how old I was. They seemed very surprised that I was still sewing for people "at my age!" I simply said, "Growing old is nothing more than a bad habit, which a busy person has no time for!"

Here's something that I cut out of the newspaper years ago that I want you to read. You'll die laughing 'cause I did! (*Editor's note: The clipping Zula mentions is on the next page.*)

—*This story originally appeared in* Tri Town Topics, *December 31, 1975, and January 7, 1976.*

Bugs in the Type

Keeping the bugs out of the type which go into printing a newspaper is a never-ending task. Typos, as they are called, are frequently the source of trouble and they also occasionally provoke a good laugh.

We always strive at The Ledger to avoid errors, and with the tremendous number of words and numbers with which you must deal in a brief period of time daily, it's probably a wonder more mistakes are not made.

This is why we laughed with our fingers crossed at a series of errors which appeared on the classified pages of a small daily newspaper in the South.

It started with the following on a Monday:

"**For Sale**—R.D. Jones has one sewing machine for sale. Phone 958 after 7 p.m. and ask for Mrs. Kelly who lives with him cheap."

On Tuesday the following notice appeared:

"**Notice**: We regret having erred in R.D. Jones' ad yesterday. It should have read: One sewing machine for sale. Cheap. Phone 958 and ask for Mrs. Kelly who lives with him after 7 p.m."

This followed on Wednesday:

"R.D. Jones has informed us that he has received several annoying telephone calls because of the error we made in his classified ad yesterday. His ad stands corrected as follows:

For Sale: R.D. Jones has one sewing machine for sale. Cheap. Phone 958 after 7 p.m. and ask for Mrs. Kelly who loves with him."

And finally this appeared on Thursday:

"**Notice**: I, R.D. Jones, have no sewing machine for sale. I smashed it. Don't call 958 as the phone has been disconnected."

My Hair, the Bane of My Existence

by
Helen Lewis

Helen Lewis was a private secretary in Chicago and New York for many years, then came "back home" to Indiana to retire. She tells of "bobbing" her hair in the Roaring Twenties.

Mama always thought I, her oldest daughter, had to look just so. She made me the most beautiful clothes and was extremely proud of my hair, light brown with red casts. I think they called it strawberry roan. It was awfully curly and came down to my waist. Back as far as I can remember, it was a pain in the neck! I could hardly stand to look at myself in the mirror without gagging. My hair, the bane of my existence!

Part of the time our family had money. Part of the time we didn't. It all depended upon whether Dad had a particularly lucrative job or if Grandfather had made a big deal in the insurance business. Sometimes we inherited money. I knew both worlds, money and no money.

We had a big house on a very fine street and we also owned a farm and horses and carriages.

I was fourteen when Sister was born, so I was like an only child for many years. Mother would tell about how beautiful I was and, even as a newborn, I never cried. She'd wheel me uptown in my perambulator and park me outside the grocery store while she went in for her supplies. When she came out, people were circled around, making over that beautiful baby. I'd be kicking my feet, swinging my arms, and laughing up at them. Oh, how I loved the attention.

She'd roll me into the front yard for sunbaths. I'd laugh and chatter and coo. Dogs came up and happily barked in at me.

When Sister came along, she moaned with colic for several months and was a recluse from the start. She'd wail until Mama covered her over so people couldn't see in. If someone, recognizing Mama, uncovered Sister to have a peek, Sister would scream out as if saying, "Get out of here!"

No one ever remarked about how beautiful Sister was. Was it that I was beautiful, or was it that I had a winning personality?

That contrasting pattern followed us through life. We grew up, were good friends, married, and neither had children. I enjoyed my jobs and all the people around me. She preferred a very private environment.

One time, when I was three, my aunt came down from Chicago and she said, "Oh, Ethel"—that's my mother, Ethel— "let's do something with that girl's hair!" So Mama took me to have it cut. It came in curlier and thicker than ever!

When I was into my early teens, I was reading about girls my age getting "bobs." My father, and all other fathers I knew, refused permission to their daughters. They thought it made a girl look "fast." Skirts began to creep upwards—the first step toward the above-the-knee lengths of the twenties. Shameless!

I remember how I dreaded having all that hair washed every other Saturday. Mama put the washtub on a backless chair in the kitchen, even though we had a bathroom. The upstairs lavatory wouldn't begin to hold the thick mane. When I bent way over I'd get dizzy and think I was going to faint. It took so long to soap it with Castile soap, then rinse it good, with a final vinegar cleansing, and then it took hours for it to dry. I kept begging Mama to have it cut. I even reminded her that I'd heard an old lady say they thought very long, thick hair like mine would sap a child's strength.

Then, the ordeal of combing it all out. "Hold still, Helen Louise!" A rat's nest of tangles. I wonder now how my mother was so patient with me and my constant complaining. She brushed each strand around her finger, so I'd have the beautiful long curls. Then she took a chicken feather from where she kept them by the iodine bottle on top of the kitchen cabinet. She dipped it into the perfume bottle, then up into each ringlet, so I'd not only look beautiful, I'd smell wonderful. To this day I abhor lily of the valley!

When I was sixteen, during the "flapper age," my very, very fancy cousin, Elma, came down from big city, Detroit, to visit us in our little one-horse town. Oh, she was just so tut-tut-tut in her latest dresses above the knees and her hair cut in the new, boyish, short look, very straight, with a curl in front of each ear, like the popular star, Clara Bow, known as the "It Girl." She had the air of a princess who had somehow misplaced her crown.

Elma copied Clara's looks and styles. First the haircut. She painted her nails. She even shaved her legs!

The flappers wore their dresses above the knees, with their stockings rolled down below them. Elma'd gently roll her silk stockings down into place below her knees, then twist the corner of each one and tuck the knot into place. Said she had fashionable garters back home, but they were out of style. And here was Helen, my long silk stockings held in place with an elastic garter belt!

Elma talked of buying a pair of slacks. She wanted to platinum her hair, but she hadn't yet. Her parents admired the Clara Bow look and didn't mind the changes, so she said.

Papa complained that Elma not only had a man's haircut, she wanted to start dressing in pants! What's the world coming to?

She went around singing the same tune all week long. The words to the popular lyric shocked my parents, "Roll 'em, Girlies, roll 'em, Go ahead and roll 'em, Roll 'em down and show your pretty knees!"

One day Elma, in her genteel manner, reached into her handbag for a pack of Lucky Strikes, then took one and put it into a long cigarette holder, and held it between her fingers. As I stared in surprise, she put it to her mouth and drew deeply, blowing little smoke rings and laughing at my expense. She looked at me, so all-knowing, and said, "I started smoking when I was fourteen. I thought it was the coolest thing anyone could do!"

One afternoon we were together in my small bedroom, perched on the end of my bed. Elma was smoking furiously, lighting one cigarette from the stub of the other, always saying, "Oh, yeah?" at my fear that Mama would come upstairs. When I picked up a cigarette to smoke I felt nervous and awkward, all long arms and large, unwieldy hands. I placed it between my lips then drew in a deep breath as she touched a lighted match to it. I started to cough—oh, it tasted awful! "How can you stand it?" I asked her. "Oh, yeah?" she gave me a surprised look.

She said, walking around the room in her step-ins, "You'll get used to it. Everyone's smoking nowadays."

I envied her, as did all my friends. I pined to be, not like Clara Bow, but a duplicate of Cousin Elma!

And, here was me, Helen, sixteen, tall, and a head full of long curls, and I choked when I tried to smoke.

Sometimes, for a dance, Mama would let me pull my hair up, with some of the curls hanging down the back.

Dad was on her side, always, on the rearing of their daughter—no hair cut and watch how she dresses, Ethel!

Mama didn't mind the short skirts when the flappers came along, but Papa! One time I was going to a ball—that's what we called dances. Mama always saw to it I had a gorgeous dress. This time it was a pale blue, panne velvet, with a V-neck, cut pretty low, sleeveless, and made by a French dressmaker.

The night of the dance, I came gliding down the stairs, all elegantly dressed. Dad took a long look. "You're not going out of this house looking like that, young lady!"

I asked, innocent like, "What do you mean, Dad? This is the way everybody dresses."

"Well, you're not going that way! You've got to have some sleeves and something in that...that-there front!"

Mama, being a seamstress, found a blending color chiffon upstairs and hurriedly made little caps for the sleeves and a thing for the neck, basting them in. Dad looked it over, seeing right through the chiffon of course, and said, "Well, doesn't look much better, but I guess it'll have to do."

That's the way it was with clothes.

But hair! Sister had one redeeming feature. Her hair was the color of cornsilk and felt like thistledown. It was easy to wash and it dried quickly. How I envied her.

Whenever I looked at Cousin Elma's hair, shivers of longing swept through me. I went to work on Mama when she was in an especially good mood. Mama's shocked reaction was always the same: "Why in the world would you want to cut those beautiful curls all off?"

"Because all the girls are doing it! Even some of the mothers have their hair bobbed and they are having finger waves," I protested, thinking she might start thoughts of her own. Secretly I wondered what Papa would think of that.

"Your beautiful curls! What would your father say?" Standing there, her arms akimbo, she looked me over, she kept using the same argument, over and over, "What would Papa say?"

I'd repeat, "It's the style. Everybody has short hair nowadays. It's so easy to care for—just takes a minute to wash and dry. I'll ask Papa. If he says it's all right, can I? Can I go to the barber shop so I'll be as pretty as Cousin Elma?"

Mama was giving it some thought. "Well, we'll see. Pretty is as pretty does, I've told you a hundred times." Then, "To the barber shop! Ladies don't go in barber shops! Barber shops are always full of customers, loafers, thick smoke, foul language and off-color jokes. I don't want a daughter of mine hanging around in there!"

I approached Papa. I could see he was appalled, by the expression that spread all over his face. He roared: "Get your hair cut! What on earth for? What does your mother say?"

"Well,.she said to ask you…," I stammered. His complaints continued: "Danged frivolities. Danged foolishness. That kind of woman makes her living on her back."

Daily I felt almost a jealous rage as I watched Cousin Elma combing her hair just so, sitting there at my vanity, glorifying herself in the mirror. On my sixteenth birthday I had been given a handpainted dresser set. It was the nicest present any girl could receive. Mine was painted in blue forget-me-nots and it contained several pieces: a brush and comb, tray, a powder jar, a talcum powder shaker, a hat pin holder—I'd never use that—a hairpin box, a pin tray, and a hair receiver.

"I just love my hair," Elma'd coo in a syrupy voice, as she brushed it with a few careful strokes, with *my* birthday brush. Mama always had to do mine as it was so thick and heavy. Elma continued to blow smoke from her nostrils like a small dragon and I thought, that doesn't look very ladylike! After a while she crushed the stub of her cigarette into a saucer, which had been sneaked upstairs for that purpose. Then she opened the window wide, fanning with her nightgown, to cleanse the air of the tobacco smoke.

She always moved lightly about the room, so gracefully. Whenever we heard the stairs creak, she'd talk unusually loud to cover our misdeeds, "Would you get me your silver looking glass, please? And your brush and comb?" We'd hear Mama, or Grandma, go on to another room.

Her beaux in Detroit. That's all she could talk about. She inked initials in the palms of her hands. The postman delivered letters to her almost daily and she let me read them. She was sought after, a pretty young thing driven around at home in automobiles by boys, she let me know! She was a knock-out, putting on all those big-city airs.

"Oh, these creepy farm boys, Helen. They give me the willies!" She loathed my schoolmates who lived here in town. I told her they were not farmers. They'd been hanging around our front porch since Cousin Elma's arrival. She'd laugh, saying, "They are about as shallow as a butter dish. Just bashful, awkward boys who aren't even aware that their voices are changing!"

One day Mama and Grandma were out with their bridge-playing friends. Cousin Elma was lovingly combing her hair, her bright red fingertips shaping the spit curls just so. Earlier she had applied nail polish, then blew the nails and swung her hands in the air so the polish would dry without smearing. I had a nail buffer for my nails. Papa would never approve of painted nails!

I lamented, "Just look at you and I'm still in my baby curls. I might just as well go out in my little sailor dress and roll a hoop!"

I overheard Mama and Papa talking earlier that morning. He was cautioning Mama: "We've got to see to it Helen stays away from Elma as much as possible. I never saw a girl in all this world so infatuated with herself as that Elma! She'll ruin Helen's reputation around town here! She's as thin as a rail; needs to get some meat on those bones." They kept on talking and I went out on the front porch. I didn't know how they'd plan to keep me away from Elma when she'd be here for several weeks.

After Mama and Grandma left, Elma teasingly whispered, "Why don't we go down to the barber shop and let the barber—you know him, don't you?—let him cut your hair. When it's short it's so much more comfortable, cooler, and easier to care for. It's the latest, and everybody's doing it! Your folks will make an old maid out of you if you let them."

So away we went, to Papa's barber shop, our arms swung around each other, giggling all the way! Up ahead I saw the peppermint-striped pole. Three elderly gentlemen sat on the long bench out front. I hesitated at the door. Cousin Elma pushed me on through, "You'd better not chicken out on me!"

The barber was just finishing a shave. I was losing my nerve. One old man looked over at another, laughingly saying, "How come your hair is so white and your beard so black?" The other casually answered, "My hair is twenty years older than my beard, that's why." Everyone haw-hawed, and I forgot my uneasiness.

"Next?" the barber called out. Elma nudged me but I was hoping someone was waiting his turn before me. I slowly crawled up into the barber chair. I sat there like a sentry. Barber Joe pinned a towel around my neck. The loafers stared over the tops of their newspapers when I told him, "I want all my curls cut off and the hair shingled up the back just like Cousin Elma's there."

He pumped the chair up, looked at me, this way and that. He snipped. A length of hair fell to the floor. I had a moment of apprehension. I hoped I wasn't making a mistake. Were Mama and Papa right after all? He continued to clip away. I began to feel light-headed. I hadn't realized that my hair had weighed so much!

Up on the shelf I saw a row of shaving mugs. Where was Papa's? There was Herpicide, the hair tonic advertised to cure dandruff and grow hair on a bald head. Spittoons were scattered about, tobacco stains all over the floor, from the loafers who had missed their mark. Cigar and pipe smoke filled the air.

After the barber finished, he combed through my hair. Then he put a looking glass in my hand and turned my chair so I could see from every angle. I found myself caught up in a wave of the room's excitement! Were they approving or disapproving?

I primly reached up to feel my new hairstyle while I viewed it. Oh! It wasn't like Cousin Elma's at all! It looked like it had been whacked off. My thick, stubby hair now fanned out all over like porcupine quills! I could have died of mortification!

I reached in my pocket, took fifty cents, and paid the barber. I went running home, my arms circling my head, so no one would see me. Cousin Elma was trying to keep up, all the time wailing, "What's the matter, Helen? What's the matter?"

At home I sneaked up the back stairs. Wait till Mama sees it, I was thinking. She will have a conniption fit! After a while I could hear the family coming home, one by one.

Cousin Elma kept gazing at me in disbelief. Suddenly she just up and disappeared! Where was my support now that I needed it? After she left, the smell of her perfume and her beauty remained in the room with me. It was sickening.

I had to do something. First I tried water. That tamed it down somewhat. Then I decided to pull some bangs around on my forehead, but the hair was so kinky and stiff and wouldn't do a thing. Well, I thought, I'll get Mama's curling iron and I'll see if I can straighten out the kinks so my hair will lie down, not just stick out all over like a chopped-off whisk broom.

I took the curling iron to the bathroom and placed it over the gas jet under the water heater, until it was red hot. I took it out and started to curl a fingerful of hair above my forehead. Having never used one of the things before, I knew something was wrong when I heard a sizzle and smelled singed hair. Mama didn't have that trouble when she curled hers and Grandma's hair.

While taking a close look at the damage, the curling iron slipped down from my bangs and slid right over my left eyeball. I opened my eye and there was no sight! By squinting in the mirror, I could see a white blister and, oh, it hurt so bad!

Well, now I'd done it! I went to the head of the stairs, just ready to faint, and yelled, "Mama, hurry!"

Mama knew, the minute she heard my cry, that something terrible had happened. She tore up the stairs, took one look, and was shocked when she saw my hair sticking out every which way. She screamed, "What have you done to your hair?"

I said, "Don't bother about the hair! I've burned my eye!"

"Let me see." She looked, then fainted dead away at my feet! I'd been thinking I was going to faint, not Mama!

Downstairs Grandmother heard the klunk on the floor and came running upstairs. "What's the matter? What's the matter?"

"I burned my eye!"

"Your hair, Helen!" she shouted. "Let the hair go, Grandmother! I burned my eye—where's Papa?" I demanded. "Let me see your eye." Grandma looked, cried out, then she fainted!

Papa heard another klunk and yelled up, "What's going on up there!"

He came flying up the steps, three at a time. By now I was uncontrollable, my eye hurt so bad!

Papa saw Mama and Grandmother sprawled out on the floor. He ran to the bathroom and came back with cold, wet cloths and put them to the women's faces. They finally came to.

He saw me, Helen, there in my white cotton petticoat, my hair, and then my eye. I would never have let Papa see me in my underclothes, never—I'd be so embarrassed—but I was in such pain! He grabbed a blanket and hastily wrapped it around my ninety pounds, and with his majestic bulk, scooped me up into his arms and ran three blocks to the doctor.

Doctor Miller, hearing my wailing, rushed me in ahead of a roomful of people. He put drops into the eye to keep it from sticking to the eyelid. "I doubt," he said, "that she ever sees out of it again. We'll have to wait to know how deep it's burned." He sent us on to the nearby hospital.

After the eye healed—it took several days—I had twenty-twenty vision. Mama was still so disturbed. "I better get you to the beauty parlor to have your hair thinned and shaped so you look halfway decent again. What possessed you to go to the barber shop in the first place? That Elma, I know!"

After I was styled, I looked half-human again, but *not* like Cousin Elma.

Through the years I've always had trouble with beauticians who didn't understand my thick, curly hair and what to do with it. All my life I've been fighting to look the way I want to look, with no curls.

My hair, the bane of my existence!

—This story was originally published in Tri Town Topics, *May 8 and 15, 1975, and appeared in* Good Old Days, *January, 1980.*

The Kitchen, the Hub of the Home
The Stove, Its Heart
A Conversation Around The Kitchen Table

by
Halcie and Monroe Whitmoyer
and Marie and Ray Whitmoyer

When several family members get together, the account told "around the kitchen table" develops more fully. The Whitmoyer family is from Noblesville.

Monroe: Did anyone ever tell you about the salesman, with his team of mules, hauling a cookstove around on a wagon, giving demonstrations? He parked there on the north side of the court house square in Noblesville. Cookstove salesmen were always traveling through the country, going from house to house. Town to town.

Our family had come to town to do the shopping that Saturday. Already the stores were crowded with farmers in clean overalls and their wives in cotton print dresses. Mom was taking her eggs into the store to trade them for groceries when we saw smoke and a lot of commotion. We followed the crowd.

That salesman had a good fire going in a cookstove, up there on that wagon! A stovepipe carried the smoke up and away.

He was a hulking figure of a man, in a dark suit and a bowler hat, with a gold watch fob and chain strung across his pumpkin middle. He picked up a white cotton towel and tied it around his waist, hooked his thumbs in his vest, then, with all the charm of a midway barker at a carnival, he invited the crowd: "Step right up! I just happen to have this treasure of the kitchen, every lady's delight. A cookstove!" He pointed as he spoke, "Maleable iron and nickel-plate wonder, this wood-burning range. Look here at the curlicues and scrollwork designs on the oven door, on the front of the reservoir, and the firebox!

"It stands on these four elegantly sculptured sturdy legs." He pointed to each one, drawing his forefinger up and down them. "Towering above here is a roomy warming closet. You young ladies, pull this warming oven door down, and it makes the best book rest in case you want to read while you're doing the dishes. When you hear Mama coming, flip the oven door shut and hide your folly! Here on the right end is a reservoir which is constructed of copper so that one need not ever worry about it rusting out. It holds ten gallons of water. What great luxury of always having hot water handy for washing dishes, milk buckets, and boys' faces!

"The oven is roomy and will hold several pans of light bread or five or six pies all at once. It could happily accommodate a big fat hen, a turkey, or a large pan of oyster dressing. Now ladies, there's no end to what this oven will do! Men, a farmer's wife is judged by the appearance of her range and the meals she prepares on it, not how beautiful she is! You young bucks, a girl in the kitchen is worth two in the parlor!

"When Paw, there, comes in on a bitter, stormy day, he'll give the fire in the cookstove a coupla vigorous pokes, then toss the poker into the woodbox nearby. It is such a comfort to draw up a chair, open the oven door, stick his cold feet in, toast them good, and listen to the cat purring contentedly."

All the while, the peddler was mixing up a big batch of biscuits in a huge round dishpan. He shook flour from the sifter onto the wooden dough board, then poured out the dough onto it. He gave it a few swift pats with his floured hands. Out came the rolling pin. He held it in the air. "A widow maker!" he laughed, and continued rolling and patting until he got the right thickness.

"Never trust a skinny cook. You know the kind: she has to walk twice in one place to make a shadder. For dessert, she'll give ya a pickle 'stead of pumpkin pie! The old farmer says—he was always a-braggin' about th' cook's meals, he meant his wife, of course—'A plump wife and a big barn never did any man harm.'" He quickly cut round circles with a biscuit cutter, put them on black cookie pans, then into the oven they went.

How he enjoyed his curbside audience! While the biscuits were baking he kept up his humorous commentary. "Folks often ask me, a high school graduate, why I turned from the scholarly road to selling cookstoves. Wanderlust. Just wanderlust.

"Women, let those little girls of your'n stand up aside ya to learn to cook early." He opened the oven door, looked in, then closed it, shaking his head and smiling approvingly. "But I'm a firm advocate of the theory that one adult woman in the kitchen is Heaven. Two, Hell!" You should have heard that crowd roar!

"Now," he continued, "here's a gadget all you women will want. Absolutely free, with each stove I sell today. Only today. Bread toasted by means of this long-handled wire toaster, and held near the top of the hot stove, will be a treat to any man when he comes in each morning with his buckets full of foamy white milk! Or, take off this stove lid and toast it even faster over the flame.

"There was this lady cooking for threshers. Fried chicken, mashed potatoes, slaw, all those good things. When she opened the boiling pot of potatoes, ready to pour off the water and mash them, they were the color of a walnut. A brown stocking had fell into them somehow, from a clothesline over the stove. No time to peel and cook another batch. She had to have mashed potatoes with fried chicken! Well, they tasted all right. She went ahead and mashed them. Told the men they had boiled dry and scorched. Women were forever burnin' things, especially Monday's washday soup beans! For a whole week that lady worried someone would die from her brown-dyed potatoes!"

He raised his long arms skyward, holding a pan of aromatic golden brown biscuits in each hand, the like of which no one had ever seen before. He continued joking, giving the biscuits time to cool somewhat. "Two boys, Jude Haworth and a friend, Joe, were eatin' dinner with the hay hands. The lady cut her bread holdin' it up here in her arm like this, sawin' away with her butcher knife, not down on a bread board like most women. She handed the ten-year-old boys a slice apiece, and then went on around the table. Jude nudged Joe, whispering, 'How do you like your bread, with milk?' " Joe got so tickled he had to leave the table.

The biscuits were quickly passed around to the viewers. We all reached for one. I hurried and broke mine open. Best baking powder biscuits you've ever sunk your teeth into, even Mom had to admit it. Dad, too.

Then the salesman called all interested parties to come forward and place their orders. "This is your last chance! Come right up, folks! All you women, too! I know you have been crying to have a cookstove in your kitchen. Mothers are always kitchen boss! The man wears the pants but she knows where the pockets are!"

Those biscuits sold many a man, when his wife had been unable to. Dad and Mom went up and Dad signed on the dotted line. Mom was so pleased!

That evening we were in our buggy, ready to start home. The stove salesman was heading west out of town, sitting erect and happy, whistling his tune, as his mules pulled their load.

The stoves were shipped by train and you picked them up at the railroad station. We could hardly wait for its arrival! Dad went in and brought ours home on his farm wagon. It was with real pride he showed our new stove off to his family!

Ma was real blissful when Dad had it set up ready to set a fire in it. The advertisement bragged about how stout the oven door was. It showed a picture of a family all standing on the door with this caption: *The Whole Dam Family on the Beaver Dam Range. Kalamazoo, Direct to You!*

Then Dad, impulsively, jumped up on the oven door, as if to check out the truthfulness of the ad. It broke right off!

Ma was fit to be tied! Waiting all these years for an oven and now she couldn't use it until another door was ordered and delivered. Dad walked out the back door like a whipped pup.

Ma was terribly let down. I knew she'd been dreaming of juicy pies for supper. "Monroe, go get some cobs to start this fire. Right now!" Ma was still fuming. She removed the front stove lids and the cross section, placed wads of paper, cobs, and shingles at the bottom of the fire box, then put a larger stick of wood on top. She lit the paper at the bottom and replaced the stove lids, making sure all the dampers were open. As soon as the large stick of wood was burning, she adjusted all the dampers so that the stove started to heat. I liked the smell of shingles when they began burning.

Dad always got up early and built a fire, to have the oven hot for Ma to bake biscuits or corn bread for breakfast. If the wind was from a certain direction it would smoke before it started to draw real good. A woman hated to have to nurse a fire along. I have seen Ma test the heat of the stove by scattering a few drops of water on the top. If the water danced and popped, it was ready.

There was an eerie, cozy quality about the kitchen on those dark mornings, with the soft light of the coal oil lamp, the red-hot cookstove and the smell of coffee and pancakes in the air.

Many a day Ma was in the kitchen stirring rolled oats into boiling water and tossing in a few raisins for a treat. She had to get the rolled oats on early because it took them a half-hour to cook. My sister, Anna, she just hated washing the pan they were cooked in. Stuck like glue. Usually she'd pour the hot soapy dishwater into it when she finished washing breakfast dishes, and it soaked there till the next meal.

Marie: I think they peddled the Majestic Range around through the country, too. They were malleable iron ranges, and would last and last. Take a sledgehammer and hit them and they wouldn't break. But Monroe, my dad didn't jump on our oven!

The first ranges were cast iron and they'd warp. Try to fry something and all the grease would go to one end of the skillet!

The first cookstove I remember was a little iron one that Mama had. Cutest little thing you ever saw! Pa set it up on a foot and a half-square wooden box, so Ma wouldn't have to stoop over when she cooked. It was homey and so serviceable. But, no oven. She set a tin portable one on top when she needed to bake.

In time the Monarch would rust out around the oven. The Majestic didn't. Papa bought a Majestic from a peddler.

Our well water had flakes of iron in it. We had to keep a cotton cloth bag tied on the pump spout to strain that out, as much as we could, before we used it. Sometimes, after a long day of using water, the reservoir had only enough water to cover the bottom and that was red with iron rust, if it had been filled with well water. Well water, around where we lived, was very hard. Lots of iron in it.

When we lived on a farm with a cistern, we filled the reservoir with rainwater. No cistern, we used water from the rain barrel, because there was no rust in it. Lucky were the people who had a cistern full of rainwater! It was soft, but there was sediment collected from the roof after a rain.

One time, when I was eighteen, I was keeping house for Papa after Mama died, I didn't know someone had left the reservoir door cracked open and I set a plum pie down and into the water it went! Another time, I'd made two lemon pies for the Hinkle Church Homecoming. They were so pretty, with their high white meringues, beautifully browned, covering the lemon-yellow filling and the golden brown crusts! I was real proud. I took the pies out of the oven and set them on the reservoir lid. I didn't notice the lid wasn't on straight and both of them slipped down in. And, there we were, almost ready to go to church! I don't know what I did. I cried, probably. 'Course, I'd prepared other things to take: fried chicken, potato salad, and all. At that age I was out to make an impression on a very handsome young bachelor, and no better way than to bring out beautiful, tasty pies I had made myself.

The teakettle of boiling water was always there for any need. It'd boil over, water bubbles dancing all along the hot stove. Plenty of water to make a batch of starch on washday, add to a chunk of beef for dinner, or put in the washpan to scrub up with. Young girls and women stuck

their heads over the steaming spout to quickly curl their hair. And plenty for washing and rinsing dishes. The water in the reservoir stayed hot a while after the fire had gone out.

Sears, Roebuck's brand was called Acme. Montgomery Ward's was Windsor. There was a Favorite and a Hoosier, but I don't know who made them.

Even in summer the stove was going most of the day. How cozy with the heat and moisture on a cold winter washday and when ironing. But, oh, summers! Cooking for thrashers and hay hands, always big farm meals and endless days over the boiling water in the canning boiler. We'd sweat through our hair, and all our clothes! Our glasses steamed over so bad we could hardly see.

We dried everything in that oven: Corn, apples, mittens, and shoes. We warmed chilled baby pigs, lambs, and chicks.

Long underwear and socks finished drying there. Baby clothes were warmed and the baby was bathed before the opened-down door.

One time Mama brought in a bushel basket of half-grown chickens that had been caught in a sudden downpour. She wiped them off good with a soft rag, then set them to dry in a box on the oven door. We knew they had come to life when we heard them chirping and pattering around on the kitchen linoleum!

Halcie: Dad would come in from a winter day in the barn or woods, chilled to the bone. He'd push the coffeepot to the front, add a few more cobs for a quick fire, pull off his heavy felts and rubbers and draw his chair over in front of the oven. He'd let down the door, sit on a kitchen chair and stick his feet inside the oven with a grunt of comfort. He'd fill his pipe with Prince Albert tobacco, pick up the newspaper and start to read. Soon he was dozing in the chair, his pipe chest-resting.

Whenever his leather boots became wet, he'd fill them with oats and allow them to dry slowly, near the stove, so they wouldn't shrink up and get hard and crack.

Dad always knew which wood made the best heat for the kitchen stove and he sawed it into proper stove lengths.

Ray: When smoke went straight up from the chimney top and was lost to view shortly, it foretold a few days of settled weather. A clean blue smoke foretold several days of settled weather with lots of sunshine. These were the times womenfolk depended on for drying corn, beans, apples, and peaches out-of-doors. Farmers welcomed this good haymaking weather.

When the smoke came out of the chimney in a rolling pattern and floated toward the ground, it foretold falling weather. In winter, look for a heavy snow. Summer, downpours.

No smoke from a chimney the first thing of a morning led neighbors to suspect illness or injury to a widow or single occupant of the home. We knew what time to expect that first burst of morning smoke from each neighbor's chimney.

They always said if you looked up through a chimney, in the daytime you could see stars, but I never tried.

Monroe: The Methodist preacher's boy, Walter Crayler, came out one day and he and I went rabbit hunting. We got our shoes all muddy. When we got home we stuck them in the oven so they'd dry. Ma came in and saw us and scolded, "You oughten't to do that. I want to bake in there!" She didn't want her oven dirty and, also, it would take awhile to reheat.

One time Dad saw me and Ray starting a fire in the cookstove. He caught each of us by the ear and told us, "If I hear tell of either of you using coal oil on a fire, I'll tan you good!"

Walter, my cousin, was telling me something that had happened at his home. "You ought-ta seen our stove. It made the most terrible noise. I was ripped from sound sleep by the clashing of stove lids as they flew off. Pop had thrown coal oil into the stove. He didn't know there were still live coals way down inside and the thing exploded! Pop yelled and hurried to pick up the lids off the linoleum, so he could close up the stove. It was smokin' powerful when we got to the kitchen. Pop looked like a forlorned chimney sweep, all black soot save his eyes and teeth! Fire burned off his eyelashes and eyebrows and singed his hair and his wool flannel shirt. I can still smell all those burnt hair and wool odors and hear the commotion as Ma came running out of their bedroom. And I learned a lesson. Pa could have been kilt and the house burnt down. That shouldn't happen again. I'll build a fire like Ma does. Soak the cobs in coal oil, then roll them in newspaper, put them in with the rest of the kindling and wood and then strike a match."

Many a kid has been burned badly when they built up a fire with coal oil when the parents were away. Kids were bad about doing things they couldn't get away with when their parents were home.

Halcie: The kitchen was probably the most-used room, and usually the biggest in the house. It had to be large enough for the huge stove, table, and chairs, to seat a sizeable family, a wood box, a worktable, the kitchen cabinet, a pie safe, and a washstand. The men hung their heavy wool winter coats on the wall near the stove so they'd always be warm and dry. The washstand held the water bucket, washpan, and soap dish. On the door was a roller towel.

A meal's dishes were done up immediately after everyone had finished eating. Only the lazy let their dirty dishes pile up. With big families, all the plates and silverware were needed for the next meal. Dishpans, when washing and rinsing the dishes, were set on the stove or kitchen cabinet.

The warming oven, above the stove's surface, kept cooked food warm until served. Might find 'most anything else up in there, except food: Homemade potholders, tattered from so much heavy use, and showing scorch or burn marks around the edges. If they were laid too close to the stovepipe, they would catch fire. A chipped tea cup with tea leaves to be used again, and maybe a handleless cup full of bacon drippings. A crock of coarse salt for seasoning. One or two sad irons. Sometimes the men kept a pipe and tobacco and extra work gloves up there.

Marie: In summer we used wood in the stove. In winter, coal. We had to fill the firebox full of wood, to have enough to produce a hot fire while we were using it all morning. Generally, coal was too hot. A good cook could put her hand inside the oven to test its warmth. A barely warm oven for angel food cake, hot one for biscuits.

It took an hour for light bread to bake in a moderately hot oven. I'd have to keep feeding the fire for a constant heat and was very cross if boys came in and slammed the back door and made my cake fall! And, if someone opened the damper and filled the stove with coal, like a man would often do in wintertime, getting the oven too hot, oven-baked goods would invariably burn. If it was not hot enough, cakes would fall, bread would be doughy and sour, and the bottoms of the pies would be soggy. There was a knack to baking everything just right in an oven.

Halcie: We had a summer kitchen, a big room off by itself on back of the main house, with a dog trot between. We thought it was the greatest thing when we moved out there before summer's hot weather. That kept the heat off the rest of the house. We didn't move the big cookstove. There was the smaller one, four holes, and it had an oven. But it didn't have a water closet. Later we got a three-burner coal oil stove with a built-on oven. Much cooler cooking our meals and eating out there till autumn chills.

Soup beans and corn bread were a Monday washday dinner for all families. The copper boiler, for heating washwater, took up the front space.

Mama's face was always flushed deep red from bending over the fire when cooking a meal. Oh, lordy, it just makes me sick, thinking how good food tasted cooked on a cookstove and I know I can never have it again!

Some kitchens had a hard, tufted couch behind the stove or a big wooden box with a hinged, cotton-padded lid. Warmest place to take a nap or for a sick child to lie down on and listen to grown-ups.

Little tykes were always getting into the can of coal oil behind the stove, put there to start fires. We'd read frequent accounts in the newspaper where a small child drank it and died.

Mama took real pride in keeping her stove clean. Once a week she'd let the fire die down, then use stove polish and black it up good. When it was fired up the next time, it would fill the house with smoke. My eyes burn and I can cough, just thinking about it.

When we started buying bakery bread, the wax wrapper rubbed over the hot stove really made it shine. Some women used a bacon rind on their stove tops. The oil from it worked real well. I've seen Mama do it. She was so proud of her cookstove!

By the time the plastic bread wrappers came out, the wood-burning cookstove was no more. But families were using their woodburning heating stoves to cook on. What a surprise awaited them when they started to run the plastic-wrap over the hot surface. Melted right onto it!

Mama always hand-beat a lot of love into her angel food cakes! Her oven had to be exactly right before she placed the cake on the proper rack. She used a corncob fire, and she'd keep replenishing them when needed.

When baking most cakes she'd stick her hand in the oven and see if it was hot enough. She had a different method for the angel food. She'd roll tissue paper in a loose ball and put it in the oven. When it browned in ten minutes, the oven was ready. Put the cake in and bake for one hour. Some of the later-model stoves had a thermometer gauge on the oven door, but even so, most women didn't trust that.

Ray: The boys of the household carried wood to keep the fires going. It was my job to fill the woodbox back of the stove and to stack extra near the back door. Sunday morning, Ma's company on their way, she'd look at that woodbox, shout, "Raymond Whitmoyer! Are you going to fill this, or do I have to do it myself?"

Occasionally Ma sent me to the chicken coop with the dead ashes to pour in an old leaky washtub for the chickens to roll around in. She said it kept the chicken lice away. It was a distasteful job to have to sift ashes around over the contents in the toilet, but I had it to do, to keep odors down. Wood ashes are the best fertilizer for grass, garden, and fruit trees. In winter we sprinkled coal ashes out the back door in icy paths so we wouldn't slip and fall. Always, Ash Wednesday, we sprinkled ashes all around in the barn, in the barnyard, and chicken lots. Old-timers claimed it kept down diseases.

No matter how carefully you spread newspapers under the stove door, or how cautiously you lifted out the ash pan, it was impossible to empty it without spilling some ashes on the floor.

I brought in buckets of water from the pump to fill the washboiler and rinse tubs early every Monday morning. Then I had to see to it the reservoir and the teakettle were full. After the washing was done I carried the washwater out to water the flowers and garden.

I guess I did my share of sloshing water on the floor. I can feel my wet, cold, pant leg to this day when the bucket was too full and water splashed over. Ma was forever reminding me where she kept the mop.

On Tuesdays, summers, before I could go fishing or go help in the fields, I had to bring in enough wood to keep the fire hot under the sad irons for Ma to iron with. That was a long, hot job for the womenfolk. Just think, that stove had to be kept real hot, to heat the irons, summer or winter.

Marie: The handles of the irons got as hot as the iron itself, and we had to use a thick pad to hold them. In spite of this, we usually did not get through a day without getting red hands from the constant heat. Perspiration flowed down my face and over my body in the summertime.

As I learned to iron, I always had an inch-long burn on my wrist or hand. When a neighbor bought one of those new electric irons, no heating up the stove, oh, wouldn't I like to have one!

Monroe: Remember the adjustable interlocking stove lids? One lid had four sizes of holes in it. Remove the small lid in the center and you had a hole the size for a pot of coffee to set next to the open flames for quick heat. Bigger ones fit bigger pans. Sometimes one of the little lids would slip down into the open fire and what a time we had getting it out!

There was no fussing, who'll bring in the coal, when Ma announced she was making doughnuts. We had an iron pot, rounded bottom, that fit down in next to the fire, when we took the lid off the stove. That's when she'd use coal, to keep a steady fire for hot grease to fry them in.

Hedgeapple wood makes a hot fire, too, for frying doughnuts. Stove'd get so hot, steam would come bubbling up through the reservoir. First thing I knew, the stove pipe was red and the teakettle was boiling over! Dad'd come in, see all that heat, "Pretty good coal I bought, ain't it?" Then he'd sample a fresh-fried doughnut. Ma told him, it wasn't coal but hedgeapple wood.

A most exasperating problem was making fires with green wood. Had to keep poking cobs in all around it, and still it would sizzle and fry. And Ma lost patience with the stove when the wind was from the east and the stove had violent fits of smoke billowing, filling the kitchen with black smoke. She'd rush to the door for a breath of fresh air, then worry if it'd ever settle down so she could get the meal on the table in time.

Halcie: I didn't like cleaning the pot after it had sat over the open coal flame. It'd black up the bottom something awful! Get my dish towels and rags all black, would take boiling in hot soapy lye water to get them white again.

There was always a clothesline stretched across the kitchen, or a shorter one back of the stove. Hang dish towels to dry, the underwear that had to be washed out by hand, and the diapers that were hand-washed between washdays.

Besides the usefulness and cheerfulness, our cookstove fire was delightful for daydreaming. Stirring a big iron pot of apple butter, my mind would go traveling while my body remained standing alone, comfortable, cozy, watching a flame through the stovelid cracks.

Monroe: The whole family took a bath in the big round galvanized tub in front of the cookstove on Saturday night. The stove would be loaded with coal and kept hot until every member had bathed, starting with the youngest. Dad last. More water was added from the reservoir or the boiling teakettle as needed. Warm water was always available from the reservoir for those cat washes between Saturday night scrubbings.

Oh, the tragedies of badly burned or scalded children, oh, my.... Looking into a pan on the stove, or reaching up to grab a handle. Little children were always curious.

Halcie: Sometimes the stove balked. If Mama's baked goods didn't brown or were lopsided, it was Dad's job to clean the soot out, using a long-handled small stove hoe and the soot pan. After it was good and clean he'd remind Mama: "Be careful; you'll have a hot oven today."

I always knew when Ma cried out, "Drat!" the oven was too hot and burned whatever was in there, or else the stove wouldn't draw, couldn't get a good fire started, so the oven didn't heat.

The stove poker hung through the grillwork, and many a time a visiting tot grabbed it and came running across the kitchen with little black hands. The poker, made of iron, had a coiled handle at one end. The stove-lifter also had that coiled handle. I loved to lift up a lid and look in at the blazing fire.

Monroe: And naughty tykes sometimes got a fanning with the handy small stove shovel!

On a cold winter day, come in from forking manure all morning, lift the front lid up—oh, that was very warm to cold hands!

In the spring, baby chicks came in the mail. I've seen Ma put a thick layer of newspapers on the floor behind the stove, then set up table boards to make a pen. She'd put her baby chicks back there with jars of hot water for them to huddle around. The chicks would scratch and peck the rolled oats and cornmeal she sprinkled over the papers. She had a pan of warm water and would dip each chick's head into it to teach them to drink. They were so content. Ma would sit and watch them, there with all the heat from the stove, until her eyes got droopy. When the chicks got old enough to jump over the boards, they had a good start, so she moved them to the brooder house.

In the summer, that old stove turned out the best apple dumplings, cakes, cookies, and bread for the threshing crew.

Halcie: Bake day, making bread, was usually twice a week for the average family. A woman took great pride in her cooking ability. It was one sure way to get a man! In fact, usually if she could not cook she was pretty sure to be an old maid. A hustling farmer wanted to be assured of hearty meals, on time. I heard one dad advise his daughter, who had not been successful in getting her beau to pop the question, "Feed the brute!"

Pies and cakes from the bakery were looked upon with disgust by most older men and with scorn by the older women. They were expensive and they weren't as good, they claimed.

No matter what was done, a certain way the wind was from, that stove would smoke. Invariably it was a day when Mom had to get a lot of baking and cooking done. Or, the chimney would burn out when she had the clothesline full of white sheets and shirts, covering them with soot. They'd have to be washed again.

Town ladies had neighbors' smoke to worry about. Since most women washed on Monday, they respected each other.

Monroe: When gas came through we had it for lights, heat, and cooking. We had gas until they took the line up from the well west of us where Ray Clark's farm is, up until when the gas played out. Then we had to go back to coal and wood. That was hard! A lot more work, dirtier, so much slower, and not the even heat.

Dad had put a gas burner in our cookstove. He made it out of a piece of pipe he drilled holes in. The gas flowed up through. In the wintertime this would freeze up, pretty near every morning if it was real cold. It wasn't the gas that froze; it was water in the line. It would generally freeze at the same place, a dip in the line. Dad would go up and blow the well off about every day. That way it would let the water out so it wouldn't freeze near as bad. If you let that go three-four days in the winter, then come real bad weather, count on it freezing bad.

Dad put a gas burner in an old Airtight wood stove to heat with. It sent out waves of heat. Coming home after Sunday night church services or a Christmas program, the house was warm. When we burned wood in it, it'd go out before we got back. We'd all huddle around the stove warming our fronts first, then turning around and warming our backs. On each side of the stove was a fender to prop our feet up to warm them. None of the newer, more modern parlor stoves could warm my feet like that one did. Then when the gas started getting weak, playing out, that's when Dad got a coal Kalamazoo Base Burner. After the evening chores were done, supper over, I looked forward to its warmth and sitting back watching the lovely glow from the Isinglass windows as they cast reflections all around the front room. Put me to sleep every time!

He'd give a dollar a month for gas, per stove, and ten cents a room per light for gas. The gas well belonged to Judge Neal, the landlord. Judge didn't let anyone else use it except his hired man and Dad. He told Dad that if he'd take care of the well, he'd let him have it cheap.

We generally had just one light in each room. We watched that one in the living room. Liquid stuff would accumulate in the light, run down on the carpet, and burn it. Yes, we had holes burned in the carpet from that stuff! It wasn't a fire-burn, more like an acid-burn.

Ray's dad had gas under his butchering tools. Oh, that was nice and easy to adjust the flame for even heat. Us others used wood and had to keep replenishing it.

Halcie: When the gas played out, we all had to go back to burning wood and coal. Back to the coal oil lamps. Why, we could hardly see our hands in front of us!

I remember filling my dress tail with wood chips as I came from the toilet, on by the wood pile, hurrying back to get a fast fire. We did keep the barnlot cleaned up better, having to pick up trash to build fires with.

Monroe: Dad told me when they struck gas in the 1890s, you know where the old interurban bridge was across White River there at Noblesville? On the east side of the river, just north of that bridge, they struck a gusher and in some manner it caught on fire. Dad said it shot flames thirty feet in the air! People that lived in Indianapolis could see that blaze twenty-five miles away! The interurban ran excursions up from Indianapolis with cars of people who wanted to see it.

Finally they got hold of a man somewhere who specialized in putting gas fires out. He had on some kind of asbestos uniform, I imagine it was, and they threw water on him as he walked into the fire to fix it.

Whoever bought Mabel and Walter Burger's house didn't get the chimney flue in good and gas fumes escaped. Walter had to drag Mabel out in the middle of the night. They both almost died.

Goldie Craig had gas up there on Tenth Street where she owned a tourist home. Some newlyweds were staying overnight. They got gassed and the bride died. A bride one day, a corpse the next.

Some inexperienced people would install a gas heater, not realizing it had to be vented out. The gas would burn all the oxygen out of the air and suffocate people. Yes, sir, gas had so many advantages but was also very dangerous!

Marie: Along came other kinds of cookstoves. One fellow told about his mother's Lone Star gasoline stove that burned white gas. The gas drained out of the tank into the burner. Light it, it'd blaze to the ceiling, then turn it down after awhile. Said it used to scare the living daylights out of him, but it didn't bother his mother.

There were coal oil stoves with three open burners to cook on and then a built-in oven on the side. They were a pretty green and tan, not black. They didn't throw off much heat. When jelly, milk, or starch boiled over, the flames and smoke rolled to the ceiling, making a terrible odor, blackening the walls. Awful to clean up!

The stove had to be set perfectly level in order for the oil to drain in properly and the flame to burn right. You lit the stove as you would light a lamp, and when combustion started, the flame became a blue color. It was easily adjusted by turning it up or down.

Sometimes these stoves sprung a leak and that could be dangerous. Or they'd get the coal oil can mixed up with the can of gasoline. That was disastrous! The back porch on Mrs. Wright's new farmhouse burned off when a coal oil stove exploded. They got the fire stopped before the house burned down.

Halcie: Here's a Sears advertisement for a gasoline stove in this old catalogue: "If all stoves were as honestly made there would be no such thing as a gasoline explosion. Don't use cheap gasoline! Cheap gasoline clogs the burners and is more dangerous than gunpowder or dynamite. Our stove uses less gasoline than any other and it costs less to run it with seventy-four degrees deodorized gasoline than others with the cheap, dangerous, unsatisfactory low degree gasoline. Needlepoints on the valves are made of German silver wire; they will never rust or corrode, and they will always insure a steady drip. Tanks are so constructed they cannot be removed for filling until all valves are closed...."

Marie: Ray and I had a wood range until 1940, until we bought an electric stove so our daughter could bake her cakes for the 4-H club. That was wonderful! Automatic, instant, heat-controlled oven and burners!

Monroe: There's nothing like a cob-filled cookstove reaching out a welcome when you come in at night at the first cold snap.

As one man said, "There is no more beautiful spectacle on earth than that of a happy woman in the act of cooking dinner for those she loves."

And, there's nothing as wonderful in my whole life as the kitchens that always smelled so good and the food that came off Ma's and my wife's cookstoves!

—*This story originally appeared in* Tri Town Topics, *April 14, 21, and 28, 1977, and is included in* Cicero, Indiana: 1834-1984.

The Path Out Back

by
Lois Kaiser and Lois Costomiris

Lois Kaiser, wife of the author's cousin, Albert, and author Lois Costomiris, vividly recall the days "with a path." Lois and Albert's son, Larry, illustrated this book.

Kaiser: Older folks are often reliving the known-but-seldom-mentioned incidents of everyday life as it was back then. There were many things to laugh about!

I just can't recall the first bathroom I ever saw. The Millers, they lived on River Road at Strawtown, and the Finleys, whom my dad worked for, they were considered very well off—had such nice homes, yet they had outside toilets.

Costomiris: I remember two houses, built before the 1920s. Henry Heinzman's, near us, constructed by John Zelt for his wife, Belle, a fine country home with a furnace in the basement, a bathroom upstairs, and hardwood floors throughout.

Aunt Ada and Uncle Sam Illyes had a beautiful modern country home over near Riverwood. All the rooms were heated by a furnace, with just the one big register in the living room. They had a bathroom upstairs, hardwood floors throughout, and an ice box with ice to use in the summer!

When a new house was built, the very first bathrooms were upstairs, near the bedrooms. At that time there were very few modern homes, even in town.

Aunt Ada had a family dinner one Sunday. The boy cousins, using this new thing, the bathroom, found two packages of chocolate candy, Ex-Lax, in the medicine cabinet. They divided it up, which resulted in comedy effects!

Kaiser: Our toilet was on the river bank, fenced in, and we never had any problems with anyone pushing it over at Halloween.

I was in the third grade, at Strawtown School, when one of my mittens slipped down into that old four-holer. I cried and bawled and carried on while watching it down in that yawning hole! Gladys Gatton, my sister, four years older than I, knew how precious those new mittens were to me. Alerted to the occasion, and always taking care of me, Gladys had someone stay at the closed door till we got back.

We took off to Ollie Stage's Store across the road. He let us borrow that long-handled arm he took cans from the grocery shelves with. Back at the toilet, Gladys reached it down in there, got my mitten out, took it in to the schoolroom and wrapped it in a scrap of yellow tablet paper she took from the wastebasket, then she returned the long-handled arm back to Ollie, after she rinsed it off good under the outdoor pump. At home that evening, Mom washed it real good, then laid it up in the warming oven to dry overnight. I wouldn't have given a thought to throwing it away or just leaving it there. I'd have had to go bare-handed the rest of the winter, always putting that hand in my coat pocket, or probably Mom would have pulled a heavy old wool sock over it. These weren't only my mittens, they'd be handed down to the next-in-size until they were worn out.

One thing that wouldn't be rescued, however, was that pencil that rolled down the hole. It was a long way to the bottom of the pit. A child had only one pencil, and it was cherished.

At school there was one toilet for the girls and one for the boys, built the same. They were like the ones at the fairs or park, wooden guard of solid boards around the outside so no one could see in. We went in and came out the back.

The seats were of two heights: one in the center about twelve inches high, for the young children, and the others about eighteen inches high, for older students. Seemed I always had to use adult accommodations and try not to jackknife!

Get up there and little bottom'd go down inside, why, it'd scare you to death. I never did know anyone who lost their hold and fell in. In winter it was so cold and the biting, cutting wind whistled up through on those bare backsides! First thing of a morning, after a big snow, we'd use the sawed-off broom to sweep the accumulation off the seats. No broom, we'd use our mittened hands.

Boys would sneak up behind, bang on the wall and yell, "I can see you!" We girls would all jump up and scream. The teacher finally put a stop to it by making the boys stay at the schoolhouse while we girls were out there.

Different students brought catalogues or newspapers to use for toilet paper, like we did at church and at home. When we were having company we cut eight-inch newspaper squares and stacked them just so. Sometimes Mom bought a roll of toilet paper at the store, it was an expense we couldn't afford, and the unused portion—after everyone had gone home—was kept in the pantry until we had company again. Oh, to have toilet paper to use all the time!

If a bad storm came up and blew open the toilet door, the catalogue got soaked through. Wintertime, those pages would freeze together. We'd have to go to the house in a hurry to find newspaper. Or, the pet goat would work open the door and go in and chew the catalogue to bits.

In winter, real bad weather, we had to put all those clothes on to go outside—our boots, coats, hat, and mittens. It was an awful distance way out there, especially in deep snow. A toilet in those winter days was a place to do what one had to do and leave, not a place to rest and talk or read the catalogue.

The side ledge was a good place to park our mittens or scarf, so they wouldn't fall down the hole. One time, family gathering, a visiting uncle left his cigar stub on the ledge. I don't know how he could have smoked that thing.

Remember how the boys in the family hated it when someone tore the sporting goods section out of the catalogue first—or the pages with all the guns?

At school, if I had to be excused, I raised my hand, and oh, that was so embarrassing. The teacher would nod and I'd try to slip out unnoticed.

Sometimes, when I was older, I made it up with my best friend, saying, "I'm going to be excused" or maybe she'd write a note for me to come and we'd go visit a little bit, usually early fall or spring. It was a convenient temporary escape from the boredom of seat work, but if the stolen minutes stretched too long, the teacher would send someone out to get us. Next time we'd have a hard time convincing the teacher we really needed to go! I guess we didn't make a habit of it or the teacher would have caught on.

I never saw a bad word on the walls. There'd be the "Jane loves John," "Jane + John," "Jane hates John," "True Love," hearts drawn all around.

It was tradition, on the last day of school, the girls in the seventh and eighth grade went over and looked in the boys' toilet and those big boys came over and looked into ours. They were exactly alike, I'm sure. It was exciting when I was old enough to go see the boys' toilet.

There was a difference, however. Boys, with their pocketknives, carved their names and dates. Naughty words were scribbled everywhere, providing entertainment for those who followed. The boys' facility also served as a safe haven to smoke rabbit tobacco and to bandy words that did not appear in our school readers.

Costomiris: In winter, my sister, Virginia, two years younger than I, she and I took turns emptying the pot when we got home from school, as part of our chores. There was never time before the bus came of a morning. One evening something happened at the head of the stairs. I can hear that racket yet, the clank-clanking of the pot as it hit every step on the way down. The pained look on Mom's face! Virginia let out an awful howl. I was glad I hadn't done it! I felt sorry for Mom having to clean it up!

Kids were always spilling things. We soon learned to be careful and not pour the pot's contents on the toilet seat after we had to scrub it off ourselves!

Emptying the slop jar was a summer morning ritual, usually performed before breakfast, and not my favorite chore. Then the pot was rinsed at the well with water and left exposed to the sunlight, or, in winter, returned to the house.

Virginia, confused with back or front yard, always set it on a little knoll in the front, in full view of anyone driving up our long lane.

Pots could be purchased in two colors, either gray-blue speckled enamel or snow-white, each with matching lids. Often the lid was forgotten back in the toilet.

It had a wire bail with a wooden handle. The bail creaked as you walked along. How nice to live in the country—no close neighbors to see or hear it!

One man saw a popular actress of the day, in the town of Atlanta, north of here, who was performing in the Chautauqua. An aristocratic lady! The next morning, from his bedroom window across the street, he saw her coming out the back of the hotel, her pot in hand, heading for the toilet!

There was a walk of big, old, worm-eaten, two-by-eight wooden planks, from the back porch door to the toilet, always covered with mud and fresh boot tracks. It's staggering when you think of the miles of travel that must have gone over that path by the countless feet of family and friends! Planks on the ground kept you out of the mud or dew-covered grass on the way to the toilet. They were slick after a shower or in icy weather. I was always tripping where two misfits joined.

Each Monday, washday, we carried the hot sudsy wash water from the washing machine out to the toilet, and gave the floor and seat a good scrubbing.

One Saturday Ada, Virginia, and I were helping Mom get the house cleaned for a surprise birthday party for Dad on Sunday. All the Kaiser family were coming. Mom was dusting around the flowers on the front porch table and knocked off her big elephant ear begonia. Plant, dirt, and broken pot went everywhere.

Mom was never one to let an accident throw her, except when we broke one of her good dishes. Then she cried. She looked at the begonia, then went out and sorted through the trash pile. She found a discarded old slop jar, replanted the flower, and placed it back on the porch table.

The next day Dad and our uncles sat on the porch, in chairs, and the porch swing. I overheard Uncle Luther's teasing remark about Ethel's clever Old White Owl begonia container. Dad answered, laughing, that it was just another use for Keetheepee. I was so embarrassed!

Family dinners, the girl cousins were expected to help their mothers do up the dishes after the meal. On Mother's side there were those who went to the toilet to get out of helping, and they stayed and stayed. But on Dad's side, we all hurried with the dishes, so we could tear out and play.

Kaiser: There was this very large, imposing, meticulously groomed lady, much given to feathers, lace, and furbelows, who gave the impression of never having lifted a hand in her life. Up from Indianapolis, I guess. Ringed fingers flashed in the sunlight. She was always in and out of Cicero, visiting friends and relatives. One day she came up on the interurban to attend a funeral. She had on a full length sealskin coat—very few ladies had fur coats—which emphasized her very large size, wore a hat and gloves and was all gussied up. Oh, mah deah!

"My Lady" went to one of the outside toilets at a house near the town's intersection. My deah—she of the more prosperous who had a bathroom and a furnace in the city!

She'd just stepped inside when the floor broke through. Down she went to her armpits! Someone heard her cries for help and came and pulled her out. I've often wondered, how did they clean that fur coat?

In one of our toilets there were weather cracks in the seat's rim. Gladys most always got a good pinch!

After dark, go with lighted lantern, and together we stole through the darkness with extreme caution, like a chicken thief on his way to the henhouse. We watched the soft shadows dance and sway around us. I was scared! We hurried inside and quickly closed and hooked the door. I could hear the wind crying in the tall pines and a train whistle in the distance. Gladys always took so long, and I'd keep saying, to sound adult, "Aren't you ready yet? What's the matter, are your bowels all bound up?"

A toilet, outside or inside, has always been a gathering place for boys and girls, and often the center of mischief making! Steve, only about a year old, was playing around out in the grassy yard when I heard an awful, "Yip!" out of our mama dog. She was always so considerate of little kids, what happened? I decided Steve must have reached over and bit one of the dog's nipples.

When Larry was four years old, he had a mongrel puppy, his first dog. It was frisky, and Larry played with it all the time. One day I heard pitiful whimpering from down in the toilet. Hurrying there, I somehow got the feeling the pup had been pushed in! He was trying to paw his way out. That poor, crying little thing! I reached inside, lifted him up, and carried him to the back door, then hurried into the house to get a tub and some hot, sudsy water to give a bath.

There was a knock at the front door. I ignored it. Mrs. Steedman, the Methodist minister's wife, came on around back. That puppy, always friendly, kept trying to jump up on her and I kept trying to keep him off!

When I became pregnant, the neighbors knew about it the same time as we did. I had morning sickness and would make a dash for the outhouse. Most of the time I didn't make it. I'd be bent over in the tall grass, heaving it all up.

Costomiris: We had three daughters, Wanda in college, Becky in high school, and Toni in junior high, and we adopted three little boys, ages three, five, and seven. Living in our family now, everything was so new to them.

Jan Kaiser, their seven-year-old cousin, was coming for a visit from New York. They loved watching "Batman" on TV, and were so excited when their father gave them an old brooder house to have their own Batman house. They cleaned it, then played out there constantly.

Jan was thrilled with her visit to a farm. All week long they played and played, riding Old Pet, the white mare, hiding in the haymow, gathering eggs, and being Batman. But as the week wore on the boys seemed to run out of things to do and got mischievous. They shut the door and locked Jan inside the "Bat House" and ran away to the haymow.

I knew nothing about it until some days later when my mother scolded me. "Those boys!" she railed. "Why, Jan will never come to Indiana again!"

I apologized to Jan and to her mother, Rene. Rene laughed heartily. "Oh, that reminds me," she said. "When I was about Jan's age, I was a city girl and my country cousins and I went to Grandma's every summer for our vacation. These cousins, boys and girls, told me of all the horrible things that went on in that stinking toilet—big, hairy-legged spiders, bats, mud daubers, bees whose stingers inflicted pain and swelling. I'd had a bathroom all my life, and it was bad enough for me to use this putrid place, without all the tales.

"Always, before I went in, I drew a gasp of fresh air, then pinched my nose between my fingers so I could not smell what came up through. They had whispered to me that if I'd look way down, sometimes I could see rats and snakes and all kinds of wild animals. Every time, when I was in there alone, intent with the business at hand, someone would throw a stick of wood against the back of the building or they'd throw rocks and corncobs, or shower the roof with gravel, to frighten me.

"The last thing at night, before going to bed, us girl cousins made our last trip out back. We sneaked out, so the boys wouldn't know. We'd no more than settled down when we heard, in a hushed, manful voice, 'A bear's gonna git you—come up through that black hole!' It was awful!

"I was sitting out there one day, bib overalls down to my ankles, sun was shining through the long cracks so bright and warm, and I looked down in that dark pit. I was absorbed in watching a spider snare a fly. Then, there it was—a big black snake just a-weaving and wiggling around!

"I shot out of there, kangaroo leaping, my overalls hugging my ankles, and all the way to the house I was screaming to Grandma!

"The boy cousins came out then, with a long dead limb, still weaving it at me. Grandma found a peach sprout and used it!

"I got my revenge! I'd noticed a big hornet's nest in the privy, just under the shingle roof. I bided my time behind a tree 'till I saw the boys go in. Giving them just long enough to get settled good, I let fly a big rock and it hit that roof corner like a gunshot. They burst out of there in a cloud of hornets, trying to swat and hold their pants up at the same time—they'd never let me see their bare bodies! Oh, yes, they knew who'd done it!

"And," Rene concluded, "I wouldn't give a million dollars today for that memory—and neither will Jan, when she grows up!"

Kaiser: We had a club meeting at a lady member's house one afternoon. Hanging up on the toilet wall was the bank calendar. She had made Xs on certain days of the month. Her little son asked, "Mama, what's that?"

"Oh, that's just when I come across, I put a cross."

"And," he asked, "when you come around, you put a round?"

When we wallpapered rooms in the house Mom let us have all the scraps to paper the privy. It wasn't long 'till it split at the cracks between the boards and it peeled off, but for a little while it looked cheerful and so pretty.

Costomiris: If someone happened to leave the door open, the chickens got in and made a mess. We sometimes stepped barefoot in that before we saw it, and the smell and slippery feel—so bad, until we'd get a bucket of water to wash our feet and scrub it all out. Often a hen laid an egg in the corner newspaper box.

My younger sister, Virginia, had all her life been frightened of birds. Why? I enjoyed them so much. She remembered going to the toilet in a hurry one day, and it frightened an old hen so much it came at her, fighting its way. Also, there were the dirty, pesky sparrows building and tearing down their nests up in corners. She wished she could be brave like me, just throw the hen out and admire birds.

A butting billy goat caused problems, too. Ours annoyed Mom when he chewed on her washing on the clothesline in the chicken lot, near the toilet, or ate up the toilet catalogue.

Off and on there was a fighty rooster out in the chicken lot. I remember my little brother, Dick, always being chased or spurred by one on his way to the toilet. His wails went up! One Sunday we found the rooster in a big kettle of dumplings.

The kids in one family lived in terror of their buck sheep.

Mothers were detectives. "Down under" was evidence of worms—and the family members would all be wormed, as they usually passed through the family—or signs of a young girl growing up. Young kids, usually girls, learning to smoke left telltale evidence. Boys sneaked behind the barn.

One Saturday Mom bought a box of prunes, a rare treat, and when she went to cook them, the box was empty. "No one" had eaten them, but she soon learned the guilty party by the trips made out back!

When I sat on the toilet seat, as a small child, I wanted the bare flesh just above my knees to spread and flatten out like the town girls'. But the flesh around the bones of my very healthy, plump body was firm and hard and didn't give any more than a rolling pin would as it lay on the bread board.

The first thing of a morning, oh, that walk through a door full of cobwebs—and how they'd cling to my face and body! Or I'd sit down on a nest of them!

The wire clothesline was hooked to one corner of the privy, strung on around to the henhouse and then to the plum tree. I worried I'd get caught out there during a storm and either the lightening would come in on the number-nine-wire line or the wind would blow the toilet over.

After a rain, going in barefoot, imprints of the wet feet were left on the floor. My prints were of the full toe and heel sections, but only a line along the side of the arch. How I wished for a whole footprint like in catalogues!

Kaiser: The doors were just rough boards and would hardly close. Sometimes we had a leather strap with a slit in the end to fasten over a nail to hold it shut. The hinges were usually leather straps from old horse harness, and lasted for years.

One time I was visiting a friend. Theirs was a fancy toilet. I nudged the door shut with my foot, hoping at the last moment the outside hook wasn't standing up so it would drop into the eye and trap me inside. If the fastener was a wood latch and you didn't flip it over completely, it was a long, boring wait until someone came within hearing distance.

Other toilets, but not too many, were nicely painted, set on a cement foundation, and had a star, diamond, or crescent cut-out.

Costomiris: I heard of a young fellow who was hired to build a toilet at the hired man's house. He sawed the holes straight up and down, square, with hard edges. Most were rimmed out, smoothed down, rounded in back and came around to a U in the front. The nicer ones, there where the hole was cut, they put a knob on that piece and formed a lid to put over the holes when not in use, to help keep down the odors and flies.

One poor old lady couldn't find a hammer so she used a monkey wrench when she built hers. "Well," she commented, "that dear ol' house is much better'n a bush!"

Old-timers said a toilet should be put in a straight line past the woodpile. The average woman makes four or five trips a day, and she will always gather an armload of wood on the way back. A timid woman, perhaps a new hired girl or an old maid, she starts out, she sees menfolk, she's too bashful to go direct, so she'll go to the woodpile, pick up wood, go back to the house. She watches her chance to strike out later. She might make several trips and fill the woodbox before the way clears.

Kaiser: As regular as Friday night came, most women gave their kids a laxative, whether they needed it or not. They needed to be purged! We got it if we'd been acting sickly and then it was usually castor oil! I guess maybe we really needed it, especially when we were little, we'd have a very bad cold or whooping cough, cough up that phlegm. We'd lose our appetite, wouldn't eat right, go off our feed, and a kid who doesn't eat isn't going to get well.

The doctor, or Mother, would always look at our tongues, which, if coated white, was supposed to show a stomach or bowel problem. When we took a baby to the doctor he'd ask about the stools.

Mother tried to give castor oil to us in milk or coffee. Orange juice—she knew we'd take it that way, and for years I couldn't drink orange juice without seeing those big globs of oil floating on top!

Oh, she'd stir it up real, real good, but before I could drink, it would float back to the top. And, there was that delicious orange juice that we'd just never get otherwise, all ruined with castor oil! That was enough to make me sick!

I could smell it on the juice before I tasted it. There Dad stood, and if we didn't take it right down, he'd tip our chin up, holding it tight with his big old hand, and there wasn't a thing we could do but swallow! Mom started giving us Castoria when it came on the market and it was just as effective and much more pleasant to take!

Costomiris: Mom gave us castor oil in a big tablespoon, washed down with the orange juice. Even today I can't put a tablespoon in my mouth, like when eating soup, without tasting castor oil.

Old-timers said castor oil was very healing. Good for cleansing the liver. Our little Becky was only a few months old when she had pneumonia. Dr. Ambrose gave her something very new, a penicillin shot which helped some, then she got worse. He was afraid to chance a bigger shot and was bewildered as to what to do. I walked the floor with the crying child. Would she just die? Grandmother Kepner, full of wisdom from raising eight children, said, "If that was my child, I'd give her a dose of castor oil." Give a baby castor oil? But something had to be done! Becky swallowed it right down, then licked her lips! When I changed her next few cotton diapers, they were full of phelgm and green mucus. She recovered immediately!

Uncle Jim Fetty's grandpa lived with them when he was a kid. He said one evening the whole family went to visit a neighbor. The old dog had been chilling and Mom and the sisters felt so sorry for him. They shut the dog in the house where he would be warm while everyone was away.

Late that night, coming home, Grandpa said, "I didn't remember to tell you, but I gave the dog a big dose of castor oil today. Maybe that'll straighten him out."

When they opened the kitchen door, oh, oh, you never smelled anything like it in all your life! The dog shot past them to the open door. Tell-tale trails ran all over the parents' bed, from one door to the other, to the windows, like he'd been trying to get out. Everyone felt so sorry for the dog, but this? They were all so tired, but it had to be cleaned up before they went to bed. Even though it was so cold outside, the doors were propped wide open to air out the house.

Lola Brenton said when she was five, her mother, grandmother, and she were to go to Noblesville for Grandmother to sign up for her twelve dollar-a-month pension. Just before leaving, Mother and Lola went to the toilet. A big wind blew up and Mother cried, "Lola, run for the house!" Lola got halfway and heard a big crash. An old shed had blown over on the toilet, trapping Mother inside.

A workman from the Bottle Factory was going by and heard cries, he yanked off the boards, pulled Mother out, and carried her into the house.

She didn't have any broken bones, but they called in the family, not expecting her to live till morning.

All night long they turned her in sheets, her misery was so severe. The husband painted her spine scratches with iodine, using a duck feather for a brush. He kept that bottle right up there by the chimney and brought it down and painted them several times a day. And she lived, to a ripe old age.

Kaiser: Most churches had outside toilets, even in town. Kids brought old calendar pictures to decorate walls.

When everyone modernized, got a Roosevelt out back to replace the old two-three holers, they were modern, but never as much fun. We had to take turns in it. I thought, when we finally got an inside bathroom I'd have peaceful privacy, but instead, the kids would stand outside the door and beg to come in, having to go bad. I'd see little fingers working in under the door.

Costomiris: Oh, the modern Roosevelt! Franklin D. Roosevelt took office as president of the United States when we were deep in the Depression. Financially depressed men were given jobs building that modern one-holer. It was built to specifications—the cement foundation and a commode-like stool, and seat, with an attached pipe running up through the roof to carry away all odors. No flies! The Roosevelt reined supreme for only a few years—ten? By that time, after World War II, people were finding space in their homes, usually a pantry off the kitchen, for a bathroom.

Bud and I entertained a hundred of his World War II military fellows and their wives in September, 1987. They came from all over the U.S. to attend the 823rd Tank Destroyer Battalion's four-day reunion in Indianapolis. On Saturday they came to our house for "A Day on the Farm." They'd always wondered what this Col. Costomiris' home would be like. Most had no idea of farm living. They remembered, so well, his "white glove" army inspections! Bud, knowing the beer-drinking buddies wouldn't want to make frequent and hurried comfort trips, borrowed neighbor Myron Thompson's Roosevelt. He had had it sitting in a secluded corner where his young workers planted big fields of melons and tomatoes. Not needed now, Myron hauled it here on his farm implement trailer. One of those young fellows sat "on the throne" with the door propped open, riding down the busy highway, waving and shouting to everyone who went by!

Just recently, Josh, our grandson, who is eight, was curious about the little building sitting out there beside the shed. Grandpa said, "Go look in. It's a Roosevelt—that was a bathroom years ago." Josh came running back, "But, Grandpa, there's no bathtub!"

Many changes took place when people finally had a bathroom in the house. The catalogue went out overnight. We bought toilet paper and could only afford one roll at a time. Often we ran out and we had to resort to the faithful old back house, with its catalogue, used now only when we were working in the yard and garden.

One Sunday night a Chicago couple, Bud's father's friends, complete strangers, stopped by very late. When the wife asked where the bathroom was, I pointed it out, then cringed when I heard her spin off the paper. We always carefully used it. When her husband went in, he was soon back. No toilet paper. I had no extra roll. We used cloth napkins for company, and rags for wiping up spills. How did he manage? I'll never know. They didn't stay long.

As kids, to eat in the toilet was feeding the Devil! An apple, a cookie, or a piece of bacon left over from breakfast had to be hurriedly swallowed before entering.

When reading Westerns I always wondered how travelers managed without a toilet. I read only one account, that ladies used the expression, "go pick flowers," and gentlemen went "hunting rabbits." In the wide, flat, treeless desert, women clasped hands together and made a circle, looking out, thus discreetly covering the lady in the center. Men went behind wagons.

Kaiser: The "good old days" were interesting, but I'll tell you, we had so little of the world's comforts, and I don't want to go back to them, ever!

Costomiris: If the walls of the outdoor toilets could only talk, they'd tell a lot of stories!

—This story originally appeared in Tri Town Topics, *February 8, 15, and 22, 1979, and is included in* Cicero, Indiana: 1834-1984.

Part Three: Rainbows

Children's Happiness

When Indiana became a state in 1816 the infant death rate was nearly fifty percent. Smallpox, cholera, typhoid fever and milk sickness claimed babies and children with frightening regularity. Many even died of croup because doctors often could not reach their patients in time.

Although the situation had improved somewhat by the turn of the century, childhood still was a dangerous and difficult time, as many of these stories reveal. Disease was still a child's number one enemy.

Those who survived past age five were expected to work. Children rose early to get chores done before school, and helped again after they returned home. Household and farm accidents killed or maimed a few.

But each child was a special member of the family—usually a large clan—and knew the feeling of closeness, first as a newborn sleeping with parents, then rooming with older siblings, often sharing the same bed with one or more sisters and brothers. And this physical closeness extended into other areas of family life. Children and their parents shared not only the work, but life's pleasures as well.

It was a time when children were to be seen and not heard, when they were taught to respect their elders, be kind to others, and live by the Golden Rule.

"Rainbows are bridges to Heaven."

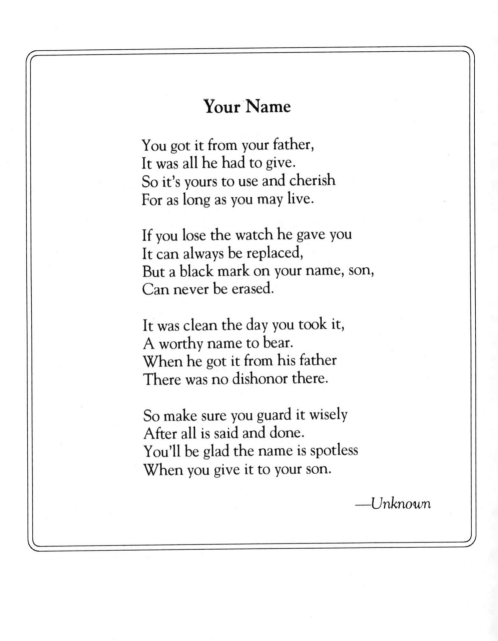

Your Name

You got it from your father,
It was all he had to give.
So it's yours to use and cherish
For as long as you may live.

If you lose the watch he gave you
It can always be replaced,
But a black mark on your name, son,
Can never be erased.

It was clean the day you took it,
A worthy name to bear.
When he got it from his father
There was no dishonor there.

So make sure you guard it wisely
After all is said and done.
You'll be glad the name is spotless
When you give it to your son.

—*Unknown*

That House of Mystery Up On the Hill

by
Amel Mongold

Although physically frail, Amel Mongold, in her eighties, had many a tale to tell as she rode along from a nursing home to spend an evening at her favorite restaurant in Noblesville.

My grandparents lived in the south end of Noblesville, down the street from us. They had a garden, chickens, an old cow Grandpa milked, and a couple pigs he fed out to butcher to provide meat for their table.

Grandma made butter and cottage cheese. All they didn't use, or give to us, they sold to neighbors.

I remember one house where Grandpa delivered a bucket of milk every morning. A Noblesville house with a shady reputation, I'd heard. Once a week he took cottage cheese, buttermilk, and a pound of butter to its residents, four pretty young ladies.

Their arrival into town had been greeted with stares of unusual interest right from the beginning. Not at all like the old folks who'd lived in that house before. I'd visited with them all the time, up to when they died. I was seven then.

Each Saturday, after the four ladies moved in, I'd beg and beg, "Please, Grandpa, please let me go with you when you deliver up there!"

"What would your mother say, Amel?" I knew what she'd say: "Indeed not!" But I could generally get around my grandparents. So I kept begging.

Finally Grandma said, in a voice extraordinarily gentle, "Oh, botheration, Paw, let 'er go." Grandma wore thick glasses, had silvery hair, and soft wrinkles. Her arthritis was bad, which caused her hands to curl like springs.

When delivering, I was never, ever allowed to go up on the porch. I watched as Grandpa went inside. I'd get so giddy. Gooseflesh prickled clear up my arms! Something was so mysterious about "That House." I couldn't imagine why all the secretiveness from everyone in our neighborhood.

That house of mystery up on the hill!

Once, waiting until Grandpa was in an extra happy mood, I hesitantly asked him about it. "Lands a livin', child, it's simply a house of pleasure. Now, git along with ya!" His lips, so funny, folded like a Japanese fan over his toothless gums.

A house of pleasure. It continued to perplex me. Did they have plays inside like at the Wild Opera House uptown? No, 'cause everyone talked on and on about those performances. And never in whispers!

And it wasn't like the Cicero Fall Festival or the circus or the county fair or even a Halloween party. Then what was it?

Babe Brown was in charge of That House. She was a young lady and the cutest thing. Babe had class, they said! She pulled every eye in her direction.

See, this was called the "red light district" by some. The railroad tracks were a few blocks down from us. Colored women ran two of those other houses on south.

Babe's seemed the most elaborate. People claimed men stopped off in Noblesville for one of two things. Probably both. A drink and a lady. These places got their name from railroad men getting off railroad cars. When they came to the porch, they hung up their lanterns, the light showing through red globes, and then went on inside. Those rows of red-light lanterns hanging there, thus the red light district.

No one would ever talk to me about them. What was this element of mystery surrounding these houses, especially Babe's?

Grandma had a dressmaker friend. I heard them, and Mama, talking one day. "There's nothing too fine for Babe," the dressmaker lady said. "She chooses the best silks and velvets and when they are made up she wears them to an advantage. She has such a graceful figure and a wealth of honey-golden hair, which is indeed her crowning glory, and large brown eyes she rolls at men. Those milk-white hands! She is easily the most beautiful woman—I won't call her a lady—that has ever lived in Noblesville!"

Mama grunted, "If she had her hands sunk deep in diapers and dishes, they wouldn't look milk-white! A scarecrow frame! Oh, yes, she has an eye for good lace, fine material, and well-cut dresses, and a wad to buy them with. Maybe I could draw looks as I walk down the street, if I had all of that!"

Oftentimes Babe came to Grandmother's for extra milk or eggs, so I got to know her pretty well. We'd sit on the front porch, Grandma and me in the swing and Babe in a rocking chair. Grandpa would come and drop down in the other rocker and rest a spell; his rheumatism was always bothering him. We'd all visit.

As Babe talked she buffed her nails and popped her chewing gum. She passed each one of us a stick of my favorite, Juicy Fruit. Oh, I wished I could buy chewing gum all the time. Grandma and Grandpa were always real friendly to Babe. Let anybody come by in pants and Babe would perk up and laugh and talk fast and bat her eyes! One time I tried to imitate Babe. Grandma scolded me, "Oh, Amel, I never ever saw nothin' equalin' it. A little mimic. My soul and body!"

Babe smelled so good of talcum powder, I guess it was. She always wore such beautiful clothes, looking like she was poured in them, some said, and her hair was just so. She came from a well-to-do family from Chicago, I heard. Her parents thought she was a secretary at the Noblesville Milling Company down here.

Once Grandma said to her, "Since you were brought up in Chicago, such a big city, you must find us very dull and stodgy after all your smart parties up there." But Babe just laughed and said, "I'm a-likin' it real fine here!"

I was never allowed to even walk by Babe's house. Sometimes, late in the evening, Beulah and Margaret, my best friends, and I would sneak around when Mama was visiting down at my grandparents'. Going by Babe's house I caught the scent of a cigar and the sound of a woman's laugh. We'd see well-dressed, handsome fellows. Some I recognized as businessmen from uptown. They'd park their buggies on down the street a-ways where they thought no one would know them, but folks knew every man's rig. Then they'd quickly walk up on the long porch, and hurriedly step through the front door.

Younger fellows clowned around there a lot. They were in and out often. Sometimes businessmen, in their black serge suits, got off a railroad car and they'd go up to Babe's. But, always, it was just men.

Oh, so much noise on Saturday night, it beat all. When I asked Charlie, my big brother, he was fifteen, why the young men hung around that-a-way, he laughed, said they were waiting their turn.

Their turn? To put nickels in to play the player piano? It was so loud and going all the time. I heard someone say that they also sold beer, but I wasn't to tell. The evils of gambling and drinking, our preacher preached. Was that the puzzle?

Bubba—that's what I called my brother Charlie—he'd let me tag along to the grocery when Mama wanted something. Sometimes he'd even let me hold his hand, if he thought no one was watching. He'd say we could walk past Babe's, "But don't look that-a-way. Just put your hand up to that side of your head when we go by."

"Well, then, Bubba," I questioned him, "is Babe's house a saloon? Margaret said her mother always made her close her eyes every time they passed a saloon." He said no; that's all he said.

Once I heard Bubba and his best friend, Boots, talking. They were stretched out in the grass under the apple tree, stroking our dog, Rags. I was in my room cutting out paper dolls from Mama's newest *McCall's*. Boots told Bubba he liked to sit and watch those high-stepping women lounging out in their backyard.

I just loved my brother, Bubba. He was nice to me, except when Boots came around he'd say, "You peeve me, girl. Now git on with yourself. Scat! Beat it!"

Bubba said to Boots, "I asked Paw once, 'How much does it cost?' and Paw said, 'Don't monkey around with them, Son.' I asked him if he was acquainted with any of the men who went there, but he said that we shouldn't invade their privacy by talking about them. Then Paw added, with emphasis, 'Iff'n I ketch you up there, I'll cut you a new bottom!' I knew what Paw meant, but I still wonder...."

Boots laughed out, "My paw said iff'n he ever caught me up there he'd skin me out and nail my hide to the barn door to flap there all winter! Then he further drove the point home: 'You heard what happened to the cat, don't you? He was crossin' the railroad track and the train run over his tail and cut it off. The cat looked back to see what happened and it cut off his head. The lesson you need to learn here, son, don't lose your head over a piece of tail!' "

One time I said to Mama, we were sitting on the porch shelling peas for dinner, "Mama," I said, "why don't Papa go in Babe's house like all the other men, 'cept Grandpa, of course?"

Mama set her jaw, her face as long as a fiddle—that's what Grandpa said about Mama when she got mad. She said, "Hush! That's a place of iniquity! Amel, it's a pity you can't keep your mind on what you're a-doin' there."

"Did Papa ever go to visit Babe? I mean, years ago before I was born when she lived somewhere else in town? What's the meanin' of 'iniquity?' " I could always read Mama's expression and I knew I was not to ask another question like that.

To make Mama feel better, I said, "I wish you could have pretty clothes like Babe. When she comes home from Chicago, after a visit up there, she has those elegant dresses that almost sweep the ground, and lace at her throat, and her large hats—oh, that's somethin' to behold!" Mama looked at me dead-faced.

I continued, "Mama, have you ever wished you could be someone other than who you are?" I knew she was thinking I'd say what I usually said to her, that I wanted to grow up beautiful just like Mama, have a pretty house, a handsome husband, and babies. I noticed the disappointed look on her face when I said, "When I grow up I want to be pretty, just like Babe, wear fine clothes and have all those handsome men coming to my house," and did Mama think I could? My two good friends, Margaret and Beulah, they would be there, too. And I could put toilet water on my handkerchief. Oh, wouldn't that be nice?

Mama was so furious the pod of peas she was shelling with her fingers flew way out and went rolling across the porch floor and onto the ground. "Indeed not! Not a daughter of mine! Where did you ever get such a foolish notion in your head? She's nothin' but a...a...a... Only fallen women wear perfume." Mama went on muttering that Babe was sinful and bold and shameless and a tramp.

I learned, quite young, there was no talking to Mama about Babe and That House! And I also noticed that all the women Mama's age in the neighborhood kept watchful eyes on their husbands.

When Mama's friends gathered on our porch I'd overhear bits of their conversation. They thought Margaret and I were out in the backyard playing house. It quickened our interest all the more when they started whispering. "Four very brassy women and all their masculine visitors, that house is distinctly shady, and not due just to its maple trees!"

"They draw young boys and men like a sorghum mill draws honeybees."

"That Babe. She's surely the seed of a wicked bed!"

"Victoria—I don't know the others—Victoria, her hair's red. Certainly not the color that nature intended it to be."

"Remember, nobody can make you bad unless you really want to be!"

"A house of shame!"

I thought, *shame!* What's to be 'shamed of? All those girls are always so nice and friendly to everyone when we see 'em up town. What has Mama heard that she thinks they are bad?

Whispers: "A place that furnishes illegal drinks to satisfy men's thirst and girls to satisfy their lusts."

"The Bible teaches us that God loves them no matter how much they...."

Just like I know Mama loves me when I've been naughty?

One day the discussion got very lively. The women talked on and on. There was another red-light district, they called it. Poor people lived there. Very poor. And dirty. Shiftless. Mama always said there was no call for being dirty, no matter you didn't have a cent to your name; they could use soap and water.

Most of them along there just eked out a living. One lady in particular, she had bad ways. Her large family of kids were all very slow learners at school. They quit at age sixteen.

All except one. He was brilliant and always looked much cleaner than the others. People said he had pride in himself. Dressed nice. He even went on to high school. Later he graduated from college. Hardly anyone went to college. Uh-huh, they knew whom he belonged to. Who else had enough money to finance his education and his living expenses? Uh-huh, they knew—spittin' image of.... And then I sneezed. So, I'll never, ever know!

My two friends and I were always playing house, out in the woodhouse, 'cause it was empty in the summer. We'd sweep out a corner, then arrange blocks of stovewood for furniture. Our doll babies needed constant attention.

Sometimes we played "That House on the Hill." I was Babe. Folks said Babe's blond hair came straight out of a bottle. Margaret was Victoria, 'cause Margaret's hair was red like Victoria's. We dressed up in Mama's old dresses. I put on my five-cent diamond ring and borrowed Mama's Japanese fan. We dabbed on pink perfume from bottled rosewater we'd made from rose petals. Margaret carried her mother's parasol. We walked up and down the side of the street, so ladylike. We talked. Does Babe ever want to get married and have babies? Margaret's mama said those girls weren't cut out for motherhood.

The years went by. We three friends graduated from the eighth grade. Young women came from away to work for Babe when older ones left. I continued to be captivated by the girls in That House! I began to realize single women, as well as the married ones, kept watchful eyes on their men!

I guess I was in the last year of high school when I learned the truth about Babe and her girls. The same big girl that told Margaret and Beulah and I about growing up, she told us all about Babe and her girls.

When my feller, Frank, and I walked or rode in the buggy by That House I yearned to ask him if he'd ever been inside, what it was like, but of course I didn't.

One time Margaret and I, after we'd both been married a spell, were talking. Margaret said she and her husband drove past That House one day when Babe was hurrying up the steps onto her porch. Margaret told him she had always wanted to be pretty and rich and stylish, like Babe. Her husband laughed, then said, "Well listen, kid, if you had a wiggle like that, maybe you wouldn't be a farmer's wife!"

Margaret's mother had overheard some women talking one day. They said one man in town was just crazy about Babe. He would have married her in a minute if she'd have had him. But Babe said she was afraid he'd never accept the way she had lived.

After I was married I saw to it that Frank and I, when visiting my parents and grandparents, came in from another direction, not past Babe's!

This house maintained its aura of mystery for me for over two decades. In time, I guess the law closed down the Noblesville houses with their shady reputations, and ran the women out of town.

I couldn't help but have a sad feeling in my heart. I still carry that memory of lying in my bed at night, smelling cigar and pipe smoke and listening to the loud piano music, mingled with the laughter of men and the occasional shrill voice of a woman.

I always fell asleep before I wanted to.

—Mrs. Mongold *was interviewed in the late 1970s.*

Grandma's Spring House

by
Willis McCarty

Willis McCarty was a retired farmer living near "Dog Town"—few knew it by its proper name of Omega—when he told his story in 1980. Now, at age eighty-two, he's still active. The spring house was the cooling system on a very few farms, and an enjoyable place for two active boys to play.

Grandpa built Grandma a spring house that I will never forget. It played such an important part in my boyhood. Such wonderful memories.

There was a quarter of a mile between my parents' home and Dad's parents. It wasn't far to run down there to play.

The spring house was a nice, old, brick building setting in the middle of the barnyard pasture. Grandpa's cattle and sheep kept the grass cropped all around it. Never a weed anywhere, so it wasn't a good cover for snakes or rodents that like to be around damp places. I saw a blue racer only once, and a black snake, but they were common back then.

The structure had a wall on three sides and the other was open. We went down some limestone slab steps to go through the wooden door. The roof extended ten feet both ways from the building—one end out over the spring.

Grandpa didn't fence it off. Livestock never got into it. They had no reason to crowd in for they had other cool places to go. Years later Grandpa cemented the floor, but back then it was just limestone laid down. Me and my brother, George, we would run barefoot on the slick walk, take a long slide, skidding to where we could breathe in the cool air from the interior.

The water going through there stayed a constant fifty degrees, the temperature of most of the water pumped from wells around there.

A spring-fed brook wound its way around our farm. It ran through the spring house and on down through the pasture into a tank for watering the animals. Us boys never had the hateful task of daily pumping water for the stock.

Grandma stood on the wood-plank, water-covered floor. She kept her milk, cream, butter, and the sour cream she collected to make butter in the stone-lined cement trough, and anything else, like puddings, cottage cheese, or buttermilk she wanted to keep cool. The water spun in a slow circle whirlpool, like horses on a merry-go-round.

She only had to walk about five hundred feet to it, but usually she'd send one of us boys. The milk crocks dripped water when we pulled them up. Oh, those fresh smells!

Mom had a big, old, glass jar about sixteen-by-twelve inches and it stood more than two feet high. It had been a case for a battery for the telephone exchange. They did away with the telephone exchange and somehow Dad got hold of some big jars. When full, or even half full, it was a bit awkward for us boys to handle. Grandma did that, rather than chance its getting broken. She'd swish it up out of the water where she could reach it better, skim off the cream to put into the cream crock for making butter, then take the milk on to the house to sour, to make cottage cheese.

We had a lot of plum trees and she made the best plum jelly you ever tasted! Every day us boys went out and picked up the fallen ripe plums, and she'd make another batch. She'd just keep adding to it each day, in another one of those glass jars, pouring it in when it was still liquid but not hot. I could tell the layers by the bubbly whitish foam on the edges—just a line around there. And she filled that clear full and also filled stone jars.

Several of us boys went to the woods and picked wild raspberries and blackberries. She'd usually have a separate crock for that, but if it was a small batch, she'd add it to the plum jelly. Another ribbon of color. Apple jelly was clear amber.

She kept all that down in the spring house and she'd dip out what she needed for the table, then she put the wooden lids back on. Because of the constant year-round temperature, no worry of it freezing.

Grandma made jelly rolls to send in our school lunches. She'd bake it in a big, shallow pan that was just the size of her oven. When it was done, she rolled it up like a piece of rubber, to cool, then she unrolled it flat on a kitchen towel. She spread on that plum jelly, made to perfection. She then re-rolled it and cut it into inch-size slices. I'd like to have some of that sweet, spongy jelly roll right now!

Unlike most springs, Grandma's was never affected by rains. Always a constant level. It never flooded.

The water stood six inches deep in the trough, or halfway on a gallon crock. Grandma set all sizes of milk crocks, with their contents, down in the stone-lined trough. Then she placed wooden lids on top of each one of them, and a rock on top of that so nothing could get in.

George and I decided how funny it would be if Grandma found a crawdad in her coffee cream. So, the next morning we watched in her kitchen as she carefully skimmed all the cream off the crock of milk. When she saw that old crawdad crawling around down in there she cried out, "How in the world did that crawdad get in this milk?" We both stood by her, sober-faced, peering in.

She took off as fast as she could go for the spring house, us two boys following—innocence all over our faces.

Down there she shoved crocks this way and that. We knew she was thinking, how could it have crawled in under that rock-weighted lid? She fussed, "Lawsy, what if someone had come in my kitchen and saw that in there?"

She threw out the rock-weights and had us boys bring in larger ones, took the new ones and scrubbed them clean, then muttered to herself all the way back to the house—me and George still down there doubling over with laughter!

The spring house roof was only three feet from the ground at one corner. On it were hand-split, clapboard shingles, big old things three feet long. They had weathered enough so there were no splinters. We could easily crawl up and slide down them. One or the other of us always stood watch, so we wouldn't get caught.

In the wintertime they got rough and we couldn't slide very easily. We'd get a pound of butter from the spring house and rub it on the shingles. We greased them good so we could slide better. Wonder we didn't get splinters in our hindsides, then we'd had to have confessed to our mischief.

Washday, Mother just fussed and fussed, "Where are you boys picking up all this grease and dirt? It just beats all. I've scrubbed these pants on the washboard till my knuckles are raw, and they still won't come clean!"

I wonder if Grandma ever missed her butter. If she did, she never let on.

Grandma had a cellar under the house she could have used, as most farmhouses had, but for some reason, it was always warm down there and milk products would have spoiled.

My folks had a storm cellar out a ways from the house where we went when a bad storm was blowing up or a tornado was sighted. We didn't like playing down in there as rats, mice, and snakes set up residence in it.

A neighbor, seeing us always down around that stream, remarked: "Every child should have a handy body of water to play around!" I agreed with him. We had ours, and none of the cellars ever compared to the fun we had in Grandma's spring house!

—*This story appeared in the* Tri Town Topics, *September 4 and 11, 1980, and in the* Good Old Days Spring Special, *1984.*

Great-Grandpa's Beard

Great-grandpa had a snowy beard
Of which he was quite vain;
Small Effie sat upon his knee
And stroked the ample mane.

She put her skill to practice then
And pulled the strands about,
Great-grandpa took a little nap
And Effie wandered out.

The old man wakened from his sleep
And walked across the town;
His neighbors' snickering and mirth
Brought forth a puzzled frown.

Until he glanced into a glass
And bolted toward a barn;
His beard was done in two neat braids,
And tied with yellow yarn!

—*Ethel Handcock Harp*

I Have Such Fond Memories of Childhood Christmases

by
Harriett Vestal

Harriett Vestal obtained a permit to work all through high school in the Cicero Branch Library. After years as wife of Robert, mother, grandmother, and office worker, she has come full circle. She's the energetic head librarian at Cicero, who loves people and books.

A doll was always on my Christmas list. Like most little girls, I loved them. A doll demands nothing and gives fun, comfort, and true companionship. It's such a lovable partner all day, naptime, and even in the dark of night. Some little "mothers" will chew it, drag it, throw it into the bathtub, and sometimes leave it in the hot sun or rain—I never did—yet dolly does not object and is always ready to snuggle close. She shares secrets and never divulges them. Little Mama takes it to tea parties, Sunday school, shopping, Mom's club meetings, and when it's sick she's a nurse and mother combined. Through the years I have had many dolls. I dearly loved each one of them.

Being an only child, I was around older people. I was always so anxious for them to recount stories of their childhoods, especially Christmas as it was "back then."

Grandma Lorenze used to tell me of her old-fashioned Christmases when she was happy to get an orange in the toe of her stocking, a candy cane, cookies, the practical homemade apron, and a cotton flannel nightgown. During the Christmas holidays they enjoyed parties with family and friends in neighbors' homes, went for sleigh rides, and attended church services. She'd tell me about the birth of baby Jesus. Once she remembered a little girl, four years old, saying, "Mama, don't you think it was nice of the shepherds to get all cleaned up before they went to see the baby Jesus?"

"What do you mean, dear?"

"Well, you know the song, 'While shepherds washed their socks by night. . . .' " We both laughed and laughed!

When Grandma's two little girls, Ruth, my mother, and Florence, were old enough for toys, store-bought dolls were rare and expensive. But stores sold china doll heads. Mothers or grandmothers made the cloth bodies, then attached the parts. Body patterns of newspaper were handed around from family, to friends, or neighbors. Later on, china feet and hands were also available but they broke easily.

Grandpa Lorenze, unlike most men of his generation, took special interest in choosing just the right doll head. He'd say to Grandma, "Let's go shopping early so we can find the prettiest and best one, before they are all picked over." The two little girls were left with relatives on this rare occasion.

The clerk would unroll cotton flannel or cotton batting on the glass countertop, for protection, bring out a box full of tissue-wrapped heads, and line them up to choose from.

Grandmother said Granddad would so painstakingly decide on the most expensive, if it was the prettiest. Left up to her, she would have been thinking economy and sensibility.

Ruth was four years older than Florence. Florence wanted the same china-headed doll as Ruth but my grandparents thought, at her early age, she'd have to wait until she was old enough to care for it properly. China heads, just like Grandma's china dishes, broke easily. At that time Florence got a teddy bear and doll dishes. Later she received beautiful dolls. Ruth always shared her toys with her little sister.

Grandma said the catalogues carried kid leather bodies, ready for the china head, arms, and legs to be sewn on. A small doll body, ten inches long, cost ten cents. The big twenty-four-inch dolls were forty cents. The finest bodies had jointed body parts. China heads cost a quarter to a dollar.

Grandma secretly made beautiful doll clothes in the style of the day. Long full skirts, Peter Pan collars, pantalets, and a small bead necklace. Slippers were made from felt, coat and bonnet from velvet.

As a child, I remember the long evenings before Christmas. I guess I was the happiest child alive! At night, after Dad had the milking done and we had supper over and the dishes done, the whole family gathered on chairs around the dining room table. Oh, how nice and warm, there near the chrome-plated heating stove. It was catalogue-shopping time for me. Near the light of the Aladdin lamp I'd look at the doll sections of the Sears, Roebuck, Montgomery Ward, and Alden's catalogues. There was page after page of beautiful dolls—baby dolls, mommy dolls, large and small dolls, some dressed, some not.

Dad would be reading his newspaper or a library book, and Mother would be sewing or reading. There was always a jigsaw puzzle to work and sometimes we'd pop corn, eat cold, juicy apples from the barrel in the cellar, and listen to radio programs on the Atwater-Kent.

My parents exchanged gifts. One year Mother asked for a tube cake pan to bake her angel food cakes in. Dad also got her a beautiful, blue neck scarf. Mother and I usually gave Dad a pretty tie and a flannel work shirt. Dad enjoyed hunting and fishing, and one year we got him a hunting coat.

Up on the upright piano was a dish of candy—Hershey bars, peppermints, and gumdrops. My folks believed that sweets spoiled a meal and they were reserved just for this time of day. Dad kept peppermints in his shirt pockets. When I wasn't watching, he'd take one out, pitch it high into the air, and when it was coming down, he'd observe, "Oh, look! Santy dropped something!" He'd reach way up and catch it.

Sometimes he'd call me "Bill" instead of "Harriett." I'd grin and say, "My name's not Bill!" Once I asked if he'd rather have had a boy. He hugged me, "I got just what I wanted—you!"

We planned and shared secrets. "Don't tell Mother; I'm making the kitchen shelves she wants." He'd whisper, "Don't forget to finish the pictures you're doing for Grandma and Grandpa!" I liked to draw animals and birds, mostly with crayons. Years later, I found some of them tucked between the pages of Gram's Bible and in her box of receipts! Grandma always said "receipts" instead of "recipes" like Mama and most women.

Dolls from the catalogue were ordered by number and name. Which one did I like best? Suzanne! I had her for years and years. Her bisque head was so realistic-looking. The hair was a brown, sewed-on wig. She had blue, open-and-shut eyes with eyelashes, pug nose, and rosy cheeks. The arms and legs were bisque. Her dress and bonnet were pink organdy trimmed in white lace. She had little, white-ribbed stockings with white leather slippers. Her cloth-covered body was soft and cuddly.

My doll had to be purchased early. Then, where to hide it? Our house was small, with one little closet. It had a shelf above. My parents knew Harriett would be watching up there. I learned, years later, that Suzanne was put in a cardboard box on the top of the kitchen cabinet. That's where they kept folded newspapers—reach up and get one to use to peel the potatoes on, make a fire, or cut out dress patterns.

When I sat on Dad's lap, listening to his pocket watch ticking in the breast overall pocket, he'd say, "I'm going to be talking to Santa. Anything you want me to tell him?"

The three of us walked through a wooded area near where we lived and we'd choose a tree. Not too big, but big enough. Just right. Dad cut it, placed it on the car fender and then drove slowly home. We decorated it together. Dad put the lights on. One tree, when I was four years old, had small, lighted candles. But that was dangerous, so the practice wasn't continued.

Mother wanted to celebrate Christmas and exchange gifts on Christmas Day, but Dad just couldn't wait to give me my presents.

Christmas Eve, what to do with Harriett? Dad would start his make-believe. "Come on, Harriett, you and I'll go to the bedroom so Santy can come." He'd leave the bedroom door open a crack to let the living room lamp light show through, then he'd start telling me stories in my dim room. I'd get so engrossed in his yarn, I didn't realize what was going on out there!

I'd receive two or three other presents besides a doll. Once there was a sled under the tree. Another time, black patent-leather slippers I'd been yearning for so badly. A much-wanted blackboard with colored chalks, just like the ones at school! A small rocking chair, a teddy bear, and always books!

Mother privately made me the most beautiful doll clothes. Always a new wardrobe for each of my other dolls. She stitched most of my clothes, too. She'd look at magazine pictures in McCall's, Ladies Home Journal, and Ladies Home Companion, and she made them to look just like those in the ads or the pattern section. Everything matched, and every place I went there were always comments about my beautiful clothes. Scraps from my dresses were made into doll pajamas, dresses, or aprons.

I loved my paper dolls! For a doll house I'd take the rounded clothespins, push two together, then, in the corner of the living room I'd line these around to define each of the rooms. Mother made doll furniture using small and large, heavy cardboard match boxes. For the bedroom, twin beds with little legs on them, then she wallpapered the headboards to resemble birdseye maple. Mother drew outlines for drawers on the dresser and put a pocketbook mirror over it. She made davenport and chairs out of the matchboxes, stuffed with cotton, then upholstered. Grandma crocheted little rugs out of grocery store string or yarn scraps. I played with my doll furniture for years.

Mother saved little trinkets all year long. A sucker stick, with broom straws wrapped around one end, was my broom. For a table lamp she used a section of sucker stick, then she curled cardboard to make a lamp shade.

Christmas Day was spent with one set or the other of the grandparents, Lorenze or Hiatt, and so, more presents and treats. Some I remember: a hand-knit wool scarf and mittens, book of paper dolls, candy, subscription to *National Geographic*, a toy miniature train whose track was the size of a dinner plate. Wind it up and it would go round and round. And, always books. Is it any wonder I'm sitting at my desk at Cicero's very busy library?

The gifts were individually wrapped in white tissue paper and tied with red or green wool yarn. One year, each person's name was written on a gummed sticker that Grandma labeled her glasses of jelly with. They had a red border of decorative red berries and green leaves. I was so delighted with my Harriett sticker, I stuck it up on the pantry door, as high as I could reach. All through the years that was never removed, just painted around. When I came home from college, it was still there.

Suzanne was always my favorite doll, but she was not the prettiest. Each year I received a doll to join my doll family.

All my Christmases were special. Those beloved memories will remain with me always, but not just because of the gifts. The giving, sharing, and togetherness was, and still is, an important part of the love that bound us to each other. I'm truly blessed to have had parents who loved me enough to teach me that we can enjoy the Christmas spirit all year through and not just one day.

—This story originally appeared in the Noblesville Daily Ledger, *December 26, 1983.*

We Lived Above the Interurban Depot
When Dad Was Station Master

by
Larry Venable

Larry Venable, organist at Noblesville First Friends Church, retired after thirty-five years at Peoples Bank in Indianapolis. He, wife Susie, and children, made Noblesville their home. Larry was interviewed in the summer of 1988.

My father, William E. Venable, was station master at the Noblesville, Indiana, depot when I was a boy from ages six to twelve, the years 1923 to 1929. We lived upstairs until I was in the latter part of the sixth grade. It was just recently I realized we were only there six years, yet it seems such a big part of my life that was so carefree and enjoyable.

The interurban was a very popular mode of travel in my early life. It was convenient, inexpensive, and often the only way to get around. A network of these electrically driven cars crisscrossed our state, right through our Hamilton County.

My father was a small man—five feet, six inches, light brown hair and blue eyes. He wore a cap that had a green celluloid bill with elastic strap around the back. Elastic sleeve garters were on each arm above his elbows. Dad worked by the glare of that pear-shaped bulb, as he stood behind the counter dispensing tickets from a rack on the counter.

The station was filled with men and women, waving and calling as they rushed to greet friends and relatives upon the arrival of an interurban. There were so many drummers—salesmen—stopping or passing through. They were freshly shaven, wore suits, patent leather shoes, and big smiles. Mothers never let their daughters hang around the depot because drummers liked to flirt.

The waiting room was usually full of smoke. Spittoons were placed all around. Women drew their skirts close to them to be sure they did not swish against some filthy cuspidor. I was glad Dad cleaned them, and didn't assign me to that job. I liked the ladies' sweet perfumes. There were restless and crying children, after long rides.

Dad was the janitor. He cleaned and also he fired the furnace, with coal or coke, I can't remember.

The wooden floors were oiled but I don't know how or when that was done—probably after I'd gone to bed at night. Dad scattered sawdust over the floor before sweeping it with a wide push-broom each morning. Two restrooms were in the back, one for men and one for women. There were long, molded wooden benches for ticket holders to use while waiting for the next interurban or for those persons waiting for incoming passengers. Dad didn't allow loafers.

The upstairs apartment went with the station master job. I have no idea how much Dad made a month. At that age I wasn't interested in those things. I thought we were living good.

My mother, Minnie, was tiny, redheaded; she had green eyes and she was a very quiet, easygoing lady. It took a lot to get that redhead temper up, but occasionally something did.

Grandmother Lydia Farlow, Mother's mother—we called her Grandma or Grandmother—was born in 1840 and lived with us. She was short and a bit plump, especially in the "hindquarters," as she called them. She wore her black hair parted in the middle, combed back and fastened in a knot just below the crown of her head. There were only a few gray hairs then. Later her hair was gray with a few black hairs.

In summer she wore cotton print dresses down to her ankles and long sleeves. Mother dressed much the same, except that she did wear short sleeves occasionally. Grandmother felt it was very indelicate to let a man see one's elbows. But times were changing. Both wore bibbed aprons to do the housework. Their winter dress styles were the same but their clothing was made of heavier fabrics. Underneath her dress, Grandmother wore several petticoats and an undergarment.

Grandmother had a Civil War pension check and that's about all we had to live on some of the time during the Depression in the 1930s. It runs in my mind that it amounted to twenty-seven dollars a month. It was her first husband who was a Civil War casualty. How she still hung onto it after she married again, I don't know. Her second husband paid somebody fifty dollars to go to war in his place. He died before I was born, his ailment, "compaction of the bowels."

My father's first wife was Clara Lee, from Sheridan. She died when their son, Jesse, was very young. Mother raised Jesse as her own. One great-grandson used to call her "Gatemudder."

Jesse and my two older sisters, Zelda and Vera, were grown and living away at this time, 1923, when I started school.

I had two other brothers: Al, eight years older than I, and Bob, fourteen months younger. Most people thought Bob and I were twins. Mother usually dressed us alike. When we were rich enough to have a suit with knicker pants, his were blue or gray and mine were tan—same suit. We were nearly always the same size. I was very dark and he was very fair.

Grandmother was busy all the time. She got up early and prepared breakfast. Dad was already at work. After breakfast she redded up the dishes and then she'd sit down in her little rocker with the newspaper. That was her relaxation. And she always picked the awfullest things to read. She'd say, "Oh, oh, tsk, tsk, tsk. Nasty, dirty scoundrels!" Then she'd pick another horror story. She read them to herself, but made the comments aloud.

One time she read about a freak automobile accident and she always kept it: "Talking with his hands caused J.B. Wyatt of near Swanders to sustain a painful injury a few days ago—the ligaments of his right arm being torn when he made a pointing gesture while riding in an automobile, his arm striking a bridge."

Grandmother did all the cooking. If Mother showed up to help, Grandma would say, "Now, Minnie, you just go on and I'll do this." Mother then went down and helped Dad in the office or she'd go from door to door peddling toilet goods: powder, toilet water, salves, and lotions.

Grandma sang as she washed dishes. I especially remember one: "From Greenland's Icy Mountains." Sometimes she'd sing a rhyming song: the state, its capitol, and the physical feature. It started out, "Maine, Augusta, on the Kennebec River." She learned them all when she was in school.

Grandma didn't help us with school or Sunday School lessons. Neither did Mother. They just took it for granted that we would do it, and we did. We'd catch it from the teacher the next day if we hadn't! Bob and I were good students.

Through all her years, Grandma had a lot of names to keep track of. My name was always Lawrence. Never Larry. She'd run through half a dozen or a dozen names before she got Lawrence. And I'm starting to do the same thing. If I was in trouble it was Lawrence Albert. Deep trouble: Lawrence Albert Venable!

When Bob got mad at me or I'd get mad at Bob, whoever was mad ran to Grandma. "He did this, he did that...." She just kept on rocking, "Well if he did, he just better not!"

She was a Quaker, a former member of the Poplar Ridge Church. She transferred to Noblesville First Friends Meeting and took Bob and me with her every Sunday. Dad, of course, didn't go. Mother went sometimes. We'd sit in the northeast section, me on one side of Grandma and Bob on the other. When we got restless she'd slip each of us a peppermint lozenge from a sack she carried with her. Then if we got to poking each other behind her back—did you know she wore a thimble on her finger? Oh, she'd make that crack on a head! I don't remember her doing it at home. Then, someone threw us out!

During the big Centennial Celebration, 1921, trestle tables were set up on Maple Avenue and they were all laden with food for the huge pitch-in dinner. Oh, the crowd! I rode in that parade. Auntie Bray, dressed as a pioneer Quaker woman going to First Day Meeting, rode a big dappled gray mare, sidesaddle. I was dressed in Quaker boy fashion and rode bareback, astraddle, next to Auntie Bray. The mare was so broad my legs stuck almost straight out. The day was hot. After the parade, someone lifted me down. My pants were wet with horse sweat. One of the men kidded me about wetting my pants. I was so mad, hollered at him, and kicked him in the shins.

Dad's working hours? Forever! The interurban ran all the time. I don't ever remember seeing Dad sleep. I do remember when he was upstairs, we weren't allowed to disturb him.

Sometimes he'd come running up the steps and yell at us for being rowdy. "Hold that noise!" he'd shout. I never realized we were that boisterous! He ate his evening meal with us.

I don't know how many steps, up and down. We didn't hit every one. Whenever one shoved the other down the stairs, which was often, there was a steam radiator at the bottom and we'd usually crack a head on that. Sometimes even lay it open!

Dad had his lodge and other meetings he attended at night. Then Mother took over for him, selling tickets. It seems cars ran till eleven but the ticket office wasn't always open. A person could buy a fare on the car from the conductor.

Our living quarters consisted of a living room, dining room, and a kitchen, all along the east. There were three bedrooms and two baths on the west side. We used only one bathroom. The second was a catch-all.

That upstairs was so hot in the summer, but we didn't think too much of it—just the way of life. Feather beds and feather pillows—we'd settle down in there and just sweat! Wintertime, they were so nice and warm.

Our living room furniture was imitation wicker, a twisted paper that was lacquered. There was a settee that seated two people, a rocker, and a straight chair with arms. Grandmother had brought much of her furniture with her. A kitchen safe, but no ice box. No quarter for ice. Anything that didn't get eaten at a given meal was put down in the bottom part of the ventilated pie safe and it showed up at the next meal, or until it was all gone. On hot summer days the margarine melted down into a yellow puddle in the saucer. In dry, hot weather the bread dried out during the meal. When it was rainy and much humidity, it would mold before it was eaten.

One time a piece of cream pie was left over from supper and was put down in the safe. Before going to bed Grandmother decided she wanted it. She took one bite and oh her mouth burned! She thought it had been sprinkled with red pepper. A closer look—red ants! And where did they come from so quickly?

Anything sour—cole slaw or pickles—gnats found them almost before the meal commenced.

Grandmother treasured her glass-front bookcase. Bob and I would get to wrestling and our heels would bump it and she'd come running. She also had what she called her bureau, signed and dated on the back by the maker, a man named Bond, 1840. In hers and my parents' rooms were the high headboard beds.

We had a nine-foot-by-twelve-foot Axminster carpet, so threadbare, right in the middle of the big living room. In the kitchen and dining room we had congoleum. Bob and I would play marbles on the floor, using one of the big medallions in the linoleum pattern for a ring.

Dinnertime, Grandma would give me a quarter and tell me to run around to Benson's Meat Market and get a quarter's worth of dried beef. I'd watch Ora Benson put the big chunk of beef on the slicer and run it back and forth, slicing it paper thin. Good old dried beef! Grandma mixed up baking powder biscuits—she didn't need a recipe—and they turned out so light and tender. She'd make dried beef gravy to pour over them. Oh, that was good!

Before the next meal, she'd send me for the meat and what else she might need. We always had potatoes, onions, and dry beans on hand.

We usually traded at Carter & King and McMahon's grocery stores. Most everybody in town had milk and bread deliveries.

Grandmother made potato dumplings. Those were dough rolled out and cut in inch-wide strips, then boiled with potatoes. And she'd do her own variation on that. When the cherries were ripe, cherry dumplings. Her dried peach dumplings were so rich!

For breakfast we usually had mush and milk or corn flakes. We'd have fried mush for supper.

My older sister, Vera, taught Mother to make goulash, which was just beef stew with paprika. She made that on Mondays, 'cause she could set it to the back of the cookstove and let it cook all morning real slowly.

It seemed Mother and Grandmother washed all day on Monday. Mother heated the water in a boiler on the stove. Bob and I helped carry the water before school, if we got to it, but Mother was never too strict about us getting our work done. If Dad had been around, he'd have seen to it, but he was always downstairs.

At first we had a clothes wringer operated by hand. Then we acquired an electric washer and wringer. One day I was helping. I lifted a wet sheet to the rollers and my finger got caught and started through with the sheet. I yelled. Mother came running and flipped up the lever releasing pressure on the wringer. She took me to Dr. Black. He looked it over, said the fingernail, hanging by a shred, would have to come off. Just that quickly, he pulled it off! Scared me to death! I was most concerned until he told me a new nail would grow in. It seemed to take forever and I watched its growth with much curiosity.

Every Monday throughout the year, baskets of wet clothes were hung on lines strung through the house. We didn't have a backyard to stretch clotheslines in like others in town.

Holidays were always family affairs. Grandmother was the strong personality at our place, and everybody came to our upstairs for all occasions. Big pitch-in dinners! Some rode in on the interurban, but by then most of them had their own automobiles. Vera lived in Indianapolis. Her husband, Chester Casler, so proud of his new, big, fancy car, only drove it once a week, and they'd come in it. Sister Zelda came with her husband, Daney—Lawrence Dane—and daughter, Marianne, who was a few years younger than I. They lived on Cherry Street. Jesse's family was sometimes with us. His children were around the same ages as Bob and me. Howard, the oldest, was six months older than I. In fact, when

I was born, at Grandmother's house in Carmel, Elva came and laid him in the bed with me and she named me.

There were a lot of stories told at family dinners. I'd seen pictures of the interurban wreck across the street east of the court house. People all around town were yelling "Runaway streetcar!" and scattering in every direction. Folks said that right in front of their eyes the car jumped the track and such a crash, bang, and general hullabaloo you never saw. People rushed up, shocked and full of disbelief, then stood around in little groups talking excitedly. When the car jumped the track, it plowed into an automobile parked along there, killing a five-year-old boy who was inside it, and injuring several others. On impact, it pushed the curbing six inches into the ground.

Then the next day, a young man leaned out from the rear of an interurban as it was coming across White River bridge into Noblesville. His head hit a pole near the track and he was killed instantly.

Martin Casey had his legs amputated just below the knees after being run over by the interurban, when he was nine years old. He and the neighborhood boys were dawdling along, no hurry to get to school until the bell rang, and were putting stones on the tracks. An interurban, speeding by, would run over them and make sparks fly. Also, it was customary for a kid to walk as close to the interurban or the train coming toward you and then jump off the tracks just before it passed. It drove the engineers and parents crazy. That morning Martin's feet slipped under one of the ties and he couldn't jerk them loose. He threw his body out as far from the tracks as he could but his feet were stuck. Along came the interurban and crushed his legs just below his knees. A big chunk of flesh was taken out of one hip.

Nellie, his younger sister, said there was quite a commotion at school as the word spread that Martin had been run over by the interurban and was rushed to the hospital to have his legs cut off! The doctor, who had the only automobile in town, amputated both legs below the knees.

Martin was in the hospital quite awhile, then recovered in bed at home. Kids came to visit, bringing good things to eat and gifts. One little colored boy always wanted to look where his feet had been, then big tears ran down his cheeks.

When Martin's stumps healed he was fitted with artificial limbs. The bones grew and he'd soon outgrow his wooden legs. He'd show everyone how they were fastened on a corset-like garment to his waist, to hold them on. He was always playing tricks. A new kid in the neighborhood, he'd say to him, "Kick me! Kick me on the leg, real hard!" He'd kick, in disbelief! Or Martin would slip his legs off, then go scooting around the room on his stumps.

One time Martin's little niece, never knowing about the accident, went upstairs where he was sleeping, to call him to breakfast. She came rushing down the steps, crying: "Uncle Martin's legs are on the floor!"

His parents didn't baby him—they knew he'd have to live with the artificial legs the rest of his life. He always said he could do anything anyone else could do. He held a good job, he was a good swimmer, but he couldn't dance.

Well, now, back to my story. Bob and I always came down with the same complaints. I suppose it was because we were together constantly. Mother would call Doc Sturdevant. He ran the hospital right across the street from us. One time he stepped in our front door, gave a great big "S-n-i-f-f-f-f!" then bellowed, "That kid's got chicken pox!" They said he could detect most illnesses by smelling when he walked in the door.

When I was real small someone fed me fried corn. Boy did I have a bellyache! Doc came. I opened my mouth when Doc said to stick out my tongue, and I let out a blast. Doc roared, "Hell, he's got the belly-ache! Who fed him fried corn? Give him castor oil immediately!" Oh, that awful thick yellow stuff, the cure-all for any complaint! I gagged and gagged, but finally got it down.

Doctors back then could always tell a lot by looking at your tongue, or feeling the glands in your neck.

We used to see the quarantine cards hanging on doors around town—diphtheria, smallpox, and scarlet fever. I don't think we were ever quarantined. A neighbor boy, name of Baker, died of meningitis. We'd been playing with him. The teachers sprayed and swabbed our throats every day.

George Kosto had the room south of the waiting room, next door to where we went upstairs. Store fronts had the plate glass windows with big sloping signboards. His read "Kosto's Kandy Kitchen" with a big red *KKK*. The Ku Klux Klan came and made him change that to "Kosto's Candy Kitchen"—*KCK*. George also sold newspapers and magazines. We were in and out often. We didn't seem to annoy him.

Big brother Al worked for George Kosto. I can see him throwing a batch of taffy over a hook and drawing a double-strand the length of the room, again and again, until it was snow white. When it hardened, Kosto and Al broke it into pieces with special steel mallets.

The Ku Klux Klan had parades in Noblesville. We usually knew each member, even though they were fully covered with their white robes. "That's old So-and-So—look at his shoes," or, "I know who that is by his walk."

After the Ku Klux Klan was outlawed, it became the Junior Order of United American Mechanics. Dad belonged to that. He was the warden. They burned a fiery cross. A couple times they had a minstrel show. They asked Bob and me to participate. We blacked our faces and we sang and danced.

The KKK's "Fiery Cross" was a translucent, upright cylinder with a cross painted, or printed, on it. A small electric bulb burned inside it, and a second translucent cylinder revolved between the bulb and cross, creating an illusion of flames. At the end of their meetings everyone stood around the cylinder and sang, "The Old Fiery Cross," to the tune of "The Old Rugged Cross." When Bob and I were there, we were expected to sing out with the rest. We had high, clear, strong leading voices. To this day I cannot bear to listen to that tune.

Noblesville's D.C. Stephenson, at one time grand dragon of the Ku Klux Klan, once boasted: "I am the Law!"

Beanie's Restaurant, a busy place next to Kosto's, was established around the turn of the century, and has been in the same location, North Ninth Street, all these years. Ownership has changed many times. Marcellus was the proprietor while we lived there. We'd go in and sit on those revolving stools at the counter and spin around. What an international crisis it caused when they upped the price of a hamburger, doubled it, from five cents to ten cents! Beanie Paskins was known for his good hamburgers, soup beans, and bean soup.

Mother had a big, old, heavy Howard upright piano. It took six men, in a cloud of grunting and groaning and muttered curses, to manhandle the monster to the head of the stairs. I don't suppose it was ever tuned. When the folks lived at Gray's Crossing, Mother drove out in a rig—a horse-drawn carriage—to people's homes and gave organ and piano lessons, but she didn't give lessons in town.

I could play most songs by ear after listening to them once. When I heard "Valencia" on Beanie's radio, I went right upstairs and played it. After a while, I was in Beanie's and Marcellus commented on how beautiful my playing was. I was embarrassed. I didn't know anyone outside our apartment could hear me play.

Bob also played by ear. We were always in demand as entertainers. Later I took piano lessons from Suzanna Jones. Still later, Sally Craig paid for a few lessons with Hobart Carlin. Hobart had lived in Paris many years and studied with Isadore Philippe. Sally was helping me further my musical education and at the same time getting Hobart established here in Noblesville, to build his piano-teaching clientele.

Growing up over the interurban depot, I used to hear a noise in the middle of the night that disconcerted me. "Hup-Hup-Huppp!" I'd get so scared. Something's going to get me! It was the longest time till I figured out it was the pressure pump at the water works, a block away.

The Nickel Plate railroad tracks were on Eighth Street, right behind us. At night I could hear the lonesome wail of the train whistle as it crossed the river trestle. I listened to trains switching down in the south end of town and west on Vine Street. The labored belching, the knocking, banging, back and forth of switch engines as trains were made up for their runs.

The Midland Railroad was on down farther south. There was a difference in their whistles. And we could tell when it was going to rain by the sound of the whistle. So loud and clear. Also, the smell of the strawboard, which was from Noblesville's Ball Brothers' Paper Mill. They made cardboard shipping boxes from rotted straw—whew! That odor carried way out in the country for miles on a rainy night.

All around town, especially in the fall of the year, were the sounds of coal being unloaded into basements or sheds. We had gas for cooking. Coal for the heating stove. Our coal bin was in the warehouse. Us boys would have to bring buckets of it up.

A tornado took down the top part of Logan Street covered bridge, two blocks away, called the "wagon bridge." Chick Gunion and Business Fisher were on it at the time. Business was blind. He blew up into the air, then came down into the water. Chick jumped in and pulled him out.

Business was not only blind, he was mean. With anybody, not just boys. He had a cane. Watch out, he'd lash you with it!

The interurban conductors were all nice to us. Dad, being the agent, could get us all free passes. Once Grandmother, Bob, and I went on pass clear over to Dayton, Ohio, to visit relatives. Probably a hundred miles away!

On one of these trips, my favorite diversion was going back to the restroom in the streetcar when it was traveling, raising the toilet lid and watching the tracks go by. And the sounds! Everything in there was new and different, even the squeal of the tracks as it turned corners and the wheels clickity-clack, clickity-clacking along, singing a cheerful song as they clipped off the miles. Bob and I set everything to music.

I'd make trip after trip back to the fountain, a huge five-gallon glass bottle filled with water. I'd pull a cone-shaped paper cup out of the rack, fill it, drink it, throw the cup away in the wastebasket, and go to my seat. Then I'd go back and do it all again!

I was exhilarated by the rapid motion of the car and the varied panorama through which we were swiftly passing. We sped onward at fifty miles an hour, at least, they said we did.

A note was posted on the restroom door: Please Do Not Flush At Station. If one did use the restroom in Noblesville, when the interurban was standing, it was Dad's job to go out and scoop it up. Boy, did that make him mad! I could see why they'd rather use it when the car was standing still—no swaying or jerking around. Between stations, it was flushed out onto the track. I never did hear of anyone running across that stuff out in the country.

We got a thrill heading out of town south of Noblesville when we went over the Nickel Plate train track on a high trestle. Standing in the back end, we were clear out over empty space when they made the sharp turn.

The red, wool velour cushioned seats were so itchy. Sometimes in the summertime they installed straw seats. They were slick. Going around the curve I was telling you about, I'd sli-i-i-de, then roll into the aisle!

I enjoyed ambling about, observing the other passengers and the conductor, with whom I was very impressed. I'd sit and read all the advertising cards above the windows:

Pink Pills for Pale People
Swamp Root Oil
White Beavers Cough Cream
Jayne's Sensitive Pills
Boschee's German Syrup
Arrow Shirts

I imagined myself a conductor with gold buttons on my suit. I'd pull a cord for the whistle or pull a release to halt the car. Our vacation was always too short!

Back home, now. At night, we'd hear the interurban freight cars pull into the loading dock on Clinton Street on a spur from Ninth

Street to the alley. When they hit the big concrete bunker backstop, they knew they were there—and so did we! The back of our building was a warehouse. The loading dock was the same height as the bed of the freight train. They hit that backstop; it'd shake the whole building and wake me up. They'd throw down this steel gangplank. It'd shake me awake again!

There was a two-wheel hand dray to haul the crates and cartons back and forth on the steel gangplank, and you know what a racket that makes at night! Well, probably during the day, too, but I didn't pay any attention then. I was batting around with my brother or in school.

Lon Gatewood was the driver of a big, four-wheeled, wood-and-metal dray. The wheels had wooden spokes and iron tires. The cotter pins were like big nails with sharp points. A wooden tongue extended in front by which the dray could be pulled by hand, or it could be used to hitch a horse to the dray.

When not in use, the dray was parked around in back under a big catalpa tree. If Lon wanted the dray in front he'd whistle to Dick, his horse, and Dick would bring it around.

It was fun to ride the dray. One day Lon was walking at the head of the dray with Dick. Bob and I were on the wagon bed, dancing the Charleston and singing. Bob missed his footing, he fell, and his leg caught down between the spokes. Here he was, going around and around. That cotter pin laid his leg wide open to the bone!

I was hollering, jumping up and down, "Gatewood, Stop!" But Gatewood was deaf. I thought I'd never get him stopped so I could pull Bob out of there. Then we went across the street to the hospital and had Bob sewed up. Boys are always getting sewed up one place or another, or did you know that?

Our building had steam heat from a boiler. Electricity for lights came up the interurban line. We could always tell when a car was coming 'cause the lights dimmed. Happened all the way along the line, pulling on the electricity at all houses and businesses through town and the countryside.

When they had their speed up, those interurban specials went fast right on through town without stopping. What a noise they made! They'd shake the whole building. Visitors would say, "Why, it sounds like it's coming right through to get us!"

We didn't have a telephone. They were pretty much a luxury. We couldn't afford electric lights part of the time.

When I was five years old I was out on the streets selling *Liberty* magazine for a nickel each. And I could make change! When I was seven I carried the *Indianapolis Times*. Mother was the agent. She did that to make extra money.

Winter nights, past dark, I'd sometimes get home with my feet about frozen, and my shoes, thin jacket, and pants were all caked with ice. Grandma stuck my feet in a bucket of cold water to draw the frost out. Boy would that smart!

Like most county seats, Noblesville's business section was built around the courthouse square, and around it an unbroken line of stores. The courthouse, a three-floored stone building, faced on the south, east and north, each with wide entrance doors. The interurban ran along the east side. Hitch racks to tie up horses were set along all the downtown streets.

The main thoroughfares were paved with bricks and they were kept clean by a man whose official title was street sweeper. He was equipped with a cart, a brush, and a shovel, and his job was to pick up the horse droppings—a big task! Flies aplenty!

On the north side of Logan Street, on the square, was a great big iron horse trough, shaped like a shell, four feet across, painted green. On the sidewalk side was a bubbler for people to drink from. On the street side was a small one down low for dogs. The water in the fountains around town ran all the time, night and day. Years later they installed shutoffs.

All Noblesville water came from deep wells. A huge gravity-fed pressure tank stood way up in the air behind us.

Irv Carey was the town watchman. At night he went around checking to see if all the businessmen's doors were locked and keeping track of things. A red light was atop the court house dome. Someone wanting Irv, the light was turned on.

At nine o'clock, a curfew whistle, and all the kids better be off the streets. I don't know if Irv took care of delinquents. I never stayed out late enough to find out.

A fellow lived in an apartment on the north side of the square. He had no bathroom or it didn't work. Early every morning he came down his long stairway with his shiny white pot in his hand. The squeaky noises the bail made as he walked attracted attention. He'd go to the court house restroom, empty it, then carry it back to his apartment.

The American National Bank was on the corner where it is now. Across the street was Sowerwine's Dry Goods Store, later Osbon's, then

Willits. Ousler's shoes was along there. With each pair of shoes they gave away a cricket toy. Every kid was drawn to that store just to get a free tin cricket whose click-click threatened to drive the family mad!

Until our feet toughened up, oh how hot those brick sidewalks were! School was out by Decoration Day. Bob and I each got a pair of seventy-nine-cent black lace-up tennis shoes. They had to do until school started in September. Then we got a pair of ninety-eight-cent leather high tops. New shoes were always squeaky. I liked that—everyone knew Larry Venable had new shoes!

Buying them was a big event. Shoes lined the sides of each wall in Ousler's store. The clerk had to reach these by climbing a ladder which swooshed around on a runner and was never on the side of the room where he wanted it to be. He excused himself a dozen times to move it. I suppose every boy and girl looked forward to the time they could be a shoe salesman.

Frank Ousler said he didn't know when the store was built, but recalled that his father and uncle, Charles and Lafayette Ousler, started in the shoe business there in 1895. In 1924 they were undergoing remodeling when it was discovered, with some surprise, that the sidewalls had never been plastered, but simply finished by gluing cheesecloth and paper directly to the brick. Its ceilings, like so many in town, had the patterned tin squares. After all these years, they are still up there!

Bob and I wore black, high-top shoes, and long black stockings hitched to a garter belt, of all things. It seemed we wore them forever, until we rebelled and demanded low-cut shoes and socks like everyone else—and no garter belts!

Our knickers had buckles at the knees to adjust the fit. Farm kids bragged about how much good stuff they could put in their knicker legs if they kept the buckles tight: apples, pears, or nuts. But I didn't do that. I didn't bother to buckle up.

How excited we were when Mother bought us our first pair of corduroys! Cord-u-roys—that sounded adult! Zsit! Zsit! Whistle-britches, the boys all called them because of the noise they made when our legs rubbed together as we walked.

The summers were extremely hot in Noblesville, as hot as the winters were cold. Old Scatterwater, we called him, a city employee, had a tank truck with a sprinkler on the back of it and he watered down the brick streets every evening. Also during the day when it was terribly hot and dry. He never paid any attention to anything or anyone. He just sat there all humped over, chewing on a cigar, driving that gravity-fed tank truck, spraying water out the back and sides.

Most kids went barefoot in the summer. Our sun-browned, calloused feet were always hot and dirty. We'd walk along the side of Scatterwater's truck and let the water spray on us. The water puddled in places and flies gathered but we splashed around in it, anyway. After a downpour, the streets flooded. We'd put on old clothes and go out and play in it.

After going barefoot all day we had to wash our feet before we went to bed—no getting around that!

On rainy days, Bob and I would take a board, hammer nails into it, put numbers underneath, hang it on the wall and then we'd throw can rubbers on the nails and keep our scores.

Nice days, Bob and I would go out our bedroom window—the roof sloped on the warehouse—then over to Beanie's roof, on to Walter Bordner's monument place, Pinnell & Dulin's lumberyard, and on to the National Guard Armory. We played ball up there, too, when we had a ball.

On drill nights, at the National Guard Armory, during break, the fellows'd go into the hard-packed cinder alley. They'd lay out a string line in a circle. Each pitched a quarter and whoever got the closest to the line picked up all the money. Then they'd start again.

The lights were very dim back there. Sometimes the quarters would roll away and they'd never find them. Early the next morning, Bob and I were scavenging quarters. That was our spending money!

Up on the roof were a lot of nighthawks. They are a night owl, related to the whippoorwill. They fly in the late afternoon and at dusk, uttering a high-pitched, "peent-peent." Their mouths are large and very wide to catch insects as they fly. They helped thin out mosquitoes and flies.

The birds squat perfectly still. Their color and markings made them almost invisible on the flat gravel roof and you almost stepped on them. I don't remember that they flew away even then.

The ice man had a horse-drawn wagon and we followed him around. Anyone wanting to buy ice hung the orange-colored diamond-shaped cardboard in the window. The corner that was up told him how many pounds to bring, printed in numbers—15, 25, 50 or 100. He'd chip the proper amount from a long chunk of ice, then with his tongs, he'd pick the piece up and carry it away, a trail of dripping water following him. We'd stand around and grab pieces of ice that had fallen, wipe off any dirt on our pants or shirt, then hold it, first in one hand and then the other, as our fingers got so cold. I don't recall a special taste, but it kinda quenched our thirst on a hot day, or gave us something else to do.

Across Clinton Street from the depot was the ice plant where the ice man loaded up. I made a tour of it just after the opening. The ice was always so very clear.

We crossed the train bridge over White River on foot, to go over and play at Forest Park after it was constructed. We got a thrill out of walking the railroad tracks, the ties with their shiny rails glistening in the sun. Sometimes there was a garter snake lying lengthwise on one of the rails and when he heard us coming, he quickly scurried away. As we walked across White River on the railroad trestle we always wondered what we'd do if a train came bearing down!

Out at the park, on the Nickel Plate line, we'd listen to the singing of the rails to tell us when the train was coming. Walking the rails was a favorite pastime—who could stay on them the longest? We'd totter, arms spread out, balancing us.

The river was only two, three feet deep. Sometimes we'd find a boat tied to a tree along the side. We'd be having so much fun and somehow Mother would find out we were down there—we were only three blocks from home—and she'd come running to the edge of the river, flogging around like a mother hen, trying to get us out of there. That's one of those times she'd get her red hair up!

We often swam in White River near the interurban bridge at Flat Rock and in Cicero Creek and Stony Creek. The very first swimming pool was in the river at North Ninth Street. It was filled with river water. I remember the sand burrs, a plant that grew along there. Oh, how those burrs hurt when they stuck you!

We had one-piece swim suits—our bodies covered. The next pool was across the road from the south entrance of the park. Free day was Wednesday mornings and kids flocked there to swim. It was always so crowded. Cost fifty cents to ride the toboggan slide. We saved our National Guard quarters for this. Later they built a new pool up in the park.

In the brand new Forest Park, we slid down the metal slides before they were even anchored in. They put cedar shavings on the ground around the slides and swings. And they had an ocean wave that revolved up and down and around. One time it broke when it was loaded and several got hurt.

I suppose the corkscrew slide was the most popular. It was the only one of its kind in the state, they said. We always took a supply of bread wrapper wax paper, sat on that and made several trips down the slide to make it slick as glass. We watched out for little fellows going down and we'd catch them, or we'd hold them on our laps. That corkscrew furnished much enjoyment to hundreds of kids through a period of over sixty years!

Bob and I didn't go fishing or hunting, although we did want to. Mother always said, "No, we don't need it for food."

July Fourth was a noisy time for a couple of boys, whooping and hollering. We had spit devils, little round, flat things about as big as my thumb. We'd grind them under our heels, quack, quack. We thought we'd put them on the interurban track and hear a loud noise but when the interurban rolled over them, nothing happened. We did cross a couple of nails on the track and they were flattened out. We called them our jewelry.

Nurse Frazee used to come out of the hospital. Remember her—big hefty nurse in her white uniform? She'd yell, "You boys are going to have to quiet down or I'll hafta get the police after ya! Go celebrate elsewhere!" That shut us up!

On the court house lawn, Civil War cannons pointed toward the four corners of the sky. A neat pyramid of cannonballs was set symmetrically in front of each. We even noticed the cannonballs couldn't possibly fit into those cannons! I liked to imagine myself heroically fighting the enemy. Us boys would climb all over them. We didn't worry that we might set the balls to rolling, but a lot of other people did.

There were so many birds around the square that the loafers moved from the curbs up next to the side of the building. There were always the same elderly gentlemen sitting and spitting and swapping yarns. It served as the clearinghouse of wisdom for scores of years. It was touching to me to see how the court house cement steps were hollowed out by generations of busy feet.

Zelda and Daney asked Mother to look after Marianne for a week when they were going to be away. Marianne was a few years younger than I. She idolized Bob and me, but she was just a kid to tag along, as far as two boys were concerned.

We got into our heads we'd go to the top of the court house, up into the clock tower. We watched out for Brodie White, the colored custodian. He was a real fine man, but didn't put up with any foolishness. Bob and I liked to slide down those long banisters and if Brodie caught us, he'd scold. He called us two Venable boys the Gold Dust Twins.

The court house floors were laid in diamond-shaped tiles. The wide marble stairs went up to the third story, to where we'd find a men's restroom with the trap door leading to the tower. Bob and I crawled onto the toilet tank, then through the trap door to the room above. We left Marianne to follow us—and she did!

We walked up a flight of steps, then climbed shakey wooden ladders on up and up; it seemed like several more flights to the clock tower. There was a creaking wooden floor at each landing. It was considered a test of bravery—initiation into becoming a man—to stay up there when the striker bell donged, so we waited until the clock struck. The whole place vibrated! Marianne was very brave, just shook with excitement. She probably knew if she cried she wouldn't get to go with us again.

It seems there were louvers for ventilation. At the top of the dome was a trap door which was usually open. Pigeons flew in and out at will. Oh, the dirt we waded through—up to our ankles in feathers, droppings, dried leaves, cobwebs, and dust.

My folks found out about us being up there and taking Marianne with us. Dad scolded. Mother laughed.

One boy was seen in the tower by a neighbor. The father confronted his son and he admitted being there. He said, "I wanted to carve my initials right under yours, Dad!"

Looking out our living room windows we could see the Olympia Theater. Much later it was called the Diana. We recognized many of the people as they lined up to buy their tickets at the front enclosed window.

Around the block was the American, later called the Logan Theater. I remember seeing *Birth of a Nation*. Also the Six Brown Brothers, a sax sextet, who were dressed in clown suits.

I didn't see dating couples coming in to the show on Saturday nights. That's when I was getting scrubbed, ready for church the next day.

One young lady was sweet on Al and hung around. He'd keep an eye out for her. If he saw her come into the depot he'd slip upstairs, go out the back window and slide down the gutter.

Up on North Ninth Street was the Commons. That's where much entertainment was scheduled. Pop Brown, Noblesville's mayor for a long time, owned the land. The band concerts every Wednesday night through the summer were something special. Meade Vestal was the director of the band. Everybody went. Kids running loose, yelling and carrying on.

The Chautauqua was out on Sixteenth and South Streets. They had all kinds of good music—piano, violin, and singing. Families came and camped for a week.

Then, as all good things must come to an end, so did our association with the interurban. The Depression. The Crash, they called it. Dad got bumped by somebody with more seniority and we had to move out.

I'd walk with Mother at night looking for a dwelling. As there were six of us, we needed a big one. Most every house through here had a lot of history, and some of it, as Dad said, shouldn't see the light of day! Rent for the biggest old place in town was five dollars a month. We found a nice, two-story house on Division and Tenth. It had such a beautiful curving walnut staircase. Dad became a handyman, working on automobiles, on buildings, and he'd hire out on farms.

For us, all of this was such a new experience. Evenings, families would be out on the front porch, Pa, sitting on the porch steps, smoking his cigar; Ma, in her rocker, busy with her knitting; kids swinging on the porch swing.

"Howdy, folks!"

"Evenin', Brother Lewis. See you in church tomorrow?" We were now watching a new stream of life going by!

Noblesville was still very rural. Most everybody had a barn, large gardens, some chickens, a cow, pigs, or a horse, always close to the alley. The animals were fed table scraps and purchased feed. Later, city regulations forbade livestock.

We'd hear the peddler calling out his wares and the rag man shouting, "Any old rags?"

There were fences of all types: the picket fence, plain board fences, the chain wire fence, and guard rails. Big maple trees lined the walks with welcomed shade, and unwelcome fallen leaves.

Even though people were very poor, they found time for free fun. In the spring of the year, down on Maple Avenue, they'd rope the street off and kids from all over town came evenings to roller skate. They also skated out Greenfield Pike and up on Federal Hill. We couldn't afford bicycles but we did have roller skates.

That street was roped off for Saturday night dancing. The traffic was light and the pavement was wide and smooth.

The Wild Opera House, where popular plays with famous actors and actresses once performed, was a movie theater when I knew it. The high school class plays were held there.

The K of P Hall had a good dance floor.

Until hard times of Depression days came along my childhood was pleasant and, I suppose, sheltered. Life in the early 1930s was hard for most people. A time of spending little and not wanting much. It was a constant struggle to find food, clothing, and shelter, and often we did without some of these things.

The interurban empire of tracks and equipment served the people well until the general use of autos cut down their revenues. In 1941, the tracks were taken up and the cars disposed of.

I've always enjoyed music and entertaining, but when I married Susie and we had our family, business came first.

Those years, from 1923 to 1929, when I was between the ages of six and twelve, seem to me now as I look back on them, rather an idyllic period. They likely were not all that peaceful to my parents and grandmother, but my memories of the era are good!

—*Larry Venable was interviewed in the summer of 1988.*

I'd Rather Be a Town Boy!

by
Harold Kaiser

Harold grew up in the Cicero area. After his military service, he became a "town boy." He established and spent most all of his business years at Kaiser's Realty in Carmel, where he, his wife Ermina, and son Craig, made their home.

Some of my fondest memories were those spent in Cicero with Grandma and Grandpa Voss, my mother's parents. They lived in town. What joy for this country kid to visit them!

I hated it in the country. My folks, Gladys and Luther Kaiser, were farmers. Us boys, my older brothers, Albert and Max, and I, had to go home from school every evening to do the chores and the milking. In summer there were thistles to hoe, or milkweeds to pull, fencerow growth to chop out, cows to herd, pigpens and cow and horse stables to clean, and garden and yard drudgery. Work, work, work!

Town kids, school out, a whole glorious vacation ahead! Summertime, fishing or swimming. They played every evening, gathering with their friends for a ballgame, then later, all congregate and visit under the streetlights until time to go home to bed. They'd trap or hunt in the wintertime. Most of them lived near enough to school to walk to all the functions.

Grandma's and Grandpa's Cicero house was open to everyone, like a hotel. Kids, grandkids—all the family—came and went as they pleased. If we stopped in five minutes before mealtime, Grandma always had food ready. People ate three meals a day. If Grandma didn't think she had enough, she'd grab her little purse and hop off down the street to the grocery.

They lived right in the center of Cicero, almost downtown, which made it real handy for us school kids. We'd make it our headquarters. Lots of times we'd stay overnight on the spur of the moment. Our folks were very lenient. I guess they knew we were safe at Grandma's.

Grandpa was a good grandpa. He was a short, chunky guy, and always full of life, happy, and so much fun. Grandma was the opposite—a wiry, little person, and kind of snappy. Like, if I'd say, "I don't like that, Grandma," she'd answer, "Well, eat it anyway!" It was just her nature. She was a good person.

One September, the canning factory was desperate for workers, so Grandma Voss, who had never worked a day away from home in her life, went to work. She'd been planning what she'd do with her canning check. Something new for the house, or a good coat to wear to church? Grandpa did provide for her real well.

The first day, the line of women peelers were along the belt. At recess and at noon a bell rang and each woman moved up a notch. If peelers were allowed to stay in one position, those at the top of the line would grab the select tomatoes. The ones at the end of the line had only the culls to peel. So to move up a notch each time was the only fair way. They were paid by the bucket.

The belt started rolling. Grandma was doing her job real well when the bell rang for a break. She put her little peeling knife down where she was standing. When she came back, a lady told her she hadn't moved up like she was supposed to. Grandma was confused. She just stood there and started peeling. When she was told again to move up, she said flatly, "Well! I'll just go home to my own kitchen where I can stand where I want to!" She took her little knife and headed for home.

My mother had two brothers. Her parents had thirteen grandchildren. There were four to six of us around our ages, and I suspect Grandma had some of us almost every night. Their doors were never locked. We'd go up and find an empty bed. Grandparents went on to bed early and they didn't know till morning how many would be sitting down for breakfast. We'd come and go as we pleased. We were good kids and didn't cause any trouble. Grandma was very tolerant of us but would snap her fingers if we got out of line.

Grandma Yetter, Grandma Voss's mother, lived with them until she passed away. Grandma Yetter's father had died when she was a baby. That seemed so sad. In her old age she just sat and looked out the window. She watched our every move—that kept her busy! She was usually nice to us. She'd say, "Not-not!" to us when we even looked cross-eyed!

Anything going on after school that we wanted to stay over for, we'd go to Grandpa and Grandma's and eat supper and our folks would come and get us later. Usually, after ballgames, we'd stay all night. When we were older, they started going to ballgames with us.

Both of the grandparents acted like they were so happy to have us kids. I see now it was extra work for Grandma.

Grandpa worked for the *Noblesville Daily Ledger*. He went all over the county, taking subscriptions. He knew everybody. He always dressed in a suit with vest, and a tie. His watch chain bowed across the expanse of his stomach.

He also did some part-time work passing bills. He'd hire us grandkids to help him. Grandpa would drive real slow with a carload of us boys so we could hop out along the way and deliver them. I remember one time the car was so full, so my older brother, Albert, and cousin, Walter Voss, rode on the front fenders.

The two boys would stand out there and when Grandpa wasn't looking, they'd reach down, outside the Model T, by the crank, and pull the wire choke. The Ford would chug-chug along. Grandpa would worry and study, so concerned. He'd fuss, "I don't understand what's wrong with this thing. Must be gettin' water in my gas at the station. I better say something to them about it." I don't know why Grandpa didn't catch on.

We had an outside toilet at home. Grandpa's had a bathroom. So inviting, especially in the winter. It was always warm. He also had a toilet outside connected to the sewer. Some of the younger grandchildren would throw the catalogue down there and stop it up. Then Grandpa would have to dig it out. He wasn't such a happy grandpa then!

One time Albert and Walter were staying over and the grandparents were gone. They had a coal furnace. That was so nice. At home we heated with coal stoves. Walter said, "I think it is cold in here; let's go down and fire up." They filled that furnace bowl full of coal. They didn't know any better. When everyone came home, it was so hot, a wonder the whole house didn't go up in smoke! Everyone went through the house, opening doors, throwing up windows, and fanning themselves! Grandpa took it good, but I'm sure he said a few choice words under his breath, especially about wasting fuel!

Mom did her grocery buying just once a week but Grandma went before every meal. Most town women did. I guess she didn't know how many she was going to cook for! She had a box that fit in the pantry window for keeping the food cold in the wintertime. They used an ice box in the summer. Oh, boy! Iced tea or lemonade every meal!

And they had a radio, too. After supper Grandpa would sit and listen to "Amos 'n' Andy," "Lum 'n' Abner," and Lowell Thomas. We had to be quiet. Grandma didn't listen. She was busy cleaning up the kitchen after supper, puttering around.

Grandpa Voss just loved Grandma's sugar molasses syrup she made out of white sugar, a clear, thick liquid. He put that on everything. He lived to be in his late eighties so I guess it didn't hurt him.

Now, a bit about my other grandma, Mary Kaiser, Dad's mother. Mike Mosbaugh was Grandma Kaiser's second husband, after Grandpa Kaiser died. They lived in Arcadia. He used every penny very thriftily. He worked all his yard up into garden—not an empty space of grass to mow. To tease him, we'd walk just as close to his vegetables, along the sidewalk, without actually walking on them. Otherwise we always tried to be good. I'm sure Grandma was glad when we went down the street to play.

Grandma Kaiser—we continued calling her Grandma Kaiser after she married Mike—was on pins and needles, we could tell, just because he was so nervous. Behind his back we'd mock him. He had a habit of continually sniff-sniffing, his nostrils working in and out like a bunny rabbit's. Us boys got pretty good at imitating him, behind his back of course!

Grandma Kaiser was immaculately clean—her house and herself—spotless, and in the latest style.

We as a family never went anyplace to speak of, except to Sunday school, church, and some school functions. We'd go to Indianapolis on the streetcar once a year to get school clothes, if Mom didn't send to Sears and Roebuck for them. We never had the money to go to any of the shows down there.

The big event of the year was Cicero's Fall Festival, or as some laughingly called it, "Cicero's World's Fair."

The fair was usually Thursday, Friday, and Saturday. I'd go over to Grandma Voss' on Wednesday afternoon, happily carrying my little overnight bag, and stay through the whole week of the fair because that was the big event we looked forward to from one year to the next. I'd saved my money since the last one, to have enough to ride the merry-go-round and ferris wheel—ten cents a ride— and maybe take in some of the attraction booths. I'd look around all afternoon and evening, then wait till late to spend my quota for the day, because I wanted to be sure I spent it wisely.

The fair was such an exciting time. The main street through town was blocked off and it was crowded with people. All we did was walk up and down the street, back and forth, back and forth. We waved at everybody 'cause we knew everybody. If we had enough money, we bought a bag of confetti and threw it at our friends.

How did I make money for the fair? I picked tomatoes and green beans for the canning factory. I did odd jobs for my folks—little pay 'cause they didn't have much to give me.

Mother made cottage cheese, butter, and buttermilk. I took them to town to sell. She'd give me four cents a quart for delivering and collecting. I did that Saturday mornings 'cause people wanted it for Sunday dinner.

Fair time was when Grandma's "hotel" filled up 'cause a lot of their grandchildren came. We'd go there to eat each meal. We couldn't afford to eat out. I imagine she was glad when the fair was over but she never once let on that it was an imposition.

She went to great pains to cook our favorites. Mine were fried chicken, mashed potatoes, and she made such good cole slaw. She, like my mother, was a good cook.

On the farm we only had fried chicken certain months of the year 'cause we raised our own. But Grandma went to the store and bought hers anytime she wanted them. Brought them home live, then killed and cleaned them herself, out by their barn.

And she bought us lunch meat! We seldom ever had it at home 'cause Mom would have to buy it. We had that old beefsteak and sugar-cured or smoked ham. Grandma always had bologna or big round hot dogs, ten cents a pound. She knew we liked it and we didn't get it often.

Mom made our bread. When we went to Grandma's we had light bread she bought from the store. She sliced it herself on her wooden breadboard with her big, sharp, butcher knife.

I didn't like the school lunches I had to fix and wrap in newspaper to take each day, the old steak or ham sandwiches! I wanted hot dogs or bologna. Town kids loved steak and ham, so we traded. They had grocery store chocolate-covered cookies. We had to take homemade oatmeals that I disliked so much! Again, we traded.

I promised myself, when I had a job away, I'd buy all those good things I liked to eat! During high school and after I graduated, I worked at Kroger's in Noblesville. Ed Kraus let us workers eat anything we wanted, even from the candy case. I soon got caught up!

Our farm was about a mile out west of Cicero. My brothers and I often walked to town. We'd go past the cemetery, then through that wooden covered bridge. It was frightening! And then there were always some bigger boys around who liked scaring us. Get through the eerie old bridge all right, on down the hill was the mammoth Coliseum; it was vacant most of those years. We were always afraid somebody was hiding back in there! We finally got up the hill to Cicero. When we lived over by Strawtown, I was old enough to drive—if I could get the car!

The sugar drawings drew big crowds to Cicero. I don't know why it was called the "sugar drawings," other than the main prize was always a ten-pound bag of sugar. Even the kids realized their parents were very anxious about anything we could win to help with the grocery budget. We got a numbered, printed, paper ticket with each twenty-five cent purchase. They'd give the customer one, tear off the other end, and put it in the box. On Saturday night the grocer chose a kid to reach in and draw out the winning ticket for each item. Mom won several times—sugar, coffee, a box of spaghetti, rice, dry beans, canned goods. Christmastime, they gave away a man's dollar pocket watch. Dad won it once. How happy we were!

Our family always went to town on Saturday night. No matter how busy we were on the farm, Saturday evening, five o'clock, we quit work, did up the chores, ate supper, and got ready to go to town. I don't know anything that kept us from going unless it was sickness. Saturday night was *the* night! Wintertime, if we couldn't get the car started, we'd take the horse and buggy.

We tried to be in town by seven o'clock, to get a close place to park. Mom liked to do her trading before the crowd gathered. She'd take eggs in and trade them for groceries. Sometimes, if she had extra money, she'd buy Jell-o, a rare treat! I'd carry her egg basket full of groceries to the car. Didn't even consider locking the doors. No worry someone stealing them. My folks then had all evening to visit with other people coming in to town. The streets were jammed with people.

If the weather was real bad, rainy, everyone crowded into the stores. The drugstore was the kids' hangout. I'd saved enough money to buy an ice cream sundae. That gave me the privilege of sitting at a table all evening! And then we always ended up going to Grandma and Grandpa's, the congregating place, to meet, visit awhile, then go home.

The free silent movie was exciting! It started at dark, flashed up on the side of an old brick building. We had to read all the conversation, but that didn't matter! We sat around on the ground or leaned against automobiles.

To make money for Saturday nights, I bought the little paper bags at the grocery, filled them with corn I popped, lined them up in Mom's grocery basket, took them around town, and sold them up and down the street.

All the Kaiser family gathered at our house on Decoration Day for big dinners. We lived just west of Cicero, through the covered bridge, back on the north side of the road, across from the cemetery.

All us kid cousins just loved wandering all over the cemetery. The gravestones were of considerable interest. We'd read inscriptions—I do it yet! One stated, "Beloved By All Who Knew Her. She Was Our Precious Jewel."

I knew where all the unusual ones were located. See the big, carved, marble angel over yonder—let's run and see it! Here's a baby lamb. The very big family headstones we recognized as being of the most prosperous men of the community. There were the exceedingly old, moldy stones we could hardly read, usually small slabs, settling crooked through all the years. There was a huge, carved-out stone of a Civil War soldier, standing at attention in his uniform, with musket over his shoulder. Many in and around Cicero were of German extraction. Some of the early stones had German markings that, of course, we couldn't read.

One gravestone of German markings read, "Jakob Smith, died 19 July 1896, at age fifty-eight and eight months."

Another stone, grieving angels—Deaths of two babies.

Often I'd see a husband buried with a wife on one side and the next wife on the other. Or I'd see a lonely grave off all by itself, and wonder what that story was. Several babies or little children. Young mothers dying at childbirth. A young husband, leaving a wife and several children—how did they get along? Several in one family died in the same year, days apart. An epidemic?

Always a child's curiosity: Do you reckon folks ever come back once they're dead and gone?

Us three brothers went to every funeral. I remember one lady, she'd lived in Cicero, then they moved to Indianapolis. They brought her husband back here to bury him. We were standing there to the side, just standing there, quietly looking on with the other mourners. Everyone left. She came over and said crossly, "Don't you kids bother anything here!" Meaning the flowers, I suppose. I never liked her after that.

One grave, close to Grandma and Grandpa Kaiser's, was Mary Brunner's. It never had flowers, so I decorated it.

Decoration Day morning I carried buckets full of flowers and Mom's grocery basket full of glass Mason jars across the road to the cemetery. I knew every grave, on both sides of the family. I'd sink a jar into the soil so the wind wouldn't blow it over, fill it with water from the pump, then put peonies and iris in, decorating each family grave. I'd pull strands of tall grass away from the base of the tombstones.

Mother had all kinds of flowers: iris, lilacs, snowballs, peonies—"pinies" some called them. Sometimes roses, but they usually bloomed later. Mother would worry if the lilacs would be gone.

Mom was busy frying chicken and getting a big dinner ready. She'd been at it for days. Each family brought baskets of food to add to what Mom fixed. All good cooks! I don't remember anything about the meal. My main interest wasn't food. It was playing with all those cousins!

Every year the same people came to Cicero Cemetery from all over and they got to recognizing me. One time a man approached me, said, "Would you happen to know where John's restin'? I just come to say good-bye to my old friend."

At Strawtown we lived near a very old cemetery. We could hardly read some of the stones. Several Indians were buried there. Twins died at birth, June sixth, the birthday of my cousin twins, Lois and Louis Kaiser.

We all wondered about the spelling of family names: Ours Kaiser; Kiser, Keiser, Kyser, Kayser.

Henry Bowman was Cicero's sexton. The grave-tender, he called himself. "I have over a thousand people under me," he'd say, never cracking a smile. I'd go over and help him. I was probably in his way, but he always acted like he was so glad to see me. He dug all the graves with pick and shovel. He mowed the entire cemetery with a push-walking mower. He had it looking so pretty all summer long, and especially on Decoration Day. Later he had a power push mower, but he never had a riding mower.

He'd tell me about deaths when he was a boy. "At funerals the entire church might be filled with mourners who were kin." Another time he said, "I reckon that I have more people on the other side than this one and believe me, since I've got up in years, I have been walking the straight and narrow." I couldn't imagine Henry ever doing otherwise!

At a death, a Cicero church bell would toll very slowly the person's age.

I had a cat cemetery at our house. I decided each dead cat deserved a proper burial. Henry gave me some little headstones that had broken off or had been replaced by new ones. I'd take my chisel and hammer and carve out the cat's name and the date, then set it in place.

My cousin Phyllis Voss, younger than I, we just loved playing funeral. We'd line a shoe box with tissue paper, and use that for a casket to put the cat in, then lovingly covered it with a blanket. I had a little tricycle with a truck-like bed on the back, which was the hearse. I'd put the cat in its box and we'd take it into the house. I'd play the church songs on the piano and Phyllis and I would sing. Oh, how we'd cry! I preached the sermon, standing on a goods box, holding a Sears and Roebuck catalogue which Phyllis had borrowed from the privy. I'd preach for all I was worth: "We mourn for Sister Anna because we loved her and wanted her to stay a little longer. But the dear Lord didn't see it that way. We're sorrowful and we're happy, 'cause this dear saint is with the Lord and his angels."

Then Phyllis had her part in the ceremony: "Let us bow our heads and I'll offer prayer for our dearly beloved departed friend. Lord, You have Sister Anna in your care now. She always said she wanted to go in her sleep. She didn't want to linger and be a burden."

We were also the mourners. We'd cry and cry. "She looks like she could just sit up and talk!"

"Don't she look nat'r'l? Just like she's asleep."

Mom said she'd stand kind of back, not let on so we'd know she was there, and she'd listen to the whole service and chuckle.

I always just loved playing the piano. Mom never had to make me practice. Not so with Albert and Max, who were both older than I.

The cemetery never frightened us. Kids coming out to our house at night, they were afraid. Car lights shone on some of the stones, making them appear ghost-like.

I just loved being around a cemetery. I wanted to be a funeral director, but after Ermina and I were married, Ermina said she didn't think she could live with that.

We boys had our own "swimming hole" in Cicero Creek. I haven't forgotten how it used to feel on a powder-dusty day in July when we would be so hot and wet with sweat, pulling out thistles in the hayfield, and see the town boys go singing up the side of the road to the swimming hole. It was back of our house near the old covered bridge. Boys only. When summer work let up Dad let us go swimming. We went in our birthday suits, with plenty of trees to hide us from the road traffic. Privacy ended when the W.P.A., the Depression workers, cut down those trees along the creek.

Every other Friday night, ice cream suppers in summertime and pitch-in suppers in wintertime, were special occasions for four families. Each had three children: Roy Hasketts, Jake Bells, Watt Kaisers—Watson was his name—and us, the Luther Kaisers. Bob Spaethes and sometimes Uncle Sam and Aunt Ada Illyes came. We'd switch to Saturday on ballgame nights. Wintertime we'd often have oyster suppers with salad and dessert. Chili suppers. Thanksgiving time, we'd have a Thanksgiving meal, each family taking its turn.

All my growing-up years were interesting, yet I never, ever liked living on the farm. I realized Dad and Mom enjoyed it and that was our livelihood. I remember Dad impressing on us kids to save for our old age, and we have. He said, "A father can care for seven kids but seven kids can't care for one father."

When Grandpa and Grandma Voss held their fiftieth wedding anniversary festivities, my folks marked their twenty-fifth on the same day, March first. My parents celebrated sixty-two years together and Grandpa and Grandma Voss observed their sixty-fifth! Ermina and I have now passed our fiftieth—it's hard to imagine where time has gone!

Oh, what fond memories I have of visiting my Cicero grandparents, the festivities—and all the while wishing I'd been a town boy!

—Harold Kaiser, the author's cousin and the illustrator's uncle, was interviewed in September, 1990.

Fun With the Flivvers
A Conversation Around The Kitchen Table

by
Berta and Chalmers Hoover and Jerry and John Hillard

These two couples grew up around the Noblesville area. Berta and Chalmers were farmers and still live on their homeplace. John Hillard made a career of the military, and upon retirement, he and Jerry returned to Noblesville.

Chalmers: The first car I had was a Model T Ford with just the running gears, and I traded a rifle for that! 1931—I was fifteen. I took the engine and everything else all apart and put it back together. I don't remember how many bolts I had left over, but it ran!

I didn't have money to buy oil, so Dad gave me some linseed oil. I put that in, and you talk about smoke and stink, Whew! Make a pigeon puke! Could have smelled me coming a mile away! The steering wheel had so much play in it, like steering a boat!

No tires, so I couldn't run it on the road. Dad said no need to put new shoes on a dead horse. Before long I had her running like a Swiss watch! You remember when that guy came out there to give airplane rides?

Jerry: Chalmers and I are first cousins, so I've been a party to a lot of his mischief and I've heard the family tales. Yes, I remember that. The man had trouble with his plane and glided down into Grandpa's pasture field. He worked on it there, got it to going, then he started giving rides to get some money to get him back to where he came from. It was an old single-prop seat, open cockpit, two wings, kind of like the Spirit of St. Louis. Why, airplanes were so rare, when one went over the school, everyone rushed to the windows to look out—even the teacher!

Chalmers: While he was giving rides, I was busy setting kids on my radiator, riding them around the bump-bumpy field. I didn't charge, though. We were all having fun!

Jerry: It didn't cost our family. Others paid around two-and-a-half dollars. Berta went with Grandma and I was with Mom trying to look

over the side to see what was all below. Mom kept hanging onto me—
nothing to tie us in. I could feel her pushing hard on the floorboard!

Chalmers: When I went, he took off over this hill east of the barn.
All at once, he was up in the air making a big circle. When he came
down, it was the roughest landing I ever saw! People scattering like
sparrows! He took off again, went back around, for he thought he'd
made a bad landing, circled, came down, and that time he really
bounced! Found out he had a flat tire.

From that Model T, I went to a small Model T van that looked like
a hearse. I don't know how in the world it got to be around here, but we
used it for a long time. Us boys, me and my friends, hauled all our camp-
ing stuff in it.

I was on the Federal Hill softball team in summertime. It had no
connection with the school. There was Sid Elder; Morris, Ralph, and
Glen West; Maurice and Fred Metsker; and Charlie Johnson. We had a
game down at Bethlehem one evening. Maurice owned a Model T Ford
pickup truck. It had sideboards about a foot high, and we'd lay the tail-
gate down. The truck top folded down. All piled in it to go to the games.
I'm a little older than Maurice—could buy cigarettes before he could!
One time Sid Elder, so big and fat, was sitting in the back end with his
feet dragging. Maurice come to this steep hill, the truck slowed, he
shoved down on the low pedal. The truck stopped, jerked, then plunged
forward. Sid slid out the back end, right on that gravel road. He was
wilder than a bobcat in a pen of turkeys! Going to whip Maurice! But
Maurice didn't do it on purpose. The rest of us had to dig the gravel out
of Sid's bottom and get him some other britches!

One time a low branch took off Maurice's cap right at a bad spot in
the road. We got mired down. Everyone piled out to push the truck to
high ground. After the first time we got stuck, we learned to push the
truck from some other position than behind the tires! The mud would
fly thirty feet, depending on the driver. Muddy shoes, wet clothes, good
friends—now that's fun!

Berta: The narrow dirt road past our house was ankle-deep mud in
early spring, cloudy with dust in the summer, and buried in drifts during
the winter.

Remember out on Road 32, east of Noblesville? Riding over that in
a car was like on a rollercoaster at Riverside Park. Fellows knew each
steep incline and its drop-off, and they'd go like sixty! That's where fellows took their dates, to give 'em a good scare. The fun went out of that

road when a carload of high school kids hit another head-on. Several of them were killed.

John: And they used to play "chicken." Be driving down the road, see a car coming, and hurriedly shut off lights. The idea was to see who would veer last. It was usually a near-miss. But there were some tragic accidents before they put a stop to that.

Jerry: What was it you and Maurice used to hook me up to, turn the crank, and the thing would give me a real charge?

Chalmers: That was an old motorcycle magneto—a small generator in which one or more permanent magnets produce the magnetic field.

Jerry: They used to ask me to come into the garage to show me something and said they needed my help for just a minute. "Now you hold onto these wires while we're working on this...." I got a good hold, then, pretty soon I started getting this terrible kick, couldn't let go, and I began screaming my head off! Grandma yelled out, "Chalmers, what are you doing to that girl!"

Chalmers: Yeah, we were always getting somebody on that. Had my own little shop out back in the smokehouse.

John: If you were holding on to the magneto, and had hold of someone else, as long as you had a firm grip on it, it wouldn't shock you, but if they touched something metal, it would bite! We had one hooked up on a car by the fence. If somebody came up, leaned up against the fence, put one foot up on the running board or the fender like they used to do, they'd stand there and bounce back and forth between the two!

Chalmers: They did that with this Model T Ford coil. Take one and hook it up. Nothing. Take two, boy! You could electrocute a fish! And, man, somebody came and set down on your fender, you could really take him off of there!

Jerry: People used to lean on your car fenders, or one hip propped against the car hood, when they went to the free shows in town. That'd scoot them off in a hurry!

John: Also, pull into town behind a car, someone sitting on the bumper, touch it and throw on the switch and it'd grab them!

Chalmers: Ralph West was one for always playing tricks. He had a double coil on his Model T Ford. I think the man's name was Whelchel, lived on Federal Hill. He'd got his hand in a buzz saw and had it all bandaged up. Whelchel walked up, put his good hand on Ralph's car and Ralph turned that on. It went through right to the bad hand. Boy, I thought Whelchel was going to kill Ralph!

When I went to high school some boys drove because the school bus only hauled grade-school kids, or parents hauled them back and forth. We parked there in front of the Noblesville High School on Conner Street. At noon, country kids came out after they'd eaten their sack lunch, and they sat in cars or around on fenders. You'd be sitting in your car—then give them a charge!

Jerry: The Model T Fords were bad to crank, for they kicked a lot. Those and the F12 Farmall tractors. I've seen my dad go around, give her a crank, she'd start popping, he'd jump in, and she'd die. Then he'd push up that lever a little more, run back around, crank again, run back around.

He showed Mom how to adjust the thing. He'd crank and she was supposed to pull it down right quick so it wouldn't die. She'd let it die, and he'd yell: "I told you to do it this way!" And the fight was on!

Have a carload of kids, all the squabbling and racket. Sometimes Dad would have driven only a short distance from our house when he'd pull over: "Who wants to get out and run along behind now?" The fear of being left behind quieted us.

Saturday evening, we'd be on our way to town for Mom to do her weekly shopping, us kids to go to the movie, and Dad to play cards at the pool room. We'd be driving down the road—Dad, always looking at what other farmers were doing along the way, commenting: "Well, I see Ed's got good straight corn rows an' no weeds to speak of. Looks like he's gettin' ready to paint his barn...." Mom'd yell, "I wish you'd keep your eyes on the road!" From the back seat, "Can't we please go faster—we'll be late!" A fight was on!

Chalmers: Johnny Stewart, the colored guy that lived down the road—we hardly saw colored people around our parts back then—he bought a good used Chevy and was so proud of it. He parked down by the granary and put his hound dog in the back, ready to go coon hunting.

I came along and we talked, we looked at his dog, and then he wanted to see my coon dogs. We were gone about an hour. Came back—in the distance the car looked so funny. Holy Mackerel! His coon dog had torn all the lining out of the top! A mess! Johnny just stood there looking, shaking his head, said, "My God, what's my old woman gonna say about this!" Wives had no love for coon dogs, anyway. They kept their husbands traipsing all over the woods in all kinds of weather every night during the season and they couldn't abide that coon dog's endless braying.

Jerry: He was an awful nice fellow and so was Mrs. Stewart. She used to come down, when Grandma had hay hands, to help her out. She always made chicken and dumplings. When all the men came in for dinner, there'd be big pitchers of lemonade with lots of big chunks of ice floating around in it, special for hired help. What a treat! But Johnny always had to have hot water, nothing else. Hot water!

They had a youngster that just loved to come down and play our piano. Every Sunday morning we'd find Johnny asleep in our chicken house. On his way home on Saturday night he'd be drunk, get tired, go in there, lie down, and go to sleep.

Chalmers: One morning Dad went out there and Johnny was at the back corner of our hog house. What happened, the dog was barking and he sat down there waiting for the dog to let up—didn't want to wake the whole neighborhood—and he went to sleep!

He was a really nice fellow, but he'd get boozed up, and he'd be mean. They put him in jail for two weeks over at Muncie and, no time at all, he was a trusty! They had him cooking and all. When he came home, he had a still in the back end of that Ford and I don't know how many bushels of peaches. I suppose they confiscated them over there.

He was quite a character, could write a book about him! He'd be back there on the crick and I'd be farming. I'd see him take a book, sit down on the bank, take a shoe off, and tie the line around his big toe, throw in the line, and he sat there and read till a fish bit!

We were thrashing down at our house one day and I was on the grain wagon. Somebody had killed a good-sized blue racer that they'd pulled out from under a shock of wheat. Johnny was standing on his wagon, there at the separator. Ben Harris gave that snake a whip and wrapped it around Johnny's ankles. I'm telling you, his eyes turned white! One thing a black man couldn't stand—snakes!

My next car, when I was sixteen, was a yellow '29 secondhand Roadster. My folks helped me buy it. Twenty-five dollars. Then I had to work it out. Every farm boy had a little savings—not much 'cause there wasn't any way to make money. Parents tried to hold him off, buying a car, as long as they could, afraid he'd go out and kill himself. I always got half a calf when they sold the cattle, and that was my pay for helping Dad on the farm all year. Sometimes I hired out making hay.

I don't remember girls having their own cars, or their spending money, only what they made helping neighbor women. They'd drive the family car.

Dad had a '26 Pontiac and he took my sister, Eva, and me out to the pasture field to learn to drive. He showed us the gears and all else that had to be done, then turned us loose. I didn't have any trouble but Eva took awhile.

Some drivers were recognized by their "sitting position" when driving. One fellow I knew always rode with one leg hanging out over the door. Another lolled over into his driving corner, holding the steering wheel mostly with his right hand, even with a girl along. Usually lovers sat so close together, his left arm on the wheel, the right one around his sweetie. Little boys would yell: Room for one more?"

In every neighborhood there was one guy with painted signs on the body of his car: *The Tin You Love To Touch...Peaches, Here's Your Can...Capacity: 5 gals...Come On, Baby, Here's Your Rattle...Danger, 100,000 Jolts...Don't Laugh Girls, Think How You Would Look Without Paint.*

That '29 Chevy—me and Dad had gone down to Indianapolis. I was hoping to find a car with a rumble seat, but nothing was in my price range. We came home. Went on another week, and I asked Dad again, and he said, "Well, do you think you'd like that one we saw?" He put me on the streetcar—mind you a sixteen-year-old country boy—and I went to Indianapolis, twenty miles away, to buy a car by myself!

You didn't have to have a driver's license. I think that started in '36. I was driving up through Broad Ripple and getting a lot of waves. I couldn't figure what was up till I came to a stop sign and found out my emergency brake was on and smoke was rolling out!

Had an awful lot of fun with that car. Me and Maurice were coming home around midnight on Saturday night. To turn the switch off, you pushed in and gave it a turn. We were breezing along on that road and all at once, that car cut out, came back on, cut out. Out of gas? Oh, boy, not now when nobody'd be coming along! Everybody in bed this time of night. I looked down. Maurice was asleep and had slipped in the seat, and his knee would push the key in and it would cut off; knee'd slip off, it'd take off.

Never knew when we were about out of gas—no gauge. Poke a stick down in there, bring it out, and you could tell.

Back in those days, of an evening when we got the work done, Maurice came by and we drove around and around. About dark one evening, we saw a big fire up in the northwest. That's where we headed in Maurice's car. Had the top down, Maurice and Fred were sitting in the front seat and I was behind. Low and behold, you know where the fire was? My dad's barn up at Atlanta! Noel Castor farmed that place.

We got there and the road was already lined with cars, so we took off through the pasture field. The gas pedal stayed on the floor and Maurice was hitting the awfullest hog-wallows you ever saw, and he threw me plumb out!

Went back home. Dad was asleep in bed. I told him; allowed he'd want to go up there. He grunted, rolled over, and went back to sleep. He couldn't do anything about it now.

John: Automobiles were scarce enough that it was no problem for most people in the country to match them with their respective owners.

There were all the country sounds after you went to bed at night. I always knew each of the neighbor's dogs, just by their bark. Hear something get into the chicken house—them raising Cain—Dad would be yelling for me to get up and go help him.

I'd see the auto lights sweeping dimly through the bedroom dark, the engines winding down, the squeak of brakes for a sudden stop. Then the "broooom" of first, the rising "brrrroooooming" of second, and finally the purr of third as they faded into the night.

I even came to know most of the drivers by their shifting of gears. I could tell Fred Metsker by the wild whine of his engine between shifts. He pushed to the limit before shifting to the next gear.

I always wondered where those late-night travelers were coming from and where they were going—no one traveled much after nine.

One evening a man's car broke down out by the barnyard gate. My folks were gone. Found out he was out of gas but we didn't have a gas barrel, only crude oil. I told him it would work. All I had to do was strain it through a cloth, but he didn't want to mess up his engine with that. He asked me, "How far is it to Noblesville?" I said, "They say three miles, as the crow flies." "Well, then," he said, "how far if the crow has to walk and carry a gallon of gas?"

John: Before I got my first puddle jumper, more than anything I wanted a motorcycle—oh, to kick it into life and take off with gravel spraying way out behind! Parents frowned on motorcycles! Get ourselves killed. It was a good way to show off in front of girls.

Berta: Automobiles seemed to be a curiosity or a source of annoyance to farmers' dogs. Most of them raced to the road and barked wildly as they attempted to stay abreast of the car as it passed. Many a dog got caught under the car wheel and that was the end of a good family pet.

Once in a while, someone we knew purchased a car from the local dealer and we were given test rides. It was new and shiny and smelled so wonderful; the heater, when they came out later, poured out a steady stream of warmth on our legs!

Chalmers: As in any neighborhood there was the rich man's son with the latest of everything and always had money to spend. He got a new convertible. Convertibles in our county were as rare as a September snow. He passed us in our old truck, waving and shouting. I'll never forget—Charlie Johnson gritted his teeth and said, "By-god, I wish we had that car and he had a boil on his butt!" Maurice laughed and said, in his droll way, "Charlie, don't go getting your drawers in a twist. It's sinful to say a thing like that. Remember what the Good Book tells us: Thou shalt not covet thy neighbor's ass."

Jerry: Dad used to drag us kids along on all his fishing trips, then he'd sit there and yell at us. You know how kids'll do—throw rocks, run up and down the banks making noise? We had talked Mom out of some weenies, raisins, and whatever else she had on hand. We went to the Strawtown Bridge and Dad sat all day and fished. Us kids enjoyed it. Don't know why Mom didn't go, or why Dad took us kids with him when all he did was yell at us! We enjoyed it. Never ever heard: "I don't know what to do. Tell me something to do...."

John: One time we were away three weeks and not a lock on the door. Nothing was bothered when we got back. People didn't worry a thing about intruders.

Chalmers: And they never locked their big, farm gas tanks when the tractors came out. They used gasoline pumped from a big, round, metal, elevated tank. Sometimes I'd come home, there'd be a note with the money: I got five gallons gas. Name signed. Left a dollar. Course, quite a bit later, it was a regular occurrence, especially boys with cars and no job, stealing gas. Then we put a lock on the hose.

Berta: The first car I ever remember was an old Oldsmobile when I was little. The Cicero-Noblesville road was dirt and there at Forest Park was quite a hill. One time we had the side curtains on. It was snowing so hard we had to stop and wipe snow off the windows to see out. There was one windshield wiper on the driver's side. Dad had to move it himself from the inside, when the window needed cleaning. Sometimes we all piled out and cleaned off the windshield good. Bud Costomiris had a little open-bladed fan, hooked up in the left-hand corner of the windshield, and when that was turned on, it kept the frost off the glass.

Jerry: I can still see gravel flying as we tried to get power to run up that hill. Dad's folks lived at Atlanta and we'd visit them every Sunday. Twelve miles. We'd leave real early in the morning and, that afternoon, three or four o'clock, Dad'd say, "Well, we'd better head for the poor farm." We'd all fuss, "Do we have to go so soon?" It was about dark when we got home. Long drive! Dad and the boys still had the chores and milking to do.

Berta: Each community had the ultimate scientific test of a car. Carter Hill was ours. It's gone now—at the bottom of Morse Lake. You came through this little bridge and turned, then not much level space to get a fast, running start up the hill. Only a few cars ever made it in high gear. Most had to change to low.

Chalmers: We were riding with Dale Hunt in his big old LaSalle, going fishing. Sitting back there, I never saw so much stuff in the back end of a car in my life! Log chains, hammers, buckets, innertubes, spades. Everything!

He got halfway up this hill, and instead of stopping when he couldn't make it, then slowly backing down, he started rolling, picking up speed, faster and faster, weaving across both sides of the road and everyone yelling, ready to jump out, but there were steep slopes on both sides.

He tried it again. Same thing. "Well," he said," I'm gonna have to back down again or go way around to get to the fishin' hole." So we went plumb around to get there.

Jerry, I never will forget the time you lived down in Fall Creek Township. Your folks had that two-seater Model T. You'd come out home to pick up a cookstove. The men tied it on the side of that Ford. Then you kids all wanted me to go home with you. Four of you kids, and you wanted me!

Jerry: We all piled in. The who's sitting where, and who's sitting on somebody's something, and the fussing would start. Everyone wanted Chalmers to sit by them! The folks were saying their good-byes, Chalmers started whimpering.

"Sh-sh, Chalmers, don't cry. Your folks won't let you go if you cry! What's the matter? Don't you want to go?"

"I can't unless I take my billy goat." So, we all rolled out and went running to catch that goat. Everyone piled back in, and the fussing continued, "I wanna hold Billy; sit next to me, Chalmers...." There was a lot of chattering and shifting around before we all got settled and on our way.

Down the road we went, with the stove tied on the running board, that car leaning way over like a man walks who has a short leg, kids hanging out all the windows, Chalmers holding Billy, and the fussing, "It's my turn to hold Billy now!" Chalmers parents stood at the yard gate and waved until we were gone.

Chalmers: That goat followed me every place I went. He'd run up steps, onto the porch, tear the house down trying to get in. I kept an umbrella around, raised it and—whoosh!—that goat was gone. Scared him half to death! I had a little cart and harness, and me and my goat spent hours together!

Dads were smart. When a kid started harping about wanting a pony, he'd say, "No pony." He got the boy a goat. Dads knew they'd no sooner get the boy a pony or a horse, he'd want a car. Then when he started harping for a car of his own, the dad would say, "I thought I might give you this little filly if you felt you were man enough to look after a good piece of horseflesh." That lasted quite awhile, then jawing about a car began again. By that time most boys his age were getting an old jalopy. Then Dad would say, "When you can pay cash for your own car and assume the responsibility of gas and oil, I'll give my consent." Yes, it was with a father's permission, but probably against his better judgment.

Jerry: All these guys Chalmers ran around with, when they were twelve to fourteen, in order to get away from everybody, have something to do, they built a log cabin back there along the river. Well, one day Grandma decided that since they'd all had so much fun back there, and we hadn't seen it, we'd have a family reunion in that cabin.

First thing when we walked in the door, snakes were hanging down from all the rafters! Live ones! Yes, live ones! Grandpa would never kill a snake. Said they eat rats. Droves of rats on farms! The women would have none of the snake business, so we spread our dinner along the crick.

Chalmers: It was one room, ten to twelve feet, made from trees we cut off of our farm ourselves with hand saws. Ted Kinsey and Gerald Gerrard, they helped. Charlie Johnson had a rickety spring wagon and his old white horse pulling it, and we hauled those logs in. Dad furnished some cottonwood boards for the roof sheeting. He bought the cement for the mortar and got the sand right out of the crick. We did it up right, even mortared in between the logs.

It had four little barn sash windows and a front door. The flue through the roof for the stove.

Then we decided we wanted a nice step for outside the door. There were limestone blocks on each end of where the old bridge was, on Old 32. We got one, probably three foot by five, and five inches thick. Heavy! Oh, it was heavy! We worked all Sunday getting that and putting it in the Model T. That old Ford ran down the road with its nose in the air and its tail dragging!

The cabin roof went up to a V. There was a loft but you couldn't stand up in it. That's where Charlie and Fred slept. Me and Maurice pulled our seniority and slept downstairs.

One morning we were having trouble getting Fred and Charlie up. I said, "By gosh, we'll git 'em!" We built up a big fire in the stove and then put a board up over the flue hole on the roof. Directly Old Fred and Charlie looked down through there. They were so black we couldn't see anything but their eyes!

One Sunday morning we were all smoking in there, probably cornsilks cause we never had money for cigarettes, even to roll our own. We were acting like grown-up men, blowing smoke through our nose and blowing smoke rings, sending out clouds of smoke! "Go on, have a snort!" I don't know what we were drinking—probably some hard cider.

Dad, about every Sunday morning, made a tour of the farm, looked at the cattle in the back and the fences. Directly, here he was. "Having your morning smoke, huh?" He went on.

He didn't approve—no one thought a boy should smoke till after he reached twenty-one. Smoking would stunt your growth, cause consumption, turn your teeth yellow, and make your breath stink, the women said. Some parents even made big promises of a hundred dollars, and education, if their sons abstained from smoking till they reached twenty-one. Most didn't abstain! And most weren't interested in any higher education than to graduate from high school.

All Fred and Charlie ever did was argue. We'd give them an egg apiece, back 'em back-to-back, then have 'em walk away from each other ten steps, turn around and throw. Nine times out of ten they'd miss each other, but we'd have no trouble with 'em the rest of the day.

Chewing! We had our experiences with that, too. By this time me and Maurice were old hands at it. We got busy doing something one day and after a while realized that Fred and Charlie hadn't been heard from for some time. Looked over. They were as pale as puss, tobacco juice running down the sides of their mouths!

One time Charlie took his clothes off to go swimming. We threw 'em up the tree. After the swim, rather than climb the tree, he went home naked. His dad came over after his clothes later, and I thought, oh boy! he's going to raise Cain, but he just laughed!

Berta: Noblesville was so full of people on Saturday night you couldn't hardly get down the sidewalks. Over on the east side of the square, in front of Penney's and the dime store, you'd have to push through, it was so jammed. All around the curb on the Court House lawn, men sat discussing all that went on through the week while the women did the shopping. Fellas and their girls always went to town on Saturday night and walked back and forth, back and forth! Young kids wanted to go to the movie. Young guys without dates would drive all around town, around and around.

Jerry: Every Saturday, before a date, Chalmers shined his car till it looked like a polished dime. Reflections were great in it. In fact, I saw Berta fixing her hair, looking in a fender!

Generally couples double-dated. One fellow would furnish the car and gas and the other would buy the movie tickets. Occasionally there'd be a fellow who never had a car to drive, but didn't think he should pay for the movie!

Chalmers: After we married, Berta thought she still had to go to town every Saturday night, and if I was working late in the fields, oh, she'd pout if she didn't get to go! "Well," she cried, reminding me, "you could always quit early enough when we were going together!"

Jerry: Girls were never allowed to stay out late, to get in trouble. If we were out at ten o'clock, that was bad! Only wild girls rode around with boys in cars. Or accepted rides; they were called "pick-ups."

Chalmers: I lost two-and-a-half dollars one night. I'd seen Berta uptown—that was before I'd started going with her—and I told Maurice I could pick Berta Webster up and take her home. He said I couldn't. Well, I lost my bet. Berta never did get to ride in my yellow car. I traded it in for one with a rumble seat.

We used to park up in front of the Franklin Ice Cream Store on the south side and watch girls walking along. Here's Old George Day coming down the street. "How-do. How-do." He'd tip his stiff straw hat at everyone he knew.

Berta: Franklin Ice Cream! Those long, pointed cones, and every imaginable flavor! They did a big business.

John: Rumble seats. The mother-in-law cars. You, your wife, and mother-in-law going someplace, she had to sit back there! Or, they'd put her up in front driving, pull the curtains between the seats, and the couple'd ride in the rumble seat!

Rumble seats were placed in the turtlebacks of coupes and convertibles. A door lifted up from the turtleback and was upholstered with imitation leather and springs, forming the back of the seat. A narrow seat, just large enough for two people, or a fat man and his pup!

They were designed, obviously, for the young because entering or leaving them was no easy matter. A heavy metal step was installed on the left, rear fender. Leg room was cramped due to limited space and the presence of jacks, tire chains, rubber boots, and patchings, and empty bottles and gunny sacks. It was like teetering around in space getting in. And you sat low down in—on the back floor almost.

For dates, girls always dressed up pretty, in dresses, silk stockings, and high-heeled shoes. That's why they liked to put their girl in the rumble seat! Why, you could almost see the calves of her legs as she climbed to get in.

Chalmers: It was a good place to put a drunk if you wanted to sober him up! And we kept all the tools in the rumble seat, so you had to make room for your feet. Some had a toolbox on the running board. The spare tire hooked on the back. I taught Berta to drive her mother's rumble seat car.

Jerry: Remember, Berta, when you and your mother came down to our house to visit one afternoon and she parked up in the yard? Our mothers sat in the house and talked and talked. Ready to go, no car. Looked all over the place. It had rolled back into the sweet corn patch!

Chalmers: One time I was late getting started to go see Berta. Most boys did a lot of trading, anything they had, they'd trade. I'd been down to Joe Bays' and traded for a revolver. Us fellows liked to sit on the fenders of our cars and shoot at tin cans on top of fence posts. Well, I came speeding up Tenth Street. I went through the light on change, turned west 'cause I remembered I wanted to pick up a pack of cigarettes at Heaton's Pool Room. I drove plumb over on the left side, heading west, believe me, I did, on the wrong side of the street, I was in such a big hurry! Just as I got out of that car, here's this red light behind me and there I was with that gun! The policeman fined me for coming down Tenth Street so fast! That's all.

Lovers' lanes! One time this guy was hiding, and I don't know why, 'cause it was a taxi cab and there was only one in Noblesville. We all knew who he was, there with a woman. They both hid! Forest Park, that was a good lovers' lane!

Every couple had their favorite lovers' lane. Yeah, romance rode in most of the young fellows' vehicles when couples got real serious. Romance, then the seven-month babies!

Jerry: Remember the couple who were parked in the wintertime? Someone came along and found them—dead from carbon monoxide gas. That's a deadly poison. Heaters were something new. There was a faulty something, I guess. If that wasn't bad enough, that fellow was to be married in less than a week. He'd taken his girl home, then he had picked up the town tramp. Both dead! The bride-to-be almost lost her mind, they said.

Berta: Driving with one headlight out. See one coming towards you, the first one to call out "Oh, pee diddle!" got a kiss. That's how a lot of romances got started!

John: Ever try running the car down the railroad tracks in town? I did lots of times, down Eighth Street in Noblesville. Never in the country. Before I was married. The tires on the cars were narrow, they'd stay on, weave around quite a bit, get on, and could run from one end of town to the next, unless someone caught you!

In the country where the railroad tracks cross the roads, there was usually a steep grade up and over them. It was fun to race up across that very bumpy grade! Dangerous, too. Many a boy got a goose egg on his noggin when he bounced from his seat.

Berta: Every time Chalmers' mom and I went to town to get groceries, we fixed a flat tire. I learned just about as good as any man!

Chalmers: A bunch of us FFA boys — that's Future Farmers of America — judging team, went to Purdue in '39 to judge livestock, seventy miles or so. I think we fixed nine tires going and seven coming back. The roads were so rocky, graveled all the way. Rocks cut tires bad.

John: Tubes would get pinched, too, and make holes. We had an old '29 Chevy and Dad always carried a spare axle for it. The car would twist the axle off in the back. Driving down the road and all of a sudden that one wheel quit. Dad'd back the thing up, yank the back wheel off, pull the axle out, put another in—all in five minutes! Next time we passed a junk yard, he'd go in and buy another spare.

Chalmers: I was hauling tomatoes in my '31 Chevy. Cost me nine dollars for another axle and I had five dollars left out of the crop, and after all that work raising, weeding, and picking 'em all summer!

Jerry: On gravel roads, with those older cars, boys would look for any oncoming traffic. No one in sight, they'd come up to a quick stop, lock their wheels and they'd slide along there sideways real fast! Big thrill!

John: Couldn't you lock the wheels on a Model T by pushing down on all three pedals?

Chalmers: No, just push on the reverse. The middle pedal was reverse and if the brake pedal didn't take, just use the reverse. It was hard on bands, but better than hitting someone!

John: One time this cop was checking brakes and he crawled up on the running board, leaned his head in the window and said, "Now, when I tell you to stop, I want you to stop!" I didn't have any brakes. I was driving along like he said, Cop yelled, "Stop!" I crossed my feet at an angle, hit both pedals, and the cop went flying into space!

The hoods raised up on each side, had a spring-tension hook on them. Sometimes we'd be going down the road and they'd work loose and fly up. That blinded you! We had to keep them wired down.

The radiator cap used to have a thing in it that told you when the water was hot. Remember the silver-angel hood ornaments; the fancy brass emblems on some radiators; when rear-view mirrors were optional equipment; and, the really deluxe models, which meant two taillights; the car radios that came into existence sometime in the twenties—nobody seems to know when, nor in which car the first radio was installed.

Chalmers: I can remember the first car radio I ever heard. A man from Lafayette had trouble right out in front of our house. And while they were there, they played the song that was popular: "I Looked For Gold On Treasure Island"! I thought, Oh, boy, to have a car radio!

Jerry: Radios! Us girls singing with the radio as we rode along. Best of all, the roll-down glass windows. No more trying to beat a rain, buttoning on the side curtains. As fast as we could snap one in place, then another came loose. Kids looked into the clear, convex headlights that made them look overweight and misshapen!

Chalmers: That '29 Chevy I had, with the top down and the windshield laid back, it would do seventy! With the windshield up and the top up, sixty-five is the best she'd do. I never did any racing that I remember, but every guy knew "what she'll do." Well, I was gunning it at seventy-five, windshield down, dark glasses on, and a June bug hit me square in the eye and broke my glasses. Hit harder than a rock!

Ted Kinsey had a '31 Roadster he'd lay the windshield down on. The wind would get under it and whip it up and break the windshield out every time. He broke so many they canceled his insurance!

John: Fellows used to tie a foxtail on the radiator—real sporty!

Jerry: The first heater, oh, my, those things got hot! Run you out.

Chalmers: There was a manifold heater on the Model T Fords. They didn't get to the water heaters till, I think, '31 Chevy.

John: I had a '34 Ford and it had an old South Wind gas heater in it, hooked up to the fuel pump. You turned your car on and there was a spark in it, pumped gas into the thing right off the carburetor. Soon's you started the car, that thing was sending out hot air!

Berta: Remember when boys put a potato in the tailpipe of some girl's car? It would idle but wouldn't run. Boys'd stand together on the running boards, bounce up and down to see how much they could rock a car back and forth, sideways.

People rode on running boards, too. Kids were allowed to ride on one from the end of their lane to the house, after opening and closing the big farm gate. Kids hated that job—opening and shutting the gate, so riding the running board kind of appeased them.

John: Be driving down the street, a buddy walking along, "Hop on!" and away we'd go, him hanging his head inside there, talking to the driver. My uncle had a dog that rode the running board all the time. And we had a dog that always wanted to go for a ride with us and we had to lock him in the house if we didn't want him along. Came back once and he'd torn up all the linoleum on the kitchen floor!

Chalmers: There was this young guy we all knew, and well, his elevator didn't go all the way up, if you get what I mean. He was girl-struck and of course no girl wanted to date him. Us fellows drew straws to see who'd dress up like a girl and be his date. I don't even remember who it was; not me. That guy whistled as he cleaned out his car and washed it real good. The two went on the date, that fellow was so polite and kind, they went to a movie, out of town, of course, and they had a nice time. Us other guys felt real ashamed of ourselves after that, but never told anyone of the prank we'd played.

When I first started working at the factory, it was the big shots we young punks picked on. We learned one man was going to Sheridan that night to pick up his high-stepping wife. We put Limburger cheese on the manifold heater. It got so rank in there with all those smells coming back into the car, his wife like to killed him!

Berta: A car picked up all kinds of odors—skunks, other dead animals, even wild garlic growing along the road, new-cut hay, or thrashed wheat and oats.

Chalmers: In '42 I bought a Model A Roadster with a rumble seat for thirty-five dollars. I drove it to work at the factory over at Remys for about a year, then farmed with it, pulled a mower, and there at the last I had to hold it in second gear.

That's the one Berta had loaded with stuff when we moved up here; she had Linda, a couple of years old, and Taffy, the dog. She hit the iron bridge, went under a rail, the crick was way out of its banks, and they went on in. She tore the front fender off but she and Linda were OK. We had to break the railing off the bridge to get the car out.

Berta: I wasn't scared about me and Linda or the stuff in the car. I was afraid of what Chalmers was going to say!

Chalmers: Us boys used to see how much our cars would take going through Fox Prairie when the water was high, before they'd drown out.

Road 38 used to get under water from Shanburger Hill to the bridge. Whole bottom covered with water. No way to get through so us boys would take a boat from where we lived, row across, get out and go to town to the show, come back, get in the boat, row back across, and then walk on home.

Babe McCarlin had a big Chrysler Roadster and we tried to tell him he couldn't get through. He said, "Aw, come now, this car'll go through anything." He got halfway and that was it. He had to roll his pants legs up, had his wife with him, she took off her high heels and pulled up her dress, and they both waded out. She was jawing him all the way for trying it after those boys had warned him! He left his car there till the water went down in a couple of days.

I was standing at our barn when I saw Gertrude Elder's car hit the southwest corner of the bridge. That old iron bridge fell in, and her car, two men and two women in it. I can see it yet. There was a liniment salesman going by and when I got there he was down on his knees before her, she all stretched out moaning, he had his linament pouring it into his hand, then rubbing it on Gertrude's legs! Why, I'd never seen that much bare skin on a lady in my life!

The road was then closed. Us boys went back in our woods and cut some tall trees for long poles, took old planks off the other bridge, and nailed to them. Me and Charlie set up a toll bridge. If a Model T drove up, he got to drive across for a nickel. Anything else, a dime. You'd be surprised, the big, old rich guys would turn, go clear around rather than pay. Others would say, "You fellows went to all this work, you deserve it."

One thing is sure, us boys always had a lot of fun with our flivvers!

—*This story originally appeared in* Tri Town Topics *on June 24 and July 1 and 8, 1976.*

Wintertime Neighborhood Amusements

by
Henry Bowman

Five generations of Henry Bowman's family lived and died, he sadly noted, in the farmhouse west of Cicero where he told the stories of wintertime amusements he enjoyed during his young years.

In the winter, when the weather was bad, I've heard Mother say to Dad a hundred times, "Go get a quarter's worth of crackers at the store, 'n' a coupla gallon oysters." Oh, boy—she was planning to have an oyster supper at our house!

Dad would take a big, old, clean, barn gunnysack to the grocery. I've seen him go to the crackers barrel at the store—everything came in barrels back then—and he'd scoop 'em out, weigh 'em, get that big sack half full for a quarter!

Oh, he'd pick out a pretty clean sack, shake it out good, to make sure. Had to watch he didn't get a chewed mouse hole in it or he'd lose crackers on the way home. Once in a while we'd see one of those brown cloth ravelings in the cracker dish, but Mother just pulled it out and thought nothing of it.

Don't suppose you remember those thick, little, round oyster crackers. I wish they had 'em today. Later on they started making the paper-thin ones and when you put 'em in soup, they're gone! The oyster crackers just swelled bigger and bigger. Eat one of 'em and you'd have a mouthful!

Our neighbors took turns having the oyster suppers in their homes during the cold winter months, especially celebrating birthdays that way.

Mother would send two, empty, gallon-sized lard buckets with Dad to get the oysters in. He'd buy 'em at the grocery store or the meat market—several of those stores in town.

I don't exactly remember how they were stored at the grocery. Probably a five-gallon wooden bucket like salt fish came in, or the tin, five-gallon buckets. Oysters were only stocked in winter months when it was cold.

One time, I remember it so dogged well, the men all went to town to get the oysters and crackers. They stopped in the saloon to get something to drink. When they came home they were all three sheets to the wind! No, they never forgot what they went to town for. Had the oysters. And they brought in a two-bushel wheat sack full of crackers. That storekeeper must have upended the whole barrel into that bag. We had plenty, and Mother divided 'em up with all the ladies when everyone was ready to go home.

Another time when the same gang went to town, Mother said for Dad to bring back some mustard. Just common yellow table mustard. Well, in town I reckon they got too much firewater. Dad brought Mother the mustard, a two-gallon jar full of it. And the men never did know how much they paid, or where they bought it. Probably from the tavern. They wouldn't admit to the women if they had.

These were all family men, not taken to drinking. I think, looking back, it was a treat, after spending so many hours out in the frigid weather doing winter farm work.

I never saw Dad drunk in my life. I suppose he went on a toot once in a while when he was a young fellow, but not after I got big enough to know about it. He'd always say, "Aw, shoot. It's all right if ya take a snort, if ya know when to quit." And Mother would add, "Now, Dad, we don't need no more mustard," and he'd shut right up.

Mother used a gallon of oysters, frying 'em in big black iron skillets on the cookstove. That was the most wonderful smell coming from that kitchen! Used another gallon to make oyster soup. We always had plenty of milk from our dairy herd to make it. She wanted to see a lot of oysters floating around in the big kettles of soup she made. One woman used a copper wash boiler to heat the milk, to which she added a gallon oysters, salt and pepper, and generous globs of butter.

Early that morning, Mother'd made a slew of pies—apple, cherry, cream, custard, I don't know what else. And all the time the oysters were cooking, the women laughed and cut up and had the best time.

The men sat around playing cards and smoking and, after supper, talking of the price of hogs and eggs, the weather, and complaining about eating too much. Kids, every age, were all over the house, playing. Usually a baby or two.

One by one the families went home, out into the cold, dark night. I'd see their lanterns bobbing as they walked to their mud boats, then watched those flickering lights on out of sight. I was glad when it was at our house. We didn't have to ride that long way home in a frigid wind, then go into an icy house, our teeth chattering as we took off our clothes, then crawl into a frosty bed.

Other times, on a cold snowy day, I'd look out and there'd come a neighbor and his family, from the west, in their mud boat or bobsled, early of a morning, to spend the day. Us kids and the folks were so excited to see them.

I can see Mother yet, when she knew they were coming, she'd get lard on her fingertips and smooth down her hair. Put on a clean apron. See it as plain as day. Then she hurried getting things out to cook for dinner. She'd bake up a bunch of pies, then cut off big slices of sugar-cured ham to fry and make gravy, got a big pan full of kraut from the crock in the cellar, opened cans of green beans—golly, I don't know what else. One lady sat with a big dishpan of potatoes, pealing them to mash, then they'd set the long dining room table.

The house was full of kids playing around all day long. Most families had a passel of 'em. There were four of us boys. The men would sit by the fire, swap stories, or maybe go on into town. After dinner the women talked about quiltin' or knitting and looked over Mother's dress patterns.

What I wouldn't give for a meal like that right now, and visit again all day with our wonderful neighbors!

Oh, those cold winters we had! Maybe a fellow living out west, the far end of our road, he would start to town in his mud boat, and every farm house he passed, the men'd see him coming, grab a coat and run out and flag him down, and by the time they got to town there'd be a whole mud boat load of 'em.

Most people had a mud boat to use in the winter. The more affluent, they had a mud boat and a bobsled. A mud boat had solid oak runners made of two-by-tens. When you turned with them, the whole thing turned, like a child's sled. A bobsled had a set of rear runners and also a set of front runners and had a coupling pole between the rear and front, and it had a bolster the bed fit in, to hold it onto the runner. The action was the same as a wagon. You could make a sharp turn with a bobsled. It was strictly for snow. The mud boat was used in muddy weather—oh the mud we used to have—to go out in the fields and bring in shocks of fodder and to get folks back and forth to town or church.

One time a whole gang of men went to town on the mud boat, said they needed something at the hardware store. It stood just beyond Doc

Havens' office. They sold whiskey, besides everything else. Cicero was a whiskey-drinking town back in those days—seven taverns and seven churches.

Alfred Bennett said to Dad, "I could use a drink; I'm spittin' cotton." Dad said, "I'm ready for a snort, too." Then they wondered how they were going to get around it without the other men knowing. Well, they went in the store and they bought one of those new little gallon, coal oil cans, you know the kind, with a spout and handle, and an outside shell for the can to sit in. They bought it, then had it filled with whiskey when the others weren't around.

The men all started home. Alfred and Dad didn't want anyone to know they had the whiskey. The two sat up on the front seat, Dad driving the team. Alfred cleared his throat a few times, then said, "I just got the awfullest doggone cold in my chest. Nothin' better'n coal oil." He took that can, unscrewed the lid off the spout, upended it to his mouth, took a big swig, smacked his lips, and set the can down between them on the seat as he screwed the lid back on.

Dad cleared his throat, said his had been scratchy and seemed a bad cold was coming on. He took up the can, unscrewed the cap, took a gulp or two, set it down and screwed the cap back on.

All the way home, every so often, they'd relieve the soreness of their throats. Those other guys never did catch on. You'd have thought they'd have smelled it.

Those jokers liked nothing better than to play tricks on one another. The families had such good times together, too.

Young couples made their own fun and it was cheap 'cause nobody had any money. Lack of finances didn't bother us any. The neighborhood kids had so many taffy pulls, yes they did. We always were anxious for that. We'd all be there. Each fellow took so much sugar to make up into taffy. The girls would stir it up in big stew pans, boiling it on the cookstove. After it was cooked and cooled, the boys and girls buttered their hands and then they'd pull it, stretching it way back and forth between them, till it was the right consistency, ready to eat.

And, we'd square dance, too. Roll the rug back and have a big old time!

You remember Albert Good? Well, his father, George Good, lived right down here. Him and his wife and my parents, they always went places together—fairs, farm sales, minstrels, all over.

There was an old horse-drawn huckster wagon John Folgerman drove out of Deming, then he went to Indianapolis to take the produce he'd gathered on his route through the countryside all week, and he sold it to the produce houses.

On his way home he'd go to a beer house and he'd get gallon jugs of whiskey real cheap. Often Dad and George Good ordered a gallon to split between them, for John to deliver on his route the next week.

When the huckster came past our house, it was always on a Tuesday, he'd pull in here, feed his horses, eat his dinner, sitting there as he waited for his horses to eat, usually come on in and have a cup of coffee with us and a piece of pie. Us kids looked forward to seein' him. He was a real devil!

Folgerman would tell Dad, "George ordered this gallon of whiskey last week." Dad would pick it up, look it over, then open it and take a drink. Yeah, from George's gallon!

He said to George Good one day, he said, "Pete"—he called Dad 'Pete' —"Pete ordered a gallon of whiskey for next week."

"That right?" That's how they managed getting around their womenfolk knowing who it was for.

One Tuesday, just before noon, we saw the awfullest old tramp hobbling up the road, acting drunker'n a coot. Used to see vagabonds often. Didn't think nothing about it. The hobo held a stick over his shoulder with his clothes tied into a red bandanna on the end. We watched him wobbling along till he finally turned north past John Wiles'.

Well, that wasn't a tramp. That was George Good! He'd walked all the way down there, dressed like a hobo, just so's we'd see him and think it was a bum! When Folgerman drove up that day at noon, he had an old bell he'd ring to call us out, there sat George up front there, in his beggar get-up!

"Hello, Pete!" he yelled out at Dad from under that old black, worn-out felt hat pulled down over his eyebrows. Dad never got over that—cackled about it for years! How they'd work to play a joke on the others to have a good laugh!

The neighborhood gatherings were always so enjoyable. People made their own fun—and it was always entertaining.

I'd like to re-live a few of those wonderful memories!

—*This story originally appeared in* Tri Town Topics, *January 27, 1977, and in* Good Old Days, *January, 1978.*

Fun Around the Bend at Riverwood
A Conversation "Around The Kitchen Table"

by
Esther Farmer, Leeanna Illyes, Dorothy Sprong

Esther Farmer, a young, single mother, was the author's aunt. She and her two friends, Leeanna and Dorothy, tell what it was like along White River in the thirties.

Esther: I'm ninety-six. The three of us should get a good story together here, don't you think? Let me collect my thoughts!

Back then, 1936, it wasn't easy for a single woman with two young children to find something for their total support and be nearby to keep a lookout on them. I was particular as far as my children were concerned. I wanted to know where Cledith and Marion, both in their early teens, were all the time.

I saw the Riverwood store advertised for sale. I felt, if I bought it— I could pay cash from my savings—the store would probably fill our needs quite well until the children were grown.

The three of us set about fixing it up, as a home and a business. We lived in the three big rooms across the back—a dining-living room area and two bedrooms. I cooked out front in the store.

Riverwood always held an attraction to me. I lived and worked in Indianapolis for many years. Those rich folks down there had a second home along the banks of this beautiful White River, north of Noblesville. Just to think, money enough to have *two* homes! Most were summer cottages, not year-round places to dwell in.

Riverwood and Clare, across the river, had no post office nor other businesses, except each had a store. Mail was delivered from Noblesville, three miles away.

Out front, in my store, was a huge room—probably fifty feet by fifty feet square. Porch-type windows all around. Across the back I had a counter where people came up for orders of food or groceries. See, farm folks, and most of those at Riverwood and Clare, went to Noblesville to do their trading just once a week. In-between times they'd need bread, coffee, or such, and they'd come here.

Remember Tom Bond? He and his stepdad, Mr. Castor, they walked two miles from home every morning, just for a pack of cigarettes.

Dorothy: My parents both came to Indiana from Ireland. Mother had worked in a hat shop over there. Dad was general foreman at the big Kingan slaughtering house, supervising the smokehouse. They bought a vacant lot in Riverwood. Dad could hardly wait for summer to come, and weekends. In 1924 my father started building our Riverwood cottage. We had a sixteen-family, party telephone line. Two women were always on it, talking, talking, talking.

When Bob and Maxine Langley owned the store they served big groups of people, banquet-style chicken dinners. Many groups came from Indianapolis, thirty miles away.

Saturday night square dances were held there. Everyone in the community came. Mr. and Mrs. Knable played the music, he the fiddle and she the piano.

Esther: I never had live musicians. I bought the juke box and square dance records. We had dances but I never did rent the room out—just folks coming in for an evening of fun. I had soft drinks and ice cream, and I made sandwiches.

Groups of young kids came. The Luther League from the Lutheran Church at Cicero, they spent the evening until dark, canoe riding, then came in for more fun. Yes, they danced!

Folks, up for a day to relax or go fishing, came in to buy sandwiches and soft drinks for a bag lunch. I made the sandwiches with cold lunch meat. Or, at mealtime, they'd eat at one of the tables, then stand around the nickel or dime slot machines I had. I sold gas from the pump in front.

I got my grocery supplies from Noblesville stores. Sometimes I'd call Dad, John Kepner—he and Mom lived in Noblesville and he was always anxious to help me—and he'd bring them up. My widowed sister, Ethel Kaiser, and her children, lived up over the hill on a farm west of me. Dad was always coming out to help her. She worked at Firestone, the Noblesville factory.

Then just south a half mile lived the Illyeses, my dead sister's family—the father, sons Ben and George, and two aunts who looked after them all. Dad, a retired farmer and carpenter, took a great interest seeing to the needs of each of us children.

Once every summer, Mother and Dad, all their kids and grandkids, the whole Kepner family, came for a family reunion. We held it out in the yard under the big maples if the day was sunny. If it rained, we set up more tables inside.

Others in the community planned summer reunions—holding them along the riverbanks. If it rained, they used my store.

I kept the big, coal heating stove going all winter long in the front room. Also had one in our back apartment. It was good and warm up around the stove, but when you got back a-ways, it wasn't too comfortable. Wind came in all those windows. But kids didn't mind when they got to dancing—usually just on weekends in the wintertime.

I was crazy about fishing. That made Cledie and Marion angry. They had all the care of the store. I'd catch those big carp, clean them, and put them in the freezer. When I went to town I took them to Mom and Dad. They just loved fish. I couldn't stand them!

Leeanna: Mary Webster's father—they had money and a summer home in Riverwood—was captain of the police force in Indianapolis. Mary had two sisters, Helen and Hazel. Most of us "local" girls envied them, but they were always a lot of fun, and never stuck-up.

Dorothy: Remember *Summer Girl*, the riverboat? Was it still running when you lived there?

Esther: Yes, but it was getting in a bad shape by then. I rode in it a few times.

Dorothy: They charged a quarter to ride. A band played on its bow. How wonderful that music sounded, up and down the river!

Persons not taking part in the July Fourth celebrations lined the riverbanks and leaned from the bridge to watch the long, decorated, boat parade. The day had all the usual elements. There were the sack races, horse races, horseshoe pitching, followed by a picnic-style meal out in front of the store or at individual houses, then a square dance.

Leeanna: Always, without fail, there were several light showers or a thunderstorm which brought a crashing downpour that lasted probably less than an hour—enough to dampen our spirits. Folks didn't have many places to go for entertainment, and it was a big disappointment to have showers spoil this special occasion.

Esther: There was the shiver and excitement of potential danger with the yearly fireworks. As an explosive holiday neared, when I was a child, my Mother would graphically recount the harrowing experiences of their six-year-old neighbor boy, who on July Fourth picked up a half-spent firecracker and had it go off in his hand! The father, at the kitchen washstand shaving when it happened, ran lather-faced through town carrying his screaming, bleeding child to the doctor. The boy lost an eye and his face was left terribly disfigured. From that day forward, Mother waged an increasing verbal battle against fireworks.

When I was young, children were sternly warned that there were to be no firecrackers lighted and thrown from the carriages 'cause they'd frighten the horses. One little fellow came up and said to me, "We cain't have no crackers 'cause Papa's horse got scared last year and runned off and it ruint the buggy and Mama and all the young 'uns were a nervous wreck."

On that day the roads leading to Riverwood were crowded with buggies, farm wagons and Model T Fords.

All the time I had the store no alcoholic drinks could be sold. I prepared and sold big tubs of lemonade and iced tea, a nickel a glass. Marion would chant, "Fresh cold lemonade/Made in the shade/Stirred with a spade!"

Dorothy: Folks all around had their own fireworks on July Fourth. Websters' were elaborate. There were flares, rockets, Roman candles, and pinwheels for the neighborhood bigger children. Girls squealed, giggled, and watched while the boys took charge.

In the evening the departing sun glinted on the water, making a golden pathway. It was the ideal time for a courting Romeo to take his best girl for a boat ride. The beauty of the river lent enchantment to couples in love and fostered dreams to be carried out in the future.

Naughty boys would tie firecrackers to the tails of dogs or cats, to cause a lot of commotion, and much to the disgust of any of the girls around who'd see them do it.

We, like most families, made a freezer of ice cream, each taking his turn cranking the handle of the ice cream freezer.

They had boat races and a boat parade on the water each Fourth of July. Everybody competed to have the most decorated boat. One year my daughter, Marcia, stood at the helm of ours. She won first prize as Little Bo Peep in her crepe paper costume I'd made.

You had a piano there at the store and someone was always playing it. George Illyes, Ben's brother—oh, how he could play!

Leeanna: Ben could play, too, but he needed the sheet of music to go by and he played every note. But, mention any song to George and he could play it by ear—take off playing the piano like most people who would sing songs.

Neither of them could swim and they lived on the water all their lives. I guess their guardian angel was with them.

Esther: You mentioned the piano. When I was a kid Dad traded a Jersey cow for the neighbor's piano. We had it for years and years and all us girls, my six sisters, one brother and I, learned to play on it. When our farm home burned—I was married and living away and had my own family—it burned up with the house.

The fire started on a hot, dry, summer day, family sitting around eating dinner and they smelled smoke. The flue burned out and sparks caught the wooden shingles on the roof on fire. Just took about everything. I cried and cried—all the family memories gone up in smoke! The folks rebuilt—a nice one-story bungalow.

Oh, kids could have a lot of fun if there was a lively piano player around. Singing and dancing! Cledie always wanted the crowd around and she invited them all in. We sprinkled something on the floor to make it slick. How they danced! Feet flying! Music always playing!

Esther: Marion kept begging to take me for a motorboat ride. He was such a tease and cut-up. I said, "No! When you get me into that boat, you'll fiddle with it, going around in circles, all that silliness. I won't go in it for anything!"

He assured me: "I promise you I won't be careless. You sit real still and I won't do a thing."

We went up the river so quiet and easy, he turned slowly and we came back, just as easy. He said, "Now, that wasn't so bad, was it?" But I couldn't enjoy the ride for wondering what he might do!

At the end of the dam was that big abutment. Marion would go over there, climb to the top and dive off way down into the waterway below. He was such a water dog.

I'd stand at the window and watch, wondering if he was ever coming up. When he came back I'd scold him and he'd say, "But, Mother, it's so much fun!"

Leeanna: When I was dating Ben we swam off Webster's pier. I can see those snakes yet! Little ones, no more than six inches long, would come through the water at us. Every once in a while we'd see a parent snake.

I couldn't swim to begin with, and I was petrified. But nothing bothered Mary, Hazel, and Helen Webster. They'd just swim like mermaids around them. I guess the snake dens were being disturbed. Flip the water like that—they'd swim away. In a little bit, they'd come back.

After we were married, Ben and I lived in Riverwood. Another couple and Ben and I would go out in the boat, early evening, and take the riffles—those very brisk ripples the water made. The boat would bob, up and down, up and down. Riffles? Every so often, just below the river's surface, it was like a mound in the earth. Then beyond, a deep part, where the water moved real fast. The boat came upon another riffle, the bottom would drag, water not very deep, real smooth. Then, down to the next deep spot, high water, go real fast! Since I couldn't swim, I was terrified.

How beautiful, the gorgeous sun shining on the east banks. Snakes were lying in the tree branches or hanging way down. The boys had a great time shooting them!

Dorothy: Dad and Mr. Webster made a real nice paddlewheel boat with a Dodge motor in it. They'd work on it night after night. One time all of us took it up the river. We saw wild grapes hanging so thick from the trees. Mother yelled: "Oh, stop! Let's go over there and get those grapes. Wild grapes make the best jelly!"

We were all standing up ready to reach and pick them. Oh, goodness, there were all these snakes clinging to the limbs, hanging down, eating grapes!

Remember Lucky Teeter and his Hell Drivers? He was the race car driver known throughout the United States and Europe. He did performances at the Indiana State Fair and other fairs every year. He'd line up several cars, side by side, then take off very fast in his race car, go up a steep ramp, and sail over the tops of all of them!

In 1936, Lucky and his Hell Drivers shot a Hollywood movie film in Noblesville. Noblesville schools were dismissed one afternoon to watch the spectacle on the south side of the square.

And, Lucky came to a weenie roast at our place. We strung lights all around the water's edge.

When Mary Webster graduated from high school, one of her Detroit aunts gave her a pair of lounging pajamas. The first that women wore long pants—or anything but dresses. They had the biggest green polka dots you've ever seen, bigger than a silver dollar. Newest fad! But *scandalous*!

They had a bib front, sun back, with straps that crossed over and white organdy ruffles that went all around. Big wide legs! Oh, my, how all of us other girls envied Mary and her pajamas! Every whipstitch Mary was washing them and starching the ruffles, ironing them so she could wear them again. Oh, she'd wear them everywhere, except to church! It wasn't long before Helen and Hazel had a pair, too.

Leeanna: Oh, yes, all of us other girls were envious! Not another father around would allow such as that on his daughter! But, a year or so later, we'd see more and more of them. It shocked all the locals when young ladies first appeared on the streets in their beach pajamas and were sunbathing in daring, two-piece suits!

Dorothy: "Beanie" and Mae Stage lived nearby. Mr. Webster and Dad decided they'd play a trick on Mr. Stage one Halloween. They got a pumpkin from a nearby cornfield, climbed up the side of the house and put it on the chimney.

Inside they heard Beanie—Elmer was his name—poking around at the smoking stove, fussing and fuming. He couldn't understand what was wrong. Instead of the smoke going up the chimney as it usually did—the pumpkin blocked it—thick smoke came out into the room. Finally they threw open all the doors and windows and rushed out and looked all around. Then they saw the pumpkin. It didn't take Beanie long to decide who'd played the trick on him!

Leeanna: Before Halloween, people usually put away all the things that were not nailed down, or they would find their porch chairs hanging on a telephone pole a mile away. It was just good fun.

Dorothy: Beanie had an old Model T Ford which he kept in the barn by his house. One Halloween Dad said, "I'll tell you what let's do. Let's go up and get Elmer's Ford and hide it in Heiny's barn." Mr. Heiny was the Riverwood caretaker. He mowed the park with a mower pulled by horses.

Dad and Mr. Webster pushed Beanie's car up the road. No lights or engine running or someone would have heard that.

When Elmer went out the next day, his Ford was gone. I never heard if he learned who took it or where it was.

That Halloween night I went with the Webster girls and we took our "tic-tac-toes" to rattle the windows of every house all around Riverwood. Our tic-tac-toes were wooden thread spools which we had notched and run a string through.

One place, it was dark as midnight, the man of the house sneaked around from the back and grabbed Mary. We all ran. Not Mary. She was too scared and she wet her pants, but finally got away.

Leeanna: A whole gang of people, old and young, gathered at the store every Halloween for a party. Everyone came! Ben and I were dating, we were high school age. He dressed as a woman and I as a man. I had his pipe in my mouth. You all remember he was always smoking that corncob pipe! All the boys smoked, cigarettes or a pipe. They'd guessed everyone and got down to the two of us. Someone lit a match to the pipe, tobacco still in it. I drew on it, started smoking, choking, and that smoke got up under my mask and I thought I was going to die! Couldn't get my breath and of course, had to remove the mask!

Do you remember the Webster girls' old cars? Their dad was on the Indianapolis police force. Old, unclaimed cars had to be towed away. He picked them up for little or nothing. One they called "The Old Blue Cloud." Later he got the "White Cloud." When my mother needed something from the store, I'd call up and here they'd come!

After George Illyes and Mary Webster were married, they had a little car with a rumble seat. George drove like the wind. One time Ben and I went with them. George drove through Potter's Bridge, the covered wooden bridge. There was a sudden drop-off. As he neared it, he gunned the motor. Ben and I didn't know if we were coming back down into the rumble seat or behind onto the gravel road! And, oh, remember how he went around curves! Ben was always just as cautious as George was reckless.

Esther: That was a wonderful community to live in. I just loved all those kiddies along the river. Everyone had so much good, clean fun.

Sometimes I wondered if I could keep my nose above water but, financially, in the long run, I got along pretty good.

—These three ladies were interviewed in the summer of 1984.

Photos

Photographs are from the collections of the author and Joe Roberts, Hamilton County coroner, Noblesville funeral director, and historian.

In 1914, Leonard Bradfield had the full-time job of picking up "horse apples" from the bricked streets in downtown Noblesville.

Using this vehicle, Dickie Couden was employed by the city of Noblesville in 1920 to spray water on the streets.

As a publicity stunt, clerks in the windows of the Craycraft and Osbon Dry Goods store in downtown Noblesville tossed a thousand dimes to the crowd down on the street in 1909.

Boys took time out for a little fun while posting election returns on this wooden platform, right, in Noblesville.

Below, George Kosto stands in the door of his candy store with young Larry Venable, who recalled this neighbor fondly in "We Lived Above the Interurban Depot." Kosto's Kandy Kitchen—*KKK* on the storefront—was forced to become Kosto's Candy Kitchen—*KCK*—after powerful Ku Klux Klan officials saw the signs.

Noblesville residents view the wreckage caused by an interurban that jumped the tracks in front of the Court House in 1919. A five-year-old boy was killed in the accident.

This interurban station in Noblesville was a busy place from 1903 until the last interurban car passed through in 1938. In Hamilton County, the car stopped in Carmel, Noblesville, Cicero, Arcadia and Atlanta.

The Noblesville Fire Department in 1913 had modest equipment and manpower by today's standards!

A 27053   9th Street looking North, Noblesville, Ind.

This view of Ninth Street in Noblesville, looking north, displays two sets of interurban tracks—one for northbound cars; the other

This covered bridge across White River at Logan Street in Noblesville, built in the mid-1880s, has long since been replaced with a more modern span. Until 1931, when the Conner Street bridge was completed, this wooden structure was the only bridge serving the city. Note the pedestrian walkway to the left.

Vice Presidential candidate Franklin D. Roosevelt attracted this crowd when he spoke at a 1920 political rally on the north side of the Court House square in Noblesville. Notice how horses and buggies were parked along one side of the Court House, "horseless carriages" on another side. All of the buildings in this photo are still standing.

In "Zula, Traveling Dressmaker," Zula Cammack recalls making the matching clothing for these twins, Edgar and Edna Evans, born on Christmas Day, 1907. The multiple birth was a surprise, so Zula had to quickly sew another set of baby clothes upon their arrival.

Horse-drawn bobsleds like this one in front of a Cicero home were handy for traveling in the snow. A tongue in front enabled the sled to turn like a wagon.

Cicero grade-school students pose in front of the R.E. Worley home, above, just east of Cicero. The grand house figures prominently in "Ada's Papa, Hard Shell Baptist Preacher," as it was the scene of monthly church services and many, larger Baptist meetings, held once a year.

At left are the Worley children, (from left) Sara, Floyd, Howard and Ada, around 1908.

The Opera House in Noblesville, right, is mentioned in several stories in this book. Many famous entertainers performed there during its heyday in the early 1900s.

Horse-drawn hacks similar to the one pictured above were a common means for rural children to travel to school. This one operated around Deming in 1915.

Index of Names